Vienna

D1584898

25·8·88

The Travellers' Companion series

General editor: Laurence Kelly

St Petersburg: a travellers' companion
Selected and introduced by Laurence Kelly (1981)

Moscow: a travellers' companion
Selected and introduced by Laurence Kelly (1983)

Naples: a travellers' companion
Selected and introduced by Desmond Seward (1984)

Edinburgh: a travellers' companion
Selected and introduced by David Daiches (1986)

Florence: a travellers' companion
Selected and introduced by Harold Acton and Edward Chaney
(1986)

Istanbul: a travellers' companion
Selected and introduced by Laurence Kelly (1987)

Delhi and Agra: a travellers' companion
Selected and introduced by Michael Alexander (1987)

Dublin: a travellers' companion
Selected and introduced by Thomas and Valerie Pakenham (1988)

VIENNA

A Travellers' Companion

SELECTED AND INTRODUCED BY

John Lehmann and
Richard Bassett

Constable London

First published in Great Britain 1988
by Constable and Company Limited
10 Orange Street London WC2H 7EG
Copyright © John Lehmann and Richard Bassett 1988
Set in Monophoto Baskerville 11pt
by Servis Filmsetting Ltd, Manchester
Printed in Great Britain by
St Edmundsbury Press
Bury St Edmunds, Suffolk

British Library CIP data
Vienna: a travellers companion. –
(The travellers' companion series)
1. Vienna (Austria) – History – Sources
I. Lehmann, John II. Bassett, John
III. Series
943.6'13   DB843

ISBN 0 09 465410 7
ISBN 0 09 467750 6 Pbk

Contents

The Hofburg

Contents
9

VIENNA BEYOND THE RING

Leopoldstadt

THE APPROACHES TO VIENNA

Contents

Contents

Illustrations

Acknowledgements

I wish to make acknowledgement to the following for extracts used from their editions, translations, or where copyright permission was needed:

A.D. Peters and Edward Crankshaw for *Vienna: Image of a Culture in Decline* and *The Fall of the House of Habsburg*; Laurence Pollinger, and Kurt von Schuschnigg for *Austrian Requiem*; Novello and Company Limited for *A Mozart Pilgrimage (The Travel Diaries of Vincent and Mary Novello)* transcribed and compiled by Nerina Medici di Marignano and edited by Rosemary Hughes; Henry Pleasants for *Vienna's Golden Years of Music*; Mrs G.E.R. Gedye and Mr Robin Gedye for G.E.R. Gedye's *Fallen Bastions*; Collins and John Stoye for *The Siege of Vienna*; Verlag Styria (Graz, Wien, Köln), for Evliya Celebi's *In the Empire of the Golden Apple*; Hamish Hamilton for Count Carl Lonyay's *Rudolf: the Tragedy of Mayerling*; Oxford University Press and Percy Scholes for Dr Charles Burney's *Musical Tours in Europe, 1772*; Emily Anderson and Macmillan for *Letters of Mozart and his Family*; Marcel Brion and Weidenfeld & Nicolson for *Daily Life in the Vienna of Mozart and Schubert*; Claud Cockburn and Hart-Davis for *In time of trouble*; John Murray and Osbert Lancaster for *With an Eye to the Future*; Fischer, Frankfurt, for Alma Mahler's *Memoires*; Faber & Faber and Stella Musulin for *Vienna in the Age of Metternich*; Karl Rach for *Eye-Witness Accounts of the Siege of Vienna*; Weidenfeld & Nicolson for Arthur Schnitzler's *My Youth in Vienna*; Cassell for Stefan Zweig's *The World of Yesterday: an autobiography*; Martin Secker and Warburg and Alfred A. Knopf for Ilse Barea's *Vienna, Legend and Reality*; Hellikon, Zurich for Bruno Walter's *Thema und Variationen*; and Heinemann for Robert Young's *A Young Man looks at Europe*.

It is my pleasure to thank the staff of the National Library in Vienna who were unfailingly helpful during long searches for archive material. In particular Herr Werner Rotter time and again secured access to books which would normally have been most difficult to find without expert knowledge of the Library's catalogue.

At the Military (Heeresgeschichtliches) Museum, Frau Dr Pepelka was equally cooperative. I am also grateful to Fräulein Hannelore Schmidt of the Austrian Institute in Rutland Gate, London; Herr Gottfried Pils; Mr Stephen Bela of Peterhouse; and Gertrude Felderer. Mr Michael O'Sullivan also made several intelligent suggestions.

Above all, however, thanks are due for Prudence Fay who had the formidable task of sorting out the details of a book one of whose authors had died over a year earlier while the other remained for most of the time between the capitals of Central Europe.

R.B.

Vienna 1987

Introduction

An historical retrospect

The best way to appreciate Vienna's history, is to look at its architecture. No city in the world reveals the pattern of the past so clearly, nor provides so subtle a key to the character and spirit of its modern inhabitants, in the stones, the concrete and plaster of which it is built.

If you look at a map of Vienna, you will see that the First District, the Old or Inner Town, is enclosed by the horseshoe of the Ring, the series of broad tree-planted boulevards that meets the Danube canal at both ends and marks the line of the old fortifications. This tiny kernel of the vast contemporary city stretching round it on all sides remained, up to the middle of the last century, still all there was officially of Vienna. It was separated from its suburbs not only by the city walls but also by the *glacis*, a wide belt of meadows used as military training grounds and popular playing-fields. When, however, in the 1850s and 1860s, the opening decades of Franz Josef's long reign, the fortifications were demolished and further districts incorporated as the era of bourgeois expansion and prosperity opened, the *glacis* was rapidly built over or converted into public parks. The customs barrier was then removed to the Gürtel, the series of streets that forms a roughly concentric circle outside the Ring. A friend has told me how she remembers, as a small child, helping her parents to smuggle country produce from the village of Hernals past the bored eye of the customs official on the western side. This, though not really so very long ago, sounds remote enough to a modern generation, for during the next half-century this demarcation too disappeared, as more and more suburbs merged with the city and were officially incorporated, including Grinzing and Neuwaldegg and other districts which even today seem like little country towns or villages with a distinct individuality and life. By the time Vienna was separated from Lower Austria by the new Social Democratic government in 1920 and made a province by itself among the federated provinces of Austria, it had a total extent of nearly 110 square miles and stretched from the last spurs of the Wiener Wald on the north and west, taking in the edge of the wide treeless plain beyond Floridsdorf on the further side of the Danube, to the outskirts of the village of Schwechat in the south-east – where Metternich, as the story goes, maintained that the Balkans began.

The Stefansdom, the Cathedral that seems so essentially the ancient centre of Vienna now, was, in the period before the Habsburgs, actually outside the town. The Square now known as the Hohemarkt was roughly the centre of the medieval (as well as the Roman) city, and around it, as Vienna's importance as a trade-centre increased, the early Viennese working population settled itself according to occupations, as the names of many little streets and corners show today: the cloth-workers in the Tuchlauben, the dyers in the Färbergasse, the nail-makers in the Naglergasse, and so on. The Wollzeile, further outside on the eastern circumference, was the abode of the foreigners trading in wool.

It was in the middle of the twelfth century that the Babenbergs – the then rulers of Austria – removed from the Leopoldsberg into the city itself and built their palace in what is now the beautiful baroque square of Am Hof, where there had previously been a farm-yard. And at the same time, it is interesting to remember, a monastery for Scottish and Irish Benedictines was founded, which survives as the present Schottenkirche and Schottenstift; but the Scots and the Irishmen themselves left many hundreds of years ago, having proved extremely turbulent guests, who indulged shamelessly in trading and ball-games, to the horror of the pious, and had finally to be ejected by force. By the time the Babenbergs had given place to the Bohemian kings – an interval of Czech rule which Nazi Vienna must have blushed to remember – and they, in 1276, had been succeeded by the first Habsburg Emperor, Rudolf the Founder, the earliest Roman-esque version of the Stefansdom had been built, and the city walls extended to the position they were to hold right down to Franz Josef's reign. Of this original cathedral little or nothing remains, as it was destroyed by fire in 1258. Rebuilding, continually held up by wars and financial difficulties, went on right up to the beginning of the sixteenth century; but by 1400 the church that signs Vienna for all its visitors even today, after all the splendours and formidable masses of later architecture have been added, was already lifting her long thin spire into the sky, visible from all the plains and hills around, completing the graceful symmetry of the compact little town, as it can be seen in many old prints.

But it is not the Gothic of the Stefansdom that is the characteristic note of Vienna's architecture, but baroque, as anyone will realize who explores the city. And in this fact lies half the city's history, and the key, too, to much that might otherwise be puzzling in the character and temperament of the Viennese today. For, first of all, it must be remembered that Austria has been for centuries one of the strongest fortresses of Roman Catholicism. If Renaissance is the style characteristic of the Reformation, baroque is the style of the Counter-Reformation, which advanced upon Austria after the Council of Trent in 1560 and gradually established an almost undisputed ascendancy. In this connection it is interesting to find that, even in post-war Vienna, of the 1,874,130 inhabitants, 1,475,744 gave their religion at the last census as Roman Catholicism, though no one should assume from that that the sensuous, happy-go-lucky Viennese are a particularly devout race. Second, Vienna's whole development has been conditioned by the fact that from the time of the first Habsburg to the end of the Great War, it was a Court city: the capital of the Holy Roman Empire as long as that strange and increasingly incoherent conception survived, and then of the Austrian Empire. Its official name was Haupt-und-Residenz Stadt. All the Princes and Dukes and powerful courtiers, with their retinues of attendants, gathered here, from the many lands of the Empire. Churches, palaces, and government offices dominated the town within the old walls; there was scarcely anyone living there who was not in some way connected with the Court.

It was a Court in whose ceremonial and manner of life Spanish influence had made itself deeply felt, a natural result of the original unity of the Spanish and Austrian houses of Habsburg under Charles V in the sixteenth century. An idea of the pomp of the gorgeous processions and festivals that characterized Court life can be had from hundreds of paintings and prints of the period. The other side to this Spanish influence, the elaborateness and stiffness of ceremonial, extending even to small details of social intercourse, though it was inimical to the Viennese temperament and though at various times attempts were made to loosen its hold, could still be observed, weakened but persistent, in Franz Josef's Court hundreds of years later in a

totally changed world. In other directions, Italian was the
predominant influence; Italian was the second language in
aristocratic circles, and traces of Italian can still, and by no
means rarely, be found in modern Viennese speech; the impress
of Italy was on architecture, on painting, on literature, on
cooking even; there was a large and powerful Italian colony of
aristocrats, officials, priests, bankers, merchants, artists. Both
these influences, Spanish and Italian, were encouraged as a
direct counterpoise to French influence. Austria was at that time
the great rival of France, and while the rest of aristocratic Europe
lay under the spell of Louis XIV's Court in Versailles, Vienna
chose to underline and foster its difference and independence as a
cosmopolitan centre of culture.

The third factor, which explains why it was precisely at the
end of the seventeenth century that these other two factors came
into full play in shaping Vienna, is the continual danger which
had threatened it from the Turks. No one cared to indulge in
elaborate building schemes so long as these destroyers were
hovering within striking distance. The first siege, under Sultan
Suleiman II, took place in 1529, but it was not until a century
and a half had passed that, after a second siege under Kara
Mustapha, the Turks were finally repulsed in 1683, and the
Christian shape of civilization was saved for Western Europe.

During that second siege Vienna became the nerve-centre of
Europe. For a time it seemed as if the city could not hold out.
Difficulties and disasters in the previous two decades had
resulted in one of Vienna's periodic expulsions of the Jews, and in
1679 a series of epidemics of the plague culminated in an attack,
the violence of which almost emptied the city of its inhabitants.
The Plague Column in the Graben, one of the most extravagant
baroque creations in all Austria, is the unlikely monument to this
tragic moment. Vienna's weakened forces nevertheless rallied, to
a large extent owing to the brilliant leadership of Count
Starhemberg, whose descendant 250 years later was so patheti-
cally to see in his own fight against 'Bolshevism' an image of the
great Count's exploits against Islam. Vienna held; and on 7
September the population saw the rockets go up from
Kahlenberg, and knew that the relief army commanded by the
Polish King Johann Sobieski and Duke Karl of Lothringen was
approaching. By the 12th, Kara Mustapha's so-dreaded soldiers
were retreating in the wildest confusion. Vienna's glory re-

sounded through Europe, but she herself scarcely recovered from the effects of her supreme effort until some years later when the Turks had finally been driven back to and out of Hungary.

A vast increase in the territories of the House of Habsburg outside the Holy Roman Empire followed the victory over the Turks. A series of successful campaigns ended in the addition of Hungary and Transylvania by the turn of the century, and within the next twenty years Habsburg arms had pushed a considerable way further down the Danube, conquering Slavonia and the Banat of Temesvar. Inside the Empire the territories comprising post-war Austria, with South Tyrol, Trieste and the Slovenian country south of the Drave, Bohemia, Moravia and Silesia now came directly under Habsburg rule. Vienna was therefore not merely the capital of the Holy Roman Empire that stretched as far as Arras in the north-west, but also of an overlapping dynastic Empire whose frontiers already reached to the northern Dalmatian islands in the south, and in the east cut deep into the territories which form post-war Romania.

Vienna began to feel itself more consciously a European capital, a capital with a cultural mission to fulfill: under Maria Theresa and Josef II much of the provincial, country-town character of the old Vienna disappeared. Already two things were happening which are essential to remember if one wants to understand the pattern of post-1918 events in Austria. The city, previously under Spanish and Italian influences, was now to become even more cosmopolitan, even less a German town than before, in spite of the strong tendency that appeared towards the end of the century to purify the German talked and written in Vienna of its local idiosyncrasies; French influences began to usurp the place of the Italian in art and science, and French became the favourite speech of the aristocracy. And from now on it was to think less and less of its loyalty to the Habsburgs as being an Austrian patriotism, for with such an enormous polyglot Empire growing round it the ruling House was bound to look in the first place for a *dynastic* loyalty. Already the post-1918 contradiction was there in germ, the problem that faced both Dollfuss and Schuschnigg: they wished, like so many of their countrymen, to resist the Pan-German flood, but this meant fostering a patriotism for Austria as Austria, and where was it to be found? They wished to remain independent, but with the

Habsburg Empire in ruins where was enormous Vienna to find
its *raison d'être?* From the proletariat came one answer – in a
federated Socialist Europe; but just that answer was one which
Austria's rulers could not accept.

The Turks were routed, and the great baroque era began,
when the Inner Town and the immediately surrounding districts
acquired the splendour of architecture that characterizes them
today. And what a style it is! Come to Vienna with all the Gothic
prejudices that an English education can give, but after a year or
two you must succumb to its charm. It is essentially a worldly
style, in which the gorgeous façade plays a most significant part.
In 'high baroque' churches there is none of the spirituality of
Gothic; everything is gay and sensuous, ornamentally flamboy-
ant, recklessly realistic; gaudily painted angels hang in mid-air,
backed by stucco clouds, above gold-loaded altars that can
sometimes only be compared with the most fantastic imaginable
efforts of a pastry-cook for a royal wedding. In the earliest 'early
baroque' this theatrical, exuberant note is only faintly notice-
able. It is an anonymous architecture, cautious, contenting itself
with a few well-tried Italian patterns; the Counter-Reformation
is still an undecided battle. But in 'high baroque' all is triumph
and delight, for to consolidate its victory the Church had
realized the necessity for making a popular, human appeal.

Baroque throws to the winds the canons of taste, the restraint,
the reserve of colour in favour of line which had governed the
artistic work of the Renaissance, and its wildest monuments are a
tumult of colour, a riot of movement instantaneously frozen.
Baroque architecture is also, as Viennese palaces and churches
immediately reveal, a style working in an 'exterior room'. Again
and again you find in Europe a Gothic cathedral cluttered about
with old houses coming right up to its walls, shapeless squares on
which little wandering streets suddenly open. But the supreme
baroque palace or church is placed at the most advantageous
point for all to see and admire, and is surrounded by carefully
designed levels and gardens or open spaces: it is only the centre of
a larger design. Look at Fischer von Erlach's great Palace of
Schönbrunn, built for the Habsburgs, or Lucas von
Hildebrand's Summer Palace of the Belvedere, built for the
triumphant Prince Eugene of Savoy: you will see how lavishly
the baroque architects squandered space to achieve their
masterpieces.

It is not, however, merely in one or two supreme examples that Viennese baroque is outstanding. All through the older parts of the city there are exuberantly decorated churches, wonderful palaces and merchants' houses. As you wander through the narrow, winding streets you are overwhelmed by the richness of the façades, by the sudden beauty of cool, sculptured courtyards of which you catch now and then a glimpse through open gates. Take one of the main thoroughfares of the Inner Town, the Herrengasse. As you come down from the Freyung towards the Hofburg, on the right-hand side of the street you see palace after palace, each with its own subtle variation of style. And in the Wallnerstrasse just behind, on the opposite side, there is yet another row of palaces, with exquisite and varied façade decoration: the Esterhazy Palace in particular, and the palace further down which used to be the British Consulate. In curious contrast, between these two streets, where once the gigantic Liechtenstein Palace stood, now rises Vienna's first, post-war skyscraper – the Hochhaus: ancient stares at modern across a few feet of asphalt.

If the Hochhaus is the first skyscraper proper (and a New Yorker would no doubt scorn to give it the name), the tendency in Vienna has been for many centuries towards continually higher building. In 1566 there were 1,205 houses in the Inner Town, but only one of them had more than three storeys. In 1800 the total number of houses had only increased to 1,312, but there were then 376 with four storeys and more. At that time, just before Napoleon was to occupy Vienna, there were 232,000 inhabitants. The great leap in population was to come at the end of the nineteenth century when the suburbs, which had in fact been merging with the city for many years, were legally incorporated in it.

Napoleon left his eagles over the gates of Schönbrunn, and they are still undisturbed there: perhaps no other people but the Austrians would have been so indifferent to the symbols of a foreign conquest they had avenged. But if they were indifferent to the symbols, they were not indifferent to the conquest itself. When Murat first took Vienna in 1805, the two months' occupation was endured with a certain gloomy resignation. Immediately after, however, a reaction and revival began, and when Napoleon again entered the city in 1809 he found the people sullen and bitter. There were a number of outbreaks against the French, and the violence of the repressive measures which followed them shows how anxious the conqueror was. Some names of popular heroes have come down to us: there was, for instance, a certain Eschenbach, a saddler, who was shot on the *glacis* for burying arms on his land. The great Austrian victory of Aspern was a sign of the change of spirit since Murat's occupation, and though the mood of the people relapsed again in characteristic fashion when they saw that bad leadership had thrown away all Aspern's gains, it was perhaps a warning for future ages that the Viennese have no love for foreign troops which occupy their city, under whatever guise they come.

The Vienna, then, which the delegates of Europe were to see at the time of the great Congress in 1814–15, was a feudal city neatly enclosed within its ancient walls, a city crowded with beautiful churches and luxurious palaces, rich with all the pomp and magnificence of the ruling class of a huge Empire. Its streets were cobbled and lamplit. In the back parts of the grand houses and the narrower alleys the poorer craftsmen and labourers lived, and wretchedly enough; but the main bulk of the working population, which was to form the future industrial proletariat, lived in the village suburbs, across the meadows of the *glacis*. In the further villages beyond the present Gürtel, which are all now part of what was – up to 1934 – the federal province of Vienna, lived then a population of smallholders, vine-cultivators and petty burghers. Here the charming, low, cream-walled cottages of the period can still be seen in many streets.

Some of these are famous for housing musical celebrities, for it was in the latter half of the eighteenth century that Vienna began to acquire its great reputation as a centre of music, drawing the talented young to itself from far and wide – Haydn from Lower Austria, Mozart from Salzburg, Beethoven from the Rhineland – moulding their genius to its own spirit and being transformed in its turn, so that in the work of the most out-and-out Viennese musician, Schubert, Beethoven's power can be felt beside the basic Slav and other peasant melodies. Diplomats and statesmen gathered to applaud Beethoven's concerts and dance interminably to the strains of the new waltzes which sprang in sudden bloom from the soil of Viennese artistic sensibility, which Heinrich Laube said were to Vienna what Napoleon's victories were to France, and which in a few decades were to make the names of Lanner and Johann Strauss world-famous.

Beyond the city walls on the north-east, between the Danube Canal and the Danube, the wide meadows of the Prater, formerly an imperial hunting preserve, had, a few decades before, been thrown open to the public by Josef II, and had become an extremely important playground. If Vienna was in theory a German capital, the centralizing force of the Habsburg rule had already filled it with Czechs, Poles, Croats, Slovenes, Magyars, Jews, Italians, whose mixing blood inevitably, and profoundly, modified the original Germano-Celtic stock and made the Viennese practically a race by themselves. But on the circumference of the Empire national aspirations were stirring, and the ideas of the French Revolution had left a mark which Metternich as Imperial Chancellor now set himself the task of obliterating by his all-pervading, notorious police system; an attempt which nevertheless was finally to cause the savage disturbances which swept Metternich himself away in the next phase of the city's history. A hundred years later Dollfuss, the Chancellor nicknamed 'Millimetternich', was to reintroduce such a police system, in a desperate attempt to stamp out the influence of another class-revolution in a great country near at hand, and at the same time to prevent the Pan-German completion of the nationalist break-aways which had already reduced Austria to a small, dismembered torso.

Metternich's system, repressing thought and initiative for a generation, combined with the impoverishment that followed the Napoleonic Wars to keep Vienna much as it was for many years after the Congress. It is one of the characteristic features of Vienna's history that each period of new national or class triumph is clearly marked, as clearly as the rings in a tree, in the city's appearance. Under Metternich, the great building impulse that had surged up after the rout of the Turks was finally extinguished. Typical of the desire to maintain things as they had been and of the fear of the disintegrating force of new ideas, the city walls remained untouched, though the near suburbs were pressing now right up to the *glacis* and the military value of such fortifications had already been proved out of date by the French wars. The only contributions of any real beauty which the Metternich period made to Vienna architecturally are the houses which the bourgeoisie, now gradually beginning to feel its strength, built in the outer districts, in Hietzing and Döbling and occasionally in the town itself. They are often exquisite in style, quiet miniatures of the great baroque palaces of the eighteenth century; in them the homely, unambitious spirit of the age of 'Biedermeyer' is well expressed.

The one artistic form which had a true life of its own at this time was the theatre. Raimund, Nestroy, and Grillparzer were the outstanding figures of a theatrical renaissance which seemed to flourish almost as much because of the repression as in spite of it; and though the names of the first two are scarcely known in other countries, it is because of their intensely Viennese character, the untranslatableness of so much of the wit and sentiment from its strong dialect. The censor's hand lay heavy on them, but they managed to evolve a technique of mocking at authority that became a tradition, and was still evident in the plays and cabaret sketches of Schuschnigg's Vienna.

The creative forces of society, however, could not be suppressed for ever, nor the growing national consciousness of the various races under Habsburg rule. The year 1848, sweeping over Europe like a tornado, brought violent disturbances to Vienna also. Revolution broke out in March, headed by liberal-minded students who to a large extent carried the masses with them in a wild wave of enthusiasm and popular unity, though the newly arisen proletariat had as yet no sort of organization. At first the storm was stayed by the flight of Metternich, ironically enough to a democratic England that had long completed its bourgeois revolution. In May the revolutionaries, thanks to the way in which the workers from the outer districts supported the students, managed to force a number of reforms through, in the panic of which the Court fled to Innsbruck. But the very energy of the proletarian support set in motion the break-up of the movement. The bourgeoisie began to be seriously scared of the forces they had called up from the 'lower depths', and looked with horror at the destruction of machines and factories which the misery-maddened unemployed had perpetrated, and with painful doubt at the various reforms in working conditions, the reduction in factory hours and the relief works.

In August there were violent battles in the Praterstrasse – Karl Marx happened to arrive in Vienna immediately after – in which the change in the attitude of the bourgeoisie was sharply illuminated. Tension steadily increased until October, when an attempt on the part of the authorities to send troops against the Hungarians, who had declared for national independence, provoked mutinies and the most serious risings of all. The War Minister Latour was lynched, the Court (which had meanwhile returned) fled again, and the masses seized control of the city. For twenty-six days the storm raged, but the fate of the revolution cannot but seem now to have been hopeless from the start. The chaotic aims and political immaturity of the masses were not the only fatal features of the situation. Vienna was alone, as so often before and after in her history; the Slavs of the Empire were playing a complicated game of intrigue to snatch their own advantage, if possible their freedom, from the confusion; the peasants were indifferent, even hostile, in spite of the improvement they had gained in their position; the Hungarians failed to come to the rescue, though all hopes were set on them. Nevertheless, it was one of Vienna's most heroic hours, in which the spirit of her people shines up against the craven way in which Berlin and Budapest finally yielded to the counter-revolutionary troops. One interesting feature of the 1848 revolution was the part which foreigners took in it, a feature characteristic of so many of the highlights of Vienna's history. The most progressive minds of Europe saw in the October rising the last hopes of the democratic revolution; among those who came to join her battle and help in her defence were Lieutenant Wenzel Messenhauser, the member of the Frankfurt National Assembly, Robert Blum, and the Polish General Bem. The latter escaped to carry on the battle elsewhere, but Messenhauser and Blum were shot by the victorious reactionaries. Another feature that should not be forgotten today is that the idea of an *Anschluss* of German-Austria was definitely in the minds of the liberal revolutionaries; all the German lands were to join together, but on a democratic and federal basis.

This was the first time that the people of Vienna showed that a small flame burned within them that was capable suddenly of becoming a great fire; three times already in the present century they have shown the same temper, the same quick change from apparent passivity to violent eruption, and one cannot help feeling that in the future, if stung beyond endurance, they will do so again. In 1848, though the reign of the revolutionaries was short enough, and the vengeance taken, when order had been restored by Prince Windischgraetz's loyal troops, was ruthless, they had brought about not only the flight of Metternich but also the abdication of the Emperor Ferdinand in favour of the young

Franz Josef, and the inauguration of an entirely new era.

The Habsburgs were saved, but the bourgeoisie and the subject nationalities of the Empire had nevertheless made a great stride forward historically. Vienna broke from the cultural restraint of Metternich's days; it developed rapidly as an industrial and financial centre; through the Hungarian achievement, which was crowned by the establishment of the Dual monarchy in 1867, and the resulting expansion of Budapest, through the increased agitation of the subject Slav peoples, particularly the Czechs, for independence, Vienna felt driven to assert itself palpably as the capital by swift modernization and lavish self-decoration. Moreover, after the defeat of Solferino in 1859 and the unsuccessful war with Prussia in the '60s, it became the centre of an Empire whose interests and power shifted more and more down river towards the east and south-east, while its connections with Germany and Italy were no longer as intimate as they had been in the preceding period. The Habsburgs were no longer rulers of the German Empire; as the frontiers and national content of their Empire changed owing to the new capitalist ascendancy, its nature changed also. It became a powerful modern state, industrialized and at the same time rich in raw materials, forming a very nearly self-sufficient economic unit. The industrial and financial expansion, that fêted its triumph and suffered its first terrible shock of crisis in the 1870s at the time of the World Exhibition, transformed Vienna's appearance as radically as the victory of the Counter-Revolution and the defeat of the Turks at the end of the seventeenth century. Parallel with this expansion came a prodigious increase in the population due partly to the actual extension of the city boundaries, partly to the stream of immigrants attracted from all the Habsburg lands by the industrial boom. By 1880 there were 726,000 inhabitants, and by 1890 already 1,364,000, while the proportion of the non-German element grew steadily.

Again this turn in the spiral of history has left its clear, decisive mark on Vienna's outward appearance. The old city walls were at last pulled down, and between 1860 and 1880 the Ringstrasse, with its magnificent four-fold belt of trees and its gigantic new buildings, was created, while part of the former *glacis* was built over, part transformed into parks. Building was everywhere pushed forward with a haste and reckless eclecticism of style to which many beauties of old Vienna fell victim. Round the Ring the Italian Renaissance motifs jostle with neo-Hellenic façades and neo-Gothic spires, challenging baroque for supremacy – but vainly in spite of all their massive self-confidence and grandeur. And how well the buildings of the Ring express the ideals of the nineteenth-century liberal middle-class in their panorama of moneyed culture! The new University, the State Opera House, the Burgtheater, the Stock Exchange, the Rathaus, the Parliament, the Palace of Justice, and the museums are the highlights, and in between them rows of characterless houses and shop-fronts stretch out. At the same time in all the additional districts of the city, the former suburbs, new blocks of dwelling-houses and offices sprang up, and beyond them increasing numbers of factories made their appearance and a huge industrial proletariat, composed partly of former Viennese and peasants of the suburbs, partly of the new elements that were pouring into the city, rapidly developed.

Liberal capitalism thus radically changed Vienna in form and content within a few decades; at the same time the increase of the proletariat, of its destitution and sufferings in the aftermath of the financial crisis of the 1870s, resulted in the emergence of socialist workers' parties as a powerful political factor. The simultaneous ruin of large sections of the petty bourgeoisie, and the fact that the native Viennese felt that they were being overwhelmed by the immigrants, a considerable proportion of whom were Jews from the eastern provinces, brought to the anti-Liberal, anti-Semitic Christian-Social party, with its hostility to high finance and capital, the rapid support of the 'small man' and Catholic sections of the proletariat as yet untouched by international socialism. A few years after its birth in the '90s it was in control of the municipal government, and continued so up to the outbreak of the First World War. And in that Christian-Social Vienna, a young house-painter from Upper Austria bearing the name of Hitler, down-and-out, hungry, consumed with ambition, prowled the streets by day and slept in the doss-houses at night, and listened avidly to Burgomaster Lueger's eloquence denouncing the Jews and championing the cause of the small Christian shopkeepers.

Lueger's administration was far from reactionary: his farsightedness and ambition to make a first-rate modern capital out of the city entrusted to his care were the guarantees of a progressive policy. Lueger's administrative and technical reforms put

Vienna in the very forefront of the world's great centres, and for many measures which he successfully carried through, such as the erection of a 'green belt' round the outer suburbs, London had to wait many decades. Between 1895 and 1910 he managed to bring not only the communications – trams, buses, trains – of Vienna under unified municipal control, but also her gas and electricity; he extended the city boundaries to include the suburbs on the left bank of the Danube; he completed the modernizing of Vienna's water-supply from the Styrian Alps, which made Vienna's drinking water famous throughout the world; he established the Metropolitan railway; and he regulated the course of the river Wien.

By 1914, however, the challenge of Social-Democracy had become more insistent, and its influence on the working classes in the crowded slums was steadily advancing. The Austrian Party, founded at Hainfeld in 1889, was one of the most influential in the International, and one of the most dynamic; in Viktor Adler it produced a leader of dominant intellect and character, with a European reputation. The ancient Habsburg power was weakening, and few intelligent observers believed it could survive for long without far-reaching concessions to the clamorous subject nationalities. At the same time it had been extending its territories – and its liabilities – by the annexation in 1908 of Bosnia-Herzegovina, which it had occupied thirty years before. The concessions, however, were not forthcoming; the one Habsburg who might have granted them, the Archduke Franz Ferdinand, was murdered in Sarajevo by a young Serb behind whom stood the shadowy terrorist figures of the Pan-Slav movement.

Vienna was undamaged during the 1914–18 War, but after the defeat of the Central Powers the expected breakaway of the non-German territories took place and Austria emerged from the redrawing of frontiers at Versailles as a small independent republic. Vienna had become a head without a body, a huge city of nearly two million inhabitants, a high proportion of whom had been occupied with the affairs of the lands formerly subject to the Habsburgs. The Hofburg and Schönbrunn were now empty, and became merely tourist attractions.

The government of Vienna remained under Social-Democratic control, but political antagonism between Vienna and the remainder of the truncated country sharpened. Both sides built up their para-military formations, the Viennese their Schutzbund, and their opponents in the countryside their Heimwehr, which was favoured, if not openly, by the central government under Chancellor Dollfuss. The crisis came in the early weeks of 1934, when the Heimwehr began its offensive against the Socialists in the Tyrol. Armed conflict very soon broke out in Vienna and the guns of the Heimwehr began to shell the great workers' tenements which they considered central bastions of Schutzbund resistance. Before the fighting was over and Socialist resistance destroyed, the Karl Marx Hof, the greatest of the tenement blocks the government of Vienna had built, lay in ruins.

The next four years were a tense period in Austria, under a dictatorship which came to be known as Clerico-Fascist. Beneath the surface an unremitting struggle went on between the government, the banned Socialists (and the Communists), and the banned Nazis who, supported by the Nazis in Hitler's Germany across the frontier, were growing in strength. The first attempt of the Nazis to gain power occurred at the end of July, only five months after the battles with the Socialists. The main risings were in Styria and Carinthia, but in Vienna the Nazis forced themselves into the Chancellory on the Ballhausplatz and assassinated Dollfuss. The chief reason why the rising petered out was that Hitler did not consider himself strong enough to challenge Mussolini, who had made it quite clear that he would not yet tolerate a Nazi Austria. A new Chancellor and dictator came to the helm in Austria, Dr Kurt von Schuschnigg. In a changing international situation, much complicated by the outbreak of the Spanish Civil War, Hitler's pressure on the country increased and finally reached the point where he felt strong enough to overthrow the Schuschnigg government and invade, in March 1938. The other European powers stood by, for one reason or another unwilling to intervene. From that time Vienna became, in effect, just a provincial capital in the greater German Reich, until the final defeat of the Nazis in 1945.

In the last stages of the Second World War, as the Russian forces advanced from Hungary in the east while the British and Americans were still held down in Italy, Vienna suffered severe damage from bombardment from the air and shelling from the Russian batteries coming up over the Prater: the Opera House, the Stefansdom, the Burgtheater and the Belvedere were all hit, and much random damage was also done across the city. This has all now been repaired, and the Opera House festively re-opened in a city that is once more the capital of an independent republic, whose neutrality has been guaranteed by the Four Powers who occupied it after the Armistice.

JOHN LEHMANN
1986

The traveller who visits Vienna today might expect the city, like so many in the German-speaking world, to offer only hints of its past. Berlin and Munich embrace the twentieth century with unusual vigour. In Vienna, the Habsburgs were sacrificed to Socialism nearly eighty years ago, and the metropolis which governed twenty nations is now a backwater, whose provincialism the unhappy addition of four international organizations and 25,000 diplomats has done little to dispel.

At first glance, however, the traveller is in for a pleasant surprise. If he walks across the Heldenplatz under the shadow of Semper's vast palace, continues along the Kohlmarkt and loses himself in the back streets around the Judenplatz, he will find a city very little changed from that which Gustav Mahler, Lord Frederic Hamilton or even Frances Trollope enjoyed. Thanks to an enlightened philosophy of banning cars from the town centre, it is even possible to experience the smells of an earlier world. In few capitals is the pedestrian so relentlessly reminded of the presence of horses. It may be possible to avoid a journey in a horse-drawn *Fiaker* but the rattle of their wheels and pungency of their dung are, on a hot summer's dusty afternoon, impossible to escape.

Such an air of timelessness is quickly reinforced. Step into a café and a seductive lethargy grips the soul. Regardless of the weather – dry and hot or ice-cold with a biting wind – the Viennese pile into the cafés at all hours of the day. Old habits die hard here. The difficulty experienced in leaving may be due as much to the waiter's incapacity to notice a frantic gesture demanding the bill as it is to that most Viennese of weaknesses, laziness. If the Parisian, the Florentine and the Londoner are increasingly difficult to encounter on their home ground, the Viennese, with all the vices-cum-virtues attributed to him in the following pages, is an irrepressible feature of the cafés.

The lack of purpose which afflicts so many Viennese is partly nurtured by the insidious comforts of the coffee-houses. Such institutions thrive on submissive melancholy minds, for whom there is always time to brood. As such, the coffee-house expresses the mentality of the Viennese perfectly, and the passion for inertia which afflicts both shows little sign of abating as the city approaches the twenty-first century.

The youth of the city, far from embracing the challenges of independence, prefer to worry, like their grandfathers, about pensions, titles and affairs of the heart. Talk of taking a profession seriously is met with disbelief. Rebellious punks, a virtually extinct species in the city, are treated with a horror normally reserved for the more gruesome inhabitants of the local zoo's reptile-house. Anyone who promotes change risks ostracism. Many factors, meteorological as well as psychological, have combined to produce such intense paralysis.

Acting against this listlessness before 1938, when the Nazis annexed the country, was a population of some 200,000 Jews. It is fair to say that most of Austria's achievements in the arts before the Second World War were their work. Since their squalid end, Vienna has failed to recover even a fraction of its former cultural prestige or intellectual vitality.

This event, combined with the cutting-off of the city's eastern frontiers after the First World War, has created a vacuum which cannot fail to impress the discerning traveller. If he has arrived from Salzburg, he will see immediately in the expressions and faces around the Westbahnhof a completely different type of *Homo Austriacus* to that inhabiting the Alps. Somewhere on the rail journey, perhaps near the baroque Abbey of Melk, a cultural frontier has been imperceptibly crossed and he is no longer in Western Europe. The Viennese have very little in common with the Tyroleans. Speech and history are different, and the Tyrol's heroic struggles for independence are far removed from Vienna's general aquiescence in whichever form of despotism was going.

'Vienna has never been ruled, only administered,' one Austrian politician quipped earlier this century. Years of oppression, however mild, are not exorcized in a few decades of democracy. In this Vienna, though a 'free' neutral capital since 1955, has much more in common with the capitals of Eastern Europe than it has with those of the West. It lies only a couple of hours' drive west of Budapest and considerably further east than Prague. In this way, Central Europe preserves an age-old unity and Vienna remains cloaked in its past. Cushioned by consensus politics, the city now sleeps, impervious to the West and the East.

If the excitement and drama which John Lehmann experienced during his days in Vienna have gone, much else of the past remains. The vast imperial bureaucracy has survived not only the dissolution of empire but the technological revolution of the twentieth century. The bureaucrats' baroque gestures, flattering obsequiousness and obsessive fear of responsibility can be seen in any Gasthaus near the Herrengasse palaces whose once-princely rooms now house office after office of Byzantine bureaucracy. These splendid buildings have remained surprisingly impervious to change, though their rooms now resound to rubber stamps rather than noble quadrilles.

Not that the Austrian aristocracy, humbled and enfeebled by catastrophe and Socialism, is on the defensive. The use of titles may be banned and incomes pitiful, but there are still probably more titles in Vienna than in any other city in the world. The Austrian aristocrat's silly chatter can be heard in almost any fashionable bar, for to be decorative rather than useful remains his motto.

The majority of Viennese fall into neither of these categories. Nonetheless they display traits of both, and like the architecture of the city, either garishly over-restored or sadly neglected, they seem a far from happy crowd. Vienna, however, would not be what it is without their singular bad temper enlivened occasionally by a professional charm. Along with the Vienna skyline, still dominated by the Gothic cathedral of St Stephen, it has survived the passage of time untouched.

RICHARD BASSETT

1987

The Emperors

1282	Rudolf Habsburg acquires Duchy of Austria
1440–1493	Friedrich III (first Habsburg to be crowned Holy Roman Emperor
1493–1519	Maximilian I (resident at Innsbruck)
(1519–1556)	(Charles V of Spain)
1521–1564	Ferdinand I (first Habsburg to live in the Hofburg)
1564–1576	Maximilian II
1576–1612	Rudolf II
1611–1619	Matthias
1619–1637	Ferdinand II
1637–1657	Ferdinand III
1658–1709	Leopold I
1705–1711	Josef I
1711–1740	Charles VI
1740–1780	Maria Theresa
1780–1790	Josef II
1790–1792	Leopold II
1792–1835	Franz I
1835–1848	Ferdinand I (of Austria)
1848–1916	Franz-Josef
1916–1918	Charles I

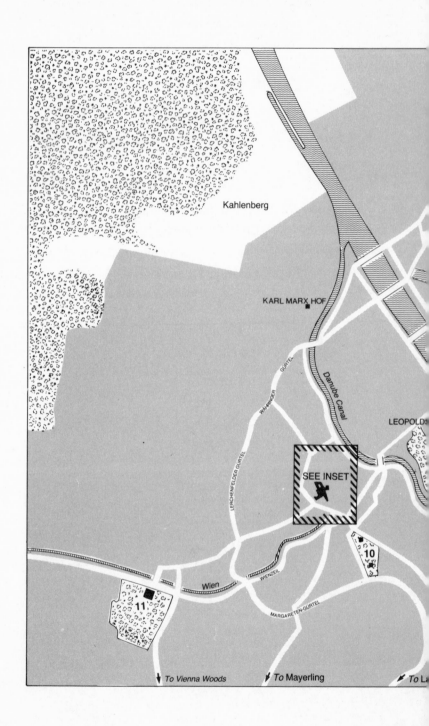

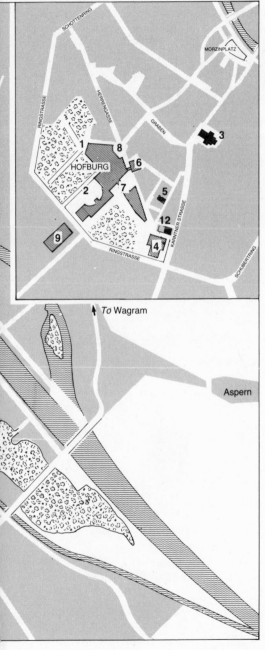

Map of the city, locating the places described

1 Ballhausplatz
2 Heldenplatz
3 Stefansdom
4 Opera House
5 Kapuzinerkirche
6 Riding School
7 Imperial Library
8 Michaelerplatz
9 Kunsthistorischesmuseum
10 Belvedere and park
11 Schönbrunn Palace
12 Hotel Sacher

The Inner City

[1] *In Austria there stands a town brightly bedecked with pretty blue flowerets; its walls are of marble; there is a green forest round it and a green forest in the midst of it, where a nightingale sings of our love.*

Medieval folksong

[2] Antonio Bonfini, official historian to Matthias Corvin, King of Hungary, is impressed by Vienna's grand houses in 1485; from Marcel Brion's *Daily Life in the Vienna of Mozart and Schubert.*

The city proper seems like a royal palace amidst the surrounding suburbs; and yet several of these vie with it for beauty and grandeur. Entering the city you might fancy yourself walking amongst the buildings of a huge royal castle, so perfect is the disposition of all the houses. Everything delights the eye of the observer; each house seems to stand more proudly thàn its neighbours. You have to pause constantly to enjoy so many beauties. The houses of the great, in particular, look like palaces. Almost every house has, in addition to its front portion, a rear building with vast peristyles covered or uncovered, offering protection from the cold winds that blow from the surrounding heights. The dining-rooms are often splendidly panelled with pine and heated with great stoves. The windows are all glazed; some of them are beautifully painted and protected with an iron trellis. The houses have bathrooms and kitchen offices, and bedrooms which can be rented. All of them are provided with cellars to store wine and provisions. The luxury of the windows and mirrors is almost equal to the splendour of olden days. So many birds sing in their cages that you fancy you are walking through a sylvan glade.

[3] An Elizabethan Englishman visits Vienna in 1593; from *An Itinerary ... by Fynes Moryson.*

(Fynes Moryson (1566–1630) was a Fellow of Peterhouse, Cambridge, and an indefatigable and extensive traveller in Europe and in the Levant. His famous *Itinerary*, covering twelve countries, and written originally in Latin, was published in English in 1617.)

After dinner we rode two miles and a halfe, through a very large plaine, fruitful of corne and pasture, with many pleasant woods, and compassed round about with mountaines, and came to Vienna, vulgarly called Wien. Neere the City on the North side the river Danow runneth by, from the East to the West, three armes whereof close together (with some ground betweene, which many times is overflowed) wee passed by three bridges, whereof one hath twenty nine arches, the other fifty seven, and the third fifteene, each of those arches being some eighteene walking paces long. Betweene the second bridge, and the third next to the City, is a pleasant grove. Wien the metropolitan City of Austria, is a famous Fort against the Turkes, upon the confines of Austria, which if they should once gaine, their horse-men might suddenly spoile the open Countries of Bohemia, and Moravia, and good part of Silesia. The Citie is of a round forme, and upon the North side there is an ascent to it upon a hil, otherwise without the wals on all sides the ground is plaine, except the West side, where mountaines lie a good distance from the City, and upon that side the Sultan of the Turkes incamped, upon the hils neere the gallowes, when in the time of the Emperour Rodolphus, hee besieged the City, or rather came to view it, with purpose to besiege it the next summer. The streets are narrow, but the building is stately, of free stone. Two Towers of the Church are curiously ingraven, the like whereof is not in Germany, except the Tower or steeple of Strasburg. The common report is, that two chiefe workemen had great emulation in building them; and that one having finished his Tower, found meanes to breake the necke of the other, lest his workemanship should excel that he had done. One of the Towers some three yeeres past, was shaken with an earth-quake, and indeed the houses of this City are many times shaken therewith, and they have a Prophecy of old, that this City shall be destroied with an earth-quake.

[4] Lady Mary Wortley Montagu finds Vienna's Inner City cramped and crowded in 1716; from her *Letters*.

(Lady Mary Wortley Montagu (1689–1762) was the daughter of the Marquis of Dorchester and wife of Edward Wortley Montagu, MP for Huntingdon, who was appointed Ambassador to Sultan Ahmed III in 1716; and it was while journeying there that they spent six months in Vienna. Intelligent and witty, she was a leader in London society, an accomplished poet, satirist and bluestocking. Her *Letters* first appeared in 1763.)

This town, which has the honour of being the emperor's residence, did not at all answer my ideas of it, being much less than I expected to find it; the streets are very close, and so narrow, one cannot observe the fine fronts of the palaces, though many of them very well deserve observation, being truly magnificent, all built of fine white stone, and excessive high, the town being so much too little for the number of people that desire to live in it, the builders seem to have projected to repair that misfortune, by clapping one town on the top of another, most of the houses being of five, and some of them of six stories. You may easily imagine, that the streets being so narrow, the upper rooms are extremely dark; and, what is an inconveniency much more intolerable, in my opinion, there is no house that has so few as five or six families in it. The apartments of the greatest ladies, and even of the ministers of state, are divided, but by a partition from that of a tailor or a shoemaker; and I know nobody that has above two floors in any house, one for their own use, and one higher for their servants. Those that have houses of their own, let out the rest of them to whoever will take them; thus the great stairs (which are all of stone) are as common and dirty as the street. 'Tis true, when you have once travelled through them, nothing can be more surprisingly magnificent than the apartments. They are commonly a *suite* of eight or ten large rooms, all inlaid, the doors and windows richly carved and gilt, and the furniture such as is seldom seen in the palaces of sovereign princes in other countries – the hangings the finest tapestry of Brussels, prodigious large looking-glasses in silver frames, fine japan tables, beds, chairs, canopies, and window curtains of the richest Genoa damask or velvet, almost covered with gold lace or embroidery. The whole made gay by pictures, and vast jars of japan china, and almost in every room large lustres of rock crystal.

[5] An eighteenth-century Englishman finds much to approve of; from *Travels in the year 1792* . . . by William Hunter.

(William Hunter, described on his title page as being 'of the Inner Temple', was probably a lawyer. His book was published in two volumes in 1798, and consisted of 'a series of familiar letters to a Lady in England'.)

Vienna, July 19, 1792.

Compared with London, Paris, and Constantinople, Vienna is not a large city; yet it is as large as, perhaps, in sound policy, any city should be. An overgrown metropolis is always a disadvantage to a country, in every point of view. It drains it of its wealth, its provisions, and its population; and is the source of dissipation, corruption, and crimes.

Vienna is agreeably situated, standing on a fruitful plain, which is watered by the Danube and several smaller rivers. It is the capital of the German dominions, and the usual residence of the emperor [*Leopold II*], who keeps a splendid court. At present he is at Frankfort, where his coronation is shortly to take place. Within the walls, which are not quite three miles in circumference, it is very confined. The houses, which are chiefly plastered and white-washed, are well built, and the streets, though narrow, are regular and well paved. At night they are lighted and watched, and passengers may walk out at all hours with the greatest security. Three of the squares are decorated with handsome monuments, which have been raised, on different occasions, at a great expence, to be erected. This regulation was enacted on account of the fortifications, which are considered as of the utmost importance, and which, indeed, have enabled the inhabitants to sustain several vigorous sieges.

Vienna has a gay and busy appearance. The streets are crowded with people, who flock in from the suburbs; and such is the concourse of strangers, that you frequently have an opportunity of seeing the habits and manners of almost every nation in Europe congregated on the same spot. Provisions are plentiful and cheap, but lodgings are expensive. The houses, in fact, are not sufficient for the inhabitants, and a different family occupies every floor.

Including the suburbs, the population of Vienna is computed to amount to two hundred and ten thousand souls. It is not ornamented with many splendid public edifices, nor are the houses of individuals distinguished, in their outward appearance, for any thing but their neatness. The churches, though numerous, are by no means remarkable for elegance of architecture, or richness of decoration. Those which are most admired are the cathedral of St Stephen, and the church of St Charles.

[6]   The perilous streets of the Inner City; from *Travels from Vienna . . . in the year 1814* by Richard Bright.

(Richard Bright (1789–1858) was a physician educated in Edinburgh and London, who wrote many medical books and became Physician Extraordinary to Queen Victoria. He had a great love of travel and on a journey through Europe he spent the winter of 1814–15 in Vienna, where the old Vienna School of Medicine was in high repute. But the Congress of Vienna then sitting engaged most of his attention.)

My apartment was large and desolate, without a carpet but provided with an earthen stove in one corner, and a little wooden bedstead in another. Such are the miserable accommodations in most of the inns at Vienna. . . .

After some time I walked into the streets, – a service of danger; for most of them are narrow, and the sides, which are paved with flat stones for the convenience of walking, and are, on that account, greatly praised throughout the whole empire, are so little elevated above the carriage tract, that the foot passenger has no safety but in the judgment of the charioteer, who frequently risks an encounter with your feet, rather than with the wheels of a passing carriage. The coachmen, however, give some warning of their approach by a species of unintelligible roar, a little in accent like the language in which a Lancashire carter converses with his team; but not less peremptory than the rapid 'by your leave' of a Bath chairman. When, by courage or good luck, I could snatch an opportunity to cast a look upwards, I observed that many of the houses were large, and handsomely built, and all of them very high; but, owing to the narrowness of the streets, there is a prevailing gloom, and it is only in a few of the more open parts that the real beauty of the buildings can develope itself. The shops display a considerable variety of goods, though frequently a square glazed case of patterns hanging at the door is the only mark by which the nature of the shopkeeper's dealings is indicated. Besides this, a small board, projecting into the street from above each door, bears some painted sign, as the Golden Fleece, the Sceptre, the Schwartzenburg Head, or the Holy Ghost.

[7] Bright admires the Canova monument in the Augustinerkirche – still to be seen there, and the finest neo-classical sculpture in Austria; from *Travels from Vienna . . . in the year 1814* by Richard Bright.

To turn, however, to what may be deemed the highest sphere in which the labours of the artist can be directed, and to an example of the perfection which it has again reached, let us contemplate one of the noblest works of Canova, the modern, the still living Phidias.

On entering the *Augustiner Kirk*, a monument, erected by Duke Albert of Saxe-Teschen to the memory of his wife, at once rivets the attention. Towards the summit of a pyramid of grey marble, an ascending angel bears on a medallion the image of the departed; beneath, the door-way of the seppulchre lies open. The lion, which should have guarded its entrance, sleeps; and the protecting genius of the disconsolate husband, wearied with watching, has rested his head upon the lion's mane, and resigned himself to melancholy. Virtue, bearing the ashes of her friend, trusting her melancholy, measured steps to the guidance of Innocence and spotless Purity, enters the unguarded vault; while Charity, supporting an aged mourner and directing with mild control the footsteps of an orphan, follows the companion of her grief towards the mausoleum of their common votary. Composed and tranquil sorrow has spread its softest influence on this mournful procession. The features are distorted by no passions; the eyes drop no tears, but the unmoistened dust, embalmed by the sweet incense of affection, will rest within the tomb, and give a sad reality to those pangs which the sculptured marble would itself have claimed.

After speaking of this sublime monument, to describe the statuary of inferior workmanship with which the open places or the fountains of Vienna are ornamented; to mention the works of Matthieli, of Donner, or of Strudel, – would be placing merit in the shade, and soliciting comparisons, which must prove injurious to the reputation these excellent artists have obtained, at a time when they are no longer able to contend for the meed of victory.

[8] The Herrengasse in the mid-nineteenth century; from *Austria . . .* by J.G. Kohl.

(Johann Georg Kohl (1808–1878) was a German scholar who became a tutor, but was obsessed by travel from his childhood. He published his first book in 1833 but it was after he had returned to Germany from St Petersburg in 1838 that he discovered his true vocation as a travel writer: 'Veni, vidi, scripsi' became his motto about a host of countries. The Golden Fleece which he mentions was the highest order of chivalry the Habsburg Court bestowed.)

The most animated parts of Vienna lie round Stephen's Place, the Graben, and the High Market; the quietest parts are the 'Burg' from the Place of the Minorities, the Herrengasse, Teinfalt Street, the back and front Schenkengasse, &c. 'Our great people live here,' said a Vienna man to me, 'and here it is still, still as a mouse.' There is not a shop in the whole neighbourhood, no busy hum of traffic. It rains jolts and thrusts in the other streets, and one is put to it to keep from under the coach-wheels and horses' hoofs. It swarms there with Croats, Slavonians, Servians, Germans, and God knows what nation besides, while nothing is to be seen in the aristocratic quarter but silent palaces, before whose doors liveried laqueys are lounging as if they were masters not only of the houses but of the whole street. In this silent quarter – the Tein quarter – are the palaces of the Lichtensteins, Stahrembergs, Harrachs, Festetics, Colloredos, Esterhazys, Trautmansdorfs, and Schönborns. Antique escutcheons are displayed before the houses, dating from

Rudolph of Hapsburg or Charlemagne, and the golden fleece
gleams from the roofs. If the little sons of these grandees clamber
over the roofs like the boys in other towns, they may gather all
manner of aristocratic reminiscences among the chimney-pots.
Here also stand the proud edifices of the Hungarian and
Transylvanian Chanceries, the States House, the Court and
State Chancery, the Bank, and several of the superior tribunals.
The whole space occupied by buildings so important to the
empire is not more than two hundred fathoms in length and
breadth; there is more than one public square of that size in St
Petersburg, and it may be safely asserted that in no other
European kingdom is the great nobility so narrowly lodged.
There are, nevertheless, buildings here stately enough, if duly
scattered, to adorn a whole capital.

[9] Childhood memories, from the turn of the century, of
Viennese baroque; from *Vienna, legend and reality* by Ilse
Barea.

(The late Mrs Barea, like many Viennese ladies, grew up in
Vienna before the events of 1938 caused her to flee to more
northern climes.)

Still later, when I went to school, I had to go through dark
narrow streets with old *Bürgerhäuser* whose window architraves
were frowning at me, and palaces whose grey fronts were heavily
scored with ornamental bands. I seem never to have looked at
any newer house, though this is a trick of memory. It was then I
began to dislike the male caryatids, supporting their balconies
with so much effort. In terms of my priggish school lore I
wondered why these old princes and counts had preferred them
to the harmonious female caryatids – the newer Pallavicini
Palace had them, in an insipid version of Greek models – who
carried their burden proudly and effortlessly. And I began to
love the stern front of the Hofburg's library wing on the
Josefsplatz; this was, I thought, true dignity and gracious beauty
in stone, unmarred by distortion. Every day I timed the last
minutes of my walk to school by the milky-white or dapple-grey
stallions of the Spanish Riding School which their grooms led
through the archway at a quarter to eight. There was dignity

and gracious beauty in living flesh. The horses figured in many of my daydreams, and even then I had the feeling that they belonged inseparably to those palace fronts.

All this was my Vienna when I was eleven years old. It fascinated me. It had an excessive influence on my taste. When the architect Adolf Loos built the first functional business and apartment house without any ornament, architrave or window frame, the 'house without eyebrows', I was as childishly incensed as any grown-up philistine that he dared put it next to the Hofburg and the old Michaelerhaus. What specially annoyed me was the idea that it had no moulding or scroll in which the snow could settle in the gentle lines I loved. But it also stirred me to thought by the tremendous implied contrast. It is my belief that in many similar and different ways the visual image of baroque Vienna has been absorbed by generation after generation of adolescent Viennese of the middle classes.

[10] Trouble in the Inner City streets in 1939; from *A Young Man Looks at Europe* by Robert Young.

(Robert Young was one of many young Englishmen who were fascinated before the war by the coming crisis in Central Europe. As the Nazis grew more powerful in Austria before Hitler annexed the country in 1938, the unrest described here became more widespread. When the Führer finally reached Vienna, scenes occurred which few who were present have ever forgotten.)

On Thursday afternoon we walked through the inner city. The Chancellery was perhaps the quietest place in all Vienna; it was significant, however, that the guards were doubled. The Volksgarten was so crowded with girls in their holiday clothes that it was almost impossible to move about. The British Consulate in the Wallnerstrasse was as staid and imperial as ever: outside the entrance two English business men were discussing a deal in Austrian timber, which would take place in the next three weeks. In was only when we returned to the Kärntnerstrasse and saw the Nazis parading on the pavement and the crowds gathering round the German travel bureau that we began to fear for the success of the plebiscite. The Nazis were more menacing than ever, the travel bureau was almost impassable: you had to step into the street in the path of motorcars if you wanted to avoid the crowd staring at the portrait of Hitler behind the plate-glass window in the travel bureau.

The travel bureau stands on the ground floor of the Bristol Hotel, in the heart of Vienna. For five years, ever since they assumed power, the Nazis made it the centre of their attacks against the Austrian constitution, while the Austrians made no move to counter the invasion which came from the heart of the city. All day long motor-cars from Germany came to a pause outside its doors and crates of propaganda were unloaded, only to be sent out later to Steiermark, Nieder-Osterreich and the Burgenland. The waiting-room of the Westbahnhof and the travel bureau in the Kärntnerstrasse were the spear-heads of the German advance: as though they intentionally reversed all previous revolutionary tactics, and contented themselves with a shop-window and the draughty annexe of a railway station rather than occupy by force the post-offices, the electricity works and the armament factories.

There was little to see during the early part of the afternoon. Vienna was outwardly unchanged. There was no excitement. Towards six o'clock we returned to the Kärntnerstrasse. As usual the Nazis were walking on the pavement, pushing into people, loudly greeting one another with the Nazi salute and a totally unnecessary 'Heil Hitler!' They made immense efforts to assume an expression which suggested that they had never seen the Nazis they met before. They stood on the edge of the pavement and talked loudly about the benefits of an Anschluss. When they reached the Stefansplatz, they turned back and greeted each other again – a process which would have been ridiculous, if there were not sixty million disciplined Germans behind them, who treated them as heroes. . . .

At six o'clock there was a clash. The Nazis were in no mood for gloves. Presumably they had received orders that the fight must be fought to a finish: it was not enough to exchange smiles and greetings in the streets. Boys of the Fatherland Front came from the direction of the Opern-Ring. Shouts of 'Heil Hitler' were drowned by shouts of 'Osterreich.' It was impossible to see what was happening. Near the German travel bureau fists were being raised, batons were crashing down, heads were bleeding and people were rolling on the ground. A girl in a torn frock flung herself away from the crowd, tripped and fell sprawling. Six or seven people walked over her. Ambulances arrived, and all the time the loud-speakers opposite the Opera were blaring Viennese waltzes.

The Hofburg

[11] The Hofburg as it looked in the time of Leopold I, *c.*1650; from *The Siege of Vienna* by John Stoye.

(The Emperor Leopold I (1685–1705) personified the spirit of the Counter Reformation in Austria. With the raising of the Siege of Vienna in 1683, the Turks were rolled out of Central Europe not only by feats of arms but also by a tide of baroque which has left its mark on the architecture of Central Europe in general and Vienna in particular.)

The scene of a Habsburg ruler's daily life in Vienna had altered comparatively little in the last fifty years. His palace, the Hofburg, occupied a large area within the wall and ramparts of the southern side of the city. If Leopold stepped out of the main doorway he saw the courtyard so beautifully depicted by a Dutch painter in 1652. Opposite was the 'new' Burg (which is almost unchanged to this day), with a massive front and a steep roof, surmounted by a cupola with a broad clock-face. To his left ran a more modern range of apartments, the so-called Leopold Wing. On his right some of the principal government offices were housed, including the Imperial Chancery and the Treasury, and probably the Emperor's library. These buildings had been extensively remodelled between 1560 and 1570; they were then barely touched until the eighteenth century.

The Burg itself enclosed a more ancient quadrangle. Over three of the four corners, towers of an antiquated style still remained, but the other had fallen down without being replaced. Near the south-east angle stood the medieval chapel, the Hofkapelle, recently redecorated by Leopold's father Ferdinand III. Probably under the south-western tower was the large hall where the Emperor, in his capacity of Archduke of Lower Austria, had received the allegiance of the Lower Austrian Estates at the beginning of his reign. The dowager Empress Eleanor lived for some time in rooms on the north front, and when she looked out of her windows she could see a formal garden of fair size which was flanked on the left by a bowling alley and a bath-house, and on the right by a ballroom. At the end of the garden ran the palace wall, and behind this stood (and stands) another building, of great importance to the court, the Stallburg or stables.

East of the Burg was an open space where horses and horsemen exercised, with a covered riding-school at one end which adjoined the main wall of the city. The view eastwards was closed by the church and library of an Augustinian foundation which the Habsburg family had patronised for many centuries. A gallery connected the convent and the palace, making it a simple matter for Leopold to go to listen to the famous preacher Abraham a Sancta Clara (a member of the order), who spared neither the humble nor the proud in hitting at the sins of the world with his redoubtable vernacular eloquence.

Such was the general aspect of the Emperor's domain in Vienna. It looked unimpressive to Italian or French visitors because money, and perhaps also the desire, for spectacular architectural expansion had been lacking here in the earlier part of the century, although the court grew bigger and needed more room. The one major improvement of recent years was certainly the Leopold Wing, (the Trakt), designed to join the older to the 'new' Burg by a building which ran immediately behind the ramparts along the line of the city wall. That part of the original palace which the Trakt now extended was also refaced, and as a result the whole south frontage of the Hofburg for the first time looked reasonably imposing. This was the target offered to the Turkish gunners in 1683, long rows of windows and a vast expanse of high-pitched roof. Leopold also put up a new theatre, a timber structure, on the rampart behind the riding-school; in 1681 he began to build a new school, planning to house his books in its upper story. This school, but no new library, was completed in the lifetime of Leopold – the greatest bibliophile among European rulers in the seventeenth century. In due course, Maria Theresa's 'Redoutensaal' and Charles VI's glorious Hofbibliothek together replaced it.

[12] Panic in the Hofburg as the Turks surround Vienna in July 1683; from *The Siege of Vienna* by John Stoye.

(Few events concentrated the attention of Christian civilization more in the late seventeenth century than the growing menace of the Turks. When in 1683, their armies laid siege to Vienna, Catholic Europe watched with bated breath. Had Vienna fallen, it is difficult to imagine that the Infidel would have not pressed further into the heart of Europe.)

'The Turk is at the gates!' was the cry; and though *we* know that each report of the day's fighting had been inaccurate, the worst fears of most people then were confirmed by the cumulative effect of so many messages and rumours. All who could prepared to quit the city immediately. The Emperor, his nerves overbearing his sense of dignity, listening to the pleas of his ministers and family, decided to sanction his own retreat from what looked like the point of maximum danger, Vienna itself.

He held a final conference at six o'clock in his private apartment. The decision to go at once was formally announced and it remained to choose the route to follow. The direct road to Linz over the Wiener Wald was proposed and rejected; the Turks would threaten it too quickly. Flight northwards to Prague, or south-west into the hilly country by Heiligenkreuz and so around to Linz, was considered. The counsellors at length advised the Emperor to cross the Danube, and then to move upstream along the farther bank towards Upper Austria.

The bustle and confusion in the Burg and the Burgplatz were by this time tremendous. The doors of the palace were left wide open, and every kind of wagon and cart or coach was being crammed with every kind of necessity and valuable which could be moved. The less fortunate, who owned or who could find no horses, made ready to walk. In the town the government tried to get each householder to send a man to work on the fortifications. It tried to requisition all the boats on the river, with their boatmen, and to send them down the Danube in order to meet the infantry regiments marching westwards from the Schütt. The conscripted labourers who had been working in Vienna downed their tools, and fled. Coming the other way, population from the outskirts packed into the city as never before, if only to pass the night in the security of the streets. Then, at about eight o'clock in the evening the Emperor left the Hofburg. A not very orderly procession made its way out of the Burggate, round the city wall to the Canal, through Leopoldstadt, and over the Danube.

[13] A meeting in 1665 between 'the hated Emperor', Leopold I, and the Turkish Pasha, Kared Mehmed; from *In the Empire of the Golden Apple* by Evliya Celebi. Translated by Richard Bassett.

(Evliya Celebi (1611–1684), a trusted adviser of the Sultan Mehmet IV, was also a brilliant Koran reciter, calligraphist, musician, Arabist, and story-teller. He travelled widely, and in 1665 came to Vienna as part of a delegation to the Emperor. Though officially attendant on the Pasha Kared Mehmed, it is clear that part of his role was to make detailed notes of Vienna's famous fortifications in preparation for the future siege of 1683.)

The meeting between the Pasha and the Emperor Leopold I was not without protocol problems. The Pasha insisted that a band of bashi-bazouks strike up as he entered the throne room and was only dissuaded by the Court Chamberlain explaining forcefully that it 'is not the custom for a band to strike up when His Imperial Majesty greets a foreign envoy'.

Through eight saloons we walked before reaching the vast throne room. As we entered, however, I was sent by my master to go and see if the Emperor would stand up to greet him. Indeed the Emperor did rise and when I told the Pasha this, he began slow steps until with the Emperor advancing ten steps, they met in the middle of the saloon.

The Pasha greeted the Emperor who took his jewelled hat from his head and acknowledged my master's greeting. Upon this, the Pasha kissed the Emperor on his breast.

Though the Emperor was King of Hungary as a young man, I doubt if the Lord God really ever created a man less endowed with Allah's gifts; he has a bottle-shaped head pointed at the top like the glove of a dervish; thick black eyebrows which are too far apart. His ears are like *Kinderkartoffeln* [very small potatoes] and he has a red nose like an unripe berry and which is the size of an aubergine from Morea.

In his broad nostrils into which three fingers could be stuck with ease, there hangs hair like a beard. His lips are like a camel, and when he talks the spit flows from his mouth. When this happens, though, dazzlingly beautiful pages rush to him with red handkerchiefs. He himself is always combing his hair and plays all the time with his comb. His fingers resemble cucumbers.

Emperor Leopold I, by an unknown artist, 1700

It is the way of Allah to make many emperors of this race like this.

[14] The Prince de Ligne, soldier, diplomat and trusted confidant of the Empress Maria Theresa, reflects on her death in the Hofburg in 1781, in a letter to Miss Caroline Murray; from *Memoirs of the Prince de Ligne*. Translated by Richard Bassett.

The most poignant epitaph for the late Empress, I heard emerging from the Hofburg, uttered by one of the Hungarian grenadiers who stood guard there. When he saw me weeping as I left her rooms in the Hofburg, he addressed me in Latin with the simple words: 'Is my King really dead?' As he said these words, he could himself barely restrain his own tears. One could see from this that though Maria Theresa was only ill for eight days, her death was two-fold.

She died first as a good Christian and then second as a great leader. For this latter role she had to thank the generals, officers and soldiers who served the State and her so loyally. She loved her army passionately.

Someone reminded me a few days ago that I had somewhere written or said that amazement preceded Maria Theresa while it followed Catherine of Russia. That is quite possible; one conquered hearts, the other won them.

The Empress possessed a lavish spirit which was both calm and impish. When she could escape the surveillance of the Emperor Josef, she would shower her troops with a generous handful of ducats. In one training camp which she inspected on a trip to her son, she allowed the soldiers to drink, sing and dance so that when they came to battle they would cry: 'Vivat, vivat regina!'

[15] Emperor Josef II, his appearance and habits; from *Memoirs of the Courts of Berlin, Dresden, Warsaw, and Vienna in the years 1777, 1778 and 1779* by N. William Wraxall.

(Nathaniel William Wraxall (1751–1831) started his career in the civil service of the East India Company, and travelled widely

in Europe on his return from India in 1772. He was elected MP
for Hindon, Wiltshire in 1780; and was a memoirist, historian
and pamphleteer.

The Emperor Josef II, Maria Theresa's gifted son, ruled
only for ten years (1780–1790) but during that time he initiated a
number of reforms which laid the basis for the Habsburgs' vast
bureaucracy which administered some twenty nations until
1918.)

Joseph the Second is rather above than below the middle size,
and in no degree inclined to corpulency. Though not handsome,
he may be accounted agreeable in his person, and when young,
he must have been elegant. Those persons who saw him on the
day of his nuptials with the Princess of Parma, assert that they
never beheld a finer youth. He was magnificently habited in the
old Spanish dress, which was calculated to add to the natural
advantages of his figure. The Countess of Pergen, who was a
spectatress of his coronation at Francfort in 1764, has declared to
me, that he appeared to her the most majestic and striking object
on which she ever looked, when he was invested with the royal
robes and Insignia; his thick hair falling down over his back in
ringlets. He had then a head of hair, such as is ascribed to Apollo
by the Poets. So bald is he now become at thirty-eight, that on
the crown of his head, scarcely any covering remains; and in
order to conceal the defect, he wears a false toupee. His queue is
very thin, but it is his own, and not an artificial one, like that of
the Great Frederic.

The Emperor's countenance is full of meaning and intelligence. I have rarely seen a more speaking physiognomy; and it is
impossible to look at him, without conceiving a favourable idea
of his understanding. His eye, which is quick, sparkles with
animation. The contour of his face is long and thin, his
complexion fair, his nose aquiline, his teeth white, even, and
good. An air of mind, spread over his features, pleases and
prejudices in his favor. The formation of his body and legs is by
no means without defect, though he is capable of severe exercise,
and of sustaining great fatigue. Nor can his state of health be
accounted such, as to afford a reasonable prospect of attaining to
very advanced age. Besides the anurism in his leg, which I have
formerly mentioned, he has another extraordinary source of
disease; it is an excrescence, of the nature of a wen, on the crown

Emperor Josef II, depicted as a Colonel of his light cavalry
regiment, with Vienna in the background, by Georg Weikert

of his head, which naturally increases in size, and may become
dangerous in process of time. Conscious of the hazard that he
must incur, if it should grow large or suppurate; he has already
consulted Brambilla his surgeon, on the subject, who means to
extract it with the knife. It is probable that the operation will not
be long delayed.

No Prince can be more indifferent than the Emperor, with

regard to all the delicacies, indulgences, and luxuries of life. Few Sovereigns devote so much time to business, and so little to pleasure or dissipation. It is very rare that he ever makes any person wait, who comes to him by appointment. 'I was accustomed,' says he, 'to pass too many hours in my father's antichamber, not to know from experience how unpleasant such a detention must be to others.' Francis by no means observed the same punctuality in giving audience. Joseph rises early, and takes for breakfast either coffee and milk, or chocolate, with which he mixes water, seldom eating any thing at that time. In order to dispatch business with more facility, he generally dines alone; his dinner being dressed in the great kitchen of the palace, for he has no private kitchen. His meal, except on meagre days, or in Lent, consists of five dishes; a soup, Bouillé, vegetables, a Fricassee, and a Roti. These are brought to his apartment in five deep dishes, placed one upon the other, as the 'Traiteurs' are used to do; and when ready, they are laid on the stove which heats the room, in order to keep them warm. The nominal hour for his dinner is two o'clock, but frequently he is so occupied, that he does not sit down till five; and he then swallows it half cold, with only a single servant to attend on him. Though he eats heartily, it is without any degree of delicacy, or selection; and he is so indifferent about every thing relating to the table, that he scarcely distinguishes game from poultry. Wine he rarely touches; and when he does, only in very small quantity. . . .

By the demise of the late Emperor [*Franz Stephen*], he succeeded, without farther form of election, to the Imperial dignity; and he was at the same time constituted by Maria Theresa, co-regent of all the hereditary dominions of the House of Austria . . . Perhaps there are moments, when the Empress Queen may regret that she has delegated any portion of her power to her son. Unquestionably they have differed in sentiment, on more than one important measure . . .

During the late Emperor's life, the number of Birth-days and Gala-days observed at Court was prodigious, amounting to near forty in a year. All the nobility, ministers, and great officers, civil as well as military, appeared at the drawing-room on those occasions; and the expence necessarily incurred by the splendid suits worn, was frequently productive of serious inconvenience. One of the first acts of Joseph, was totally to abolish both Gala and birth-days. He appointed at the same time, the first of

January, as the anniversary on which all the nobility should kiss the Empress Queen's and his hand, prohibiting any sort of notice to be taken, or any attention to be paid to all other days without exception. He even enforces the most rigid observance of this order; nor does he permit his own immediate servants and attendants to express the least mark of festivity, nor to make the slightest alteration in their ordinary dress, on his own birth-day.

Till the death of Francis in 1765, the old Spanish habit, derived from the time of the Emperor Charles the Fifth, was universally worn at the Court of Vienna, on all days of Gala or ceremony. Francis, who scarcely ever appeared in a uniform, was accustomed to change his dresses very frequently, and affected magnificence of apparel. Joseph has never worn any coat except a uniform, since his father's decease. The Spanish habit, though splendid, connected with it many inconveniencies: among others, prescription had authorized that the Aulic Counsellors never could meet for the dispatch of business, except in that dress. Of course, affairs of importance were frequently postponed, and even sacrificed to an absurd Etiquette. The present Emperor, conscious of the abuse, and of the public detriment that resulted from it, forbade the use of the Spanish dress on any occasion whatever. He commanded the Aulic Counsellors, from that time forward, to assemble in their ordinary dress, and even obliged the members to meet after dinner, as well as in the morning, for the more prompt transaction of affairs.

In external address Joseph the Second is not deficient. His manners are easy, his conversation lively, voluble, and entertaining; running rapidly from one subject to another, and displaying frequently a vast variety of knowledge. Perhaps he manifests too great a consciousness of possessing extensive information; and he may be reproached likewise with frequently anticipating the answers of the persons with whom he converses. A mixture of vanity and of impetuosity conduce to this defect. While he talks, especially if eager, he always plays with the money in his pocket. He writes with ease, perspicuity, and propriety. I have seen many of his notes, evidently composed without premeditation, addressed to persons who enjoyed his confidence, both men and women. They demonstrate feeling, enlargement of mind, and as I have thought, goodness of heart. Yet, I know from indisputable authority, that he is a profound dissembler, rarely or never speaking his real sentiments upon any point of moment. On the other hand, he certainly permits those whom he loves or esteems, to deal fairly with him, to tell him not only plain, but painful truths; and even to reprehend him on occasion with severity. . . .

In his expences and pleasures he is very economical; a quality which has generally, though not universally, distinguished superior Princes, and which must facilitate all his enterprizes or operations, whenever he ascends the throne. Neither women, nor play, nor dissipation drain his purse. I asked a lady who knows him well, whether he was supposed to have any natural children. 'I can't absolutely say,' answered she; 'but, this I can take upon me to assert, that if he has any, they will never be a charge to the State. Cinquante ducats par ann seront tout leur Appenage.' In the month of January last year, a 'Course de traineaux' was exhibited in Vienna, for the amusement of the Archduchess of Milan. A quantity of snow had been brought into the city, on the same morning, in carts, which was scattered over the streets through which the sledges must necessarily pass. The expence might amount to about six hundred florins, or somewhat more than sixty pounds. I was standing in a balcony, to view the spectacle, with two ladies of the Court. 'You have no idea,' said they, 'of the vexation that it will cause the Emperor, to throw away six hundred Florins in snow,' His attention on pecuniary points, extends to the minutest detail, and is imputed to him as a fault; but, it must be allowed that his subjects may derive no little benefit from such parsimony. . . . But, his heart is not one of those, which, like Maria Theresa's, delights in giving; and if it errs, only does so from an excess of liberality and kindness towards the unfortunate. The Emperor well knows that he is regarded as unlike her in this respect.

[16] A visit to the Imperial Library and the Arsenal in the Hofburg in 1792; from *Travels in the year 1792* ... by William Hunter.

(The Hofbibliothek or Imperial Library was designed by Fischer von Erlach and is arguably the finest baroque secular interior in Central Europe. The Arsenal at the corner of the square known as Am Hof is now the headquarters of the Vienna Fire Brigade.)

The palace of the emperor little bespeaks the residence of the first prince in Christendom. It forms two sides of a quadrangle, and is an extensive building; but the walls, which are plastered, are much out of repair, and so abominably dirty, that its appearance is (if possible) more shabby and contemptible than that of our St James's.

There are places, however, belonging to the emperor, which fully compensate for the want of a sumptuous palace; and the magnificence of the imperial library and the arsenal cannot well be surpassed. The great hall of the former is in the form of a cross. The domes and ceiling are adorned with paintings, representing the arts, and are supported by pillars in imitation of variegated marble. Under the centre dome is erected a fine statue, in white marble, of the emperor Charles the VIth, who was the founder of this noble edifice. Seventeen marble statues of the princes of the house of Austria, interspersed with antique busts (among which there is a remarkably fine one of Pyrrhus), are ranged round the hall; and those parts of the walls which are seen, are incrusted with marble. The number of volumes amounts to above three hundred thousand, besides manuscripts, of which there is a large and valuable collection, comprising, among others, the two most ancient copies that exist of Livy and Dioscorides. But the greatest rarity which this library can boast of is the original senatus-consultum, forbidding bacchanals, which passed in the year of Rome 568.

In an adjoining cabinet, amongst other curiosities, we were shewn the three following, viz.

1. A map, on which the Roman world is delineated, and which, though a copy, is the oldest extant. It is drawn on a roll of parchment, not above a foot wide, but of a great length; and the countries are represented in regular succession, without any regard to their relative situations.

2. A volume of Peruvian hieroglyphics, which was seized by the Spaniards, when they first invaded that part of America. The symbols are, I think, more whimsical than those of the Egyptians, and the colours are still very lively; owing, perhaps, to some preservative quality in the substance on which they are laid, which I was assured was human skin.

3. An orrery, which is a most wonderful and ingenious piece of mechanism, constructed according to the Copernican system, and regulated in its movements by clock-work.

In a small passage, at the bottom of the staircase, which leads to the library, there are several ancient sarcophagi. One of them was brought from Ephesus, and is adorned, in front, with a fine bas-relief, which is supposed to represent the battle between Theseus and the Amazons.

The arsenal is a spacious square building, and contains arms for four hundred thousand men. They are arranged with such surprising skill, that the devices, although formed with instruments which were invented to excite terrour and diffuse desolation, only remind us of the mildness and ingenuity of the softer arts. Besides these devices, which are varied almost without end, there are pyramids, pillars, trophies, and fortifications, which are perfectly represented by the ingenious disposal of guns, pistols, spears, swords, and other warlike weapons. Those arms, which do not contribute to the ornamental part, are concealed in cones, which, from their outward dimensions, no one would suspect to be the repositories of such immense stores. We were shewn the armours of Godfrey of Bouillon, and of the emperor Charles Vth, with the sword which he usually wore; the leathern jacket and the hat (both pierced with bullets in many places) which the great Gustavus Adolphus had on, when he was killed at the battle of Lutzen; and the helmet of prince Eugene.

In another room are ostentatiously displayed the trophies that have been gained from the different countries, with which the Germans have waged war. I felt a kind of national pride, when I was told, that they could boast of none wrested from the English.

In the court-yard there are two curious canons of an immense size; two gigantic mortars; and an iron chain; which were all taken from the Turks. The chain, which is twelve hundred feet long, is suspended, in festoons, round the walls which enclose the yard, and each link weighs from twenty-two to twenty-four pounds. It was formerly made use of by the Turks to block up the passage of the Danube near Buda.

[17] An unsatisfactory encounter in 1809 with Emperor Franz, who beneath his veneer of bourgeois *bonhomie* was every inch an autocrat; from *Memoiren meines Lebens* by I.F. Castelli. Translated by Richard Bassett.

(I.F. Castelli, a friend of the composer Schubert, who had written much anti-Napoleonic material, was forced to flee Vienna in 1809 before Napoleon and the invading French, and appealed in desperation to the Kaiser.)

The Emperor had already left the Residenz . . . I made my way to him on foot and obtained an audience. His face showed clearly his grief at the tragic fate of his country, and this gave me hope.

'Who are you?' he asked 'and what do you want?'

'A poor provincial clerk who has not even once drawn his full annual salary of 300 florins, because various taxes are still being deducted from him.'

'That is quite in order. I cannot help you there.'

'Majesty, I am asking for a very different kind of assistance. I have been proscribed by the French dictator. If I am found, I am to be handed over to a military court. I must therefore escape.'

'Of course.'

'But this is impossible, as I have no means to do so. I am therefore making so bold as to ask Your Majesty most graciously to deign to use me as an escort for one of your convoys.'

'You say you have been proscribed. And why is that?'

Humbly and sadly I handed him my work and said, 'It's all there. Please read it.'

The Emperor did so, shook his head, frowned, and then, handing me back the paper, said brusquely: 'So you have written a war-poem? And who, pray, ordered you to do so?'

[18] Antiquities at the Hofburg in 1814; from *Travels from Vienna . . . in the year 1814* by Richard Bright.

(The antiquities of the Hofburg described here are still to be seen in the Archaeological wing of the palace galleries near the Heldenplatz. Their display today, however, is considerably more formal than that described here.)

The national collection of Antiques occupies some apartments in the Imperial Palace. The statuary in this collection is very insignificant. The chief objects, worthy of any attention, are a few fine marble busts, and one or two figures; more remarkable, from the remote situation in Pannonia, and other distant parts of

Emperor Franz I; engraving by Josef Kreutzinger

the Austrian Empire, in which they have been found, and on the history of which they throw some light; than from their workmanship. The collection of small bronze figures is numerous; several of them are of exquisite design, and skilfully moulded. Some figures and busts, cut completely out of precious stones, boast of considerable beauty; and in the same cabinet, is a bowl above two feet in diameter, formed from a single mass of agate. The inimitable collection of antique cameos and intaglios, and the extensive cabinet of coins and medals, are, however, the great ornaments of this collection. Forty of the most remarkable cameos were, as is well known, excellently engraved, and published at Vienna, with descriptions by Abbé Eckhel in 1788. The whole cabinet remains unimpaired by the ravages of the war, after having been, together with the collection of minerals and natural history, three several times carried down the Danube into the Bannat, to preserve it from the plundering grasp of the French.

Of that most exquisite piece of workmanship, the cameo of the Apotheosis of Augustus, it is impossible to speak in terms of sufficient praise. It is executed on a sardonyx, of nearly eight inches square, claiming for itself the third or fourth place in point of magnitude, amongst the specimens of antiquity in this department of art, and is considered by all the principal writers upon the subject, as the first in point of design and execution. The white layer from which the figures are formed, is thin and sufficiently translucid to permit the dark stone beneath to appear through those parts, where the folds of the drapery and other lines are deeply cut. This adds great beauty and variety to the picture; while the rich dark brown of the stone, forming the ground of the design, affords a fine contrast and relief to the figures.

The subject of the design is supposed to be a flattering allegory, representing Augustus enthroned amongst the gods and filling the station of Jupiter. His wife Livia seated by his side, is figured as the goddess Rome, and near the throne are gathered Neptune, Cybele, and the goddess of abundance, attendants on his state. Germanicus and Tiberius, crowned with victorious laurels, present themselves with respectful dignity, before the august chief of the family, who receive them with tranquillity and composure, unmoved by surprise or pleasure, as conscious, beforehand, that victory must attend the footsteps of Tiberius; or unwilling to sully the purity of justice, by even the appearance of the partial smiles of favour.

Such is the principal group which occupies one half of this superb cameo. The second, which is quite unconnected, represents Roman soldiers erecting a trophy to Augustus, accompanied by prisoners of war. The sculptor, conjectured to have been Dioscorides, has succeeded, in a most astonishing manner, in giving such a grace to the principal figures, that, while gazing with admiration, the mind of the observer is never called to reflect on the difficulties which must attend every work of this nature, and whilst his eye follows the traces worn with such incalculable labour in the hardest flint, it pursues in fancy the pencil in its light and flowing course. Although there is no other gem in this collection, which approaches to the splendour of the Apotheosis of Augustus, yet there are others of extraordinary size, and some of the smaller ones of exquisite workmanship. I shall of these mention one only, which may serve as an example, and assist in stimulating, not in satisfying, curiosity.

A cameo cut in a sardonyx, of about two inches in length, represents the return of Orestes to Argos, accompanied by his friend Pylades, to revenge the death of Agamemnon, his father, by the murder of his own mother, Clytemnestra, and Ægisthus, who had usurped the throne of Argos. The murder is already perpetrated. The body of Clytemnestra, breathing her last, is depicted with all the tranquillity of death; and the soft limbs and placid sleep of a helpless woman, are finely contrasted with the force which still marks the convulsed attitude, and the clenched palms of her dying consort. The young men, amazed and disgusted at the horrid deed, stand motionless with their weapons still uplifted, turning their eyes from the objects which their bloody hands strive to conceal; whilst attending slaves evince their deep interest in the scene.

The collection of Etruscan vases includes many fine specimens. With them are several vessels of ancient glass, and a large display of figured glasses and enamels; shewing the great variety and extent to which this manufacture had been carried by the ancients. . . .

The Imperial treasury contains a few antiques, but is more rich in modern works. Amongst these are some curious pieces of clock-work, and several of the earliest watches which were made at Nuremberg, and which, from their oval form, are well known to have obtained the name of eggs; much curiously carved ivory; numerous magnificent vessels cut in crystal; others worked from blocks of jasper and agate; most splendid cups and lamps formed from solid masses of rich lapis-lazuli, and a vessel ten inches in height, by four in diameter, cut from a clear topaz. Such objects, equally wonderful as productions of nature as of art, form a grand display, and, with a large assortment of crowns, sceptres, and jewelled ornaments, make up the chief attractions of the treasury. One small apartment is, however, well worthy of attention, as containing a very extensive collection of the early labours of Raffaelle, while he was employed as a designer on Italian pottery.

[19] Musical manuscripts in the Imperial Library in 1829; from *A Mozart Pilgrimage, being the travel diaries of Vincent and Mary Novello* . . . transcribed and compiled by Nerina Medici di Marignano, and edited by Rosemary Hughes.

(Vincent Novello (1781–1861) is chiefly remembered for his editions and arrangements of musical works, though he was also a composer, an organist of distinction, and well known in literary as well as musical circles of the time. He and his wife Mary travelled to Vienna in 1829 to present a sum of money, which had been raised by subscription, to Mozart's sister, Mme Sonnenberg, then in straitened circumstances; also to collect material for a Life of Mozart, whom Novello idolized. Their separate diaries of this journey were found in 1945 by their great-great-niece, and blended by her and her editor into one narrative with two voices.)

M.N. I should have mentioned that we yesterday visited the Imperial Library to see the original of the Requiem, where the Abbé had deposited it; it is shortly to be published in the exact form in which Mozart has left it, in some places only marks, in others sketches. Here were also manuscripts of Haydn, one of his Masses and the Creation. The *salle* is most beautiful, richly ornamented with gilding and statues and the dome painted.

V.N. . . . . His Excellency the Count Dietrichstein who has the superintendence of this magnificent Library . . . took every possible pains to gratify my curiosity and interest, not only respecting the MSS of Mozart, but relative to the other music contained in this princely collection which is indeed one of the very finest and most extensive I ever visited. Haydn original MS of Mass in B flat, No. 16; sketches by ditto: Fugue 'et vitam' No. 1, ditto of Creation (very interesting and curious). Finely illuminated Missals. Hofheimer sacred music.

There is here a copy of Mozart's early opera 'Ascanio in Alba,' the only Copy I ever could meet with. I inquired also for his other Operas 'Il Ré Pastore', 'La finta Giardiniera', 'Sulla' [*Lucio Silla*], 'Mitridate', but they had not any Copies and as I have now made researches and inquiries in almost every part of Germany by different channels, without being able to find these, I fear these *germs* of Mozart's incomparable Genius are now irreparably lost.

The 'Ascanio' is bound in two Volumes, one for each Act. The introduction is in D major and I should have been delighted to have appropriated the whole day to the examination of this Opera, but before I could turn to the 2nd Movement I was called to look at some other curious MSS, with which invitation I own I complied very reluctantly. There was a good collection of Handel's work in Score (Arnold's Edition, not Walsh's).

[20] A formal presentation at the Hofburg in 1819; from *More letters . . . Impressions of Vienna 1819–1829* by Martha Wilmot.

(Martha Wilmot (1775–1873) belonged to an Anglo–Irish clan of some distinction with links to the Establishment. She and her sister Catherine as girls spent some years in Russia as the protégées of the formidable and famous Princess Dashkov who had helped Catherine the Great to power, and their letters and diaries of this period were later published. In 1812 Martha married the Revd William Bradford, and they had three children. In 1819 he was appointed Chaplain to the British Embassy in Vienna, from where Martha wrote long and lively letters to her family in Ireland.

The Austrian court even at the beginning of the nineteenth century still ordered its activities along the lines of the strictest Spanish etiquette. A hundred years later, the future Edward VII, visiting Vienna as Prince of Wales, was to remark, 'Lord, this Court is stuffy.')

At five where do you think I went. Why, to the Palace to make my very best curtsey to the Empress. This had been arranged only a day before, but the *exact* dress I wore at L^y Stewart's was the proper thing there, with the addition of Lappets which dear Mrs Frazer lent me, and as my dress was without soil, nothing could have been better. Willy came with me as far as the Antichamber, then left me to my fate, which was to be met by the Empress's Grande Maitresse, a very goodnatured mannered

The Hofburg in 1835 – the Leopoldinischentrakt

Lady, to converse with her and two other Ladies who were to be presented likewise for about five minutes, and then to be ushered by her into the Presence Chamber where the Empress met us nearly at the door, and after saying a few words to each in the most gracious and most unaffected manner, she walked up to the sofa at the top of the room, seated herself, and invited us all to sit down, conversing with the most perfect ease and condescension with all, and positively more universal in her attentions to each than almost any Lady in her drawingroom is. . . .

You must know this is a very important ceremony for anybody who goes into society in this town of pride and ceremony and ettiquette, as without it there are many things from which a person is excluded. And at the same time it is a privilege granted only to 300 people in Vienna and Strangers. All Merchants, Bankers, in fact a large portion of truly respectable and highly educated people are excluded, but the fact is, we could not retain our place in the circles where we move without having been presented, and I am delighted the jobb is over tho' there was nothing tremendous in it at the time.

[21] New Year's Day at the Hofburg in 1815, and the customary greetings to the Emperor Franz; from *Travels from Vienna ... in the year* 1814 by Richard Bright.

Grand Court days, such, for instance, as New-year's-day, when every person who has been presented to the Emperor and Empress makes a point of attending, afford, perhaps, even a more splendid exhibition than the entertainment just described. The Court is usually held in the evening, beginning about seven o'clock, and breaking up about ten. On these occasions, a long and handsome suit of apartments is thrown open; the floors of which are not concealed by carpets, but are richly inlaid with various devices. Several of them, occupied as antichambers, and lined with guards and pages, lead to the hall, out of which lofty folding doors open into the principal saloon. There the Hungarian Guards, in their richest uniforms, are stationed. On entering the saloon, a much more dazzling scene of magnificence displays itself. The room is large, but its extent is somewhat lost in consequence of its great height. The roof is supported by pillars in imitation of finely polished marble, which reflect the lustres by

which it is lighted. It is beyond my powers to describe the gay
and splendid variety of dresses which were here displayed. A
large proportion of the men wore military uniforms, but such
uniforms as even a Russian would fear to wear in the field by the
side of a friendly Cossack. So interwoven with gold – so clasped
with jewels – such diamond plumes – and such embroidered stars
and orders, – that they bore the appearance of being the
substantial fruits rather than the honourable testimonials of
victorious arms. The few who were not in uniform, were little
inferior in the richness of their embroidered suits, and added
much to the variety of the scene. The ladies were generally in
white, with gold and silver points and spangles; their heads
dressed with much simplicity, but richly adorned with diamonds. The Empress and the ladies were seated; the men
conversed, standing together in the middle of the room, while a
large party of dancers marched round and round, to the sound of
music, in a quiet, graceful polonoise. And here an observer might
read in the countenances of emperors and of kings, the same
difficulties of conversation, the same free or embarrassed
address, which are occasionally met with in the intercourse of
ordinary society. After pursuing their varied windings for a time,
as if discontented with the narrow limits of their sphere, the
dancers would venture, under the conduct of their gallant
general, Prince Schwartzenburg, to explore the endless suit of
apartments, 'till the music, almost dying on the ear, warned
them to return. The thoughtful card-players let fall their cards,
and even Prince Talleyrand raised his mouth, for a moment,
above his handkerchief, to see the gay troops of royalty pass on.

[22] A masked ball in the *Redoutensaal* at the Hofburg in
1836; from *Vienna and the Austrians 1836–7* by Frances
Trollope.

(Frances Trollope (1780–1863), mother of the novelist Anthony
Trollope, herself was a novelist and writer. Her comments on
American society in *Domestic Manners of the Americans* (1832)
which followed her visit to the continent, though extremely
successful at home, won her the dislike of Americans. Following
her husband's financial ruin and death, she 'wrote to travel and

travelled to write', ending her days in Italy in financial comfort
brought about by a string of successful novels.

Redoutes, or masked balls, have always been a regular feature
of the social calendar in Vienna. In the past, ordinary citizens
mingled with the Imperial family and Viennese high society.
Between New Year's Eve and Lent the Viennese still attend
them, to enjoy the inimitable delight of the waltz.)

Who has not heard of the Redoutes of Vienna? . . . of the majestic
hall in which they are held? . . . and of the strange mélange of
which they are the resort? . . .

This unique species of amusement endures but for a short
portion of the winter season, beginning with the first day of the
year and ending with the last of the carnival. As lately as a year or
two ago it was the fashion for the very first society, including even
the ladies of the imperial family, to be seen during the carnival,
sometimes in masks and sometimes without, in the midst of this
popular amusement. . . .

It is, as I have told you, a settled thing that some one or other of
the haut ton should wind up the joys of the carnival here, by
giving a 'journée;' and these journées always end by the
company resorting at midnight to *Les salles de la Redoute:* but it is
not those alone who are admitted to the circle for whom 'la
journée' is given, who assemble there to pass the last moments
preceding Lent; every ball, public or private, high and low, on
Mardi Gras, ends at midnight, at which moment music ceases to
be heard from every orchestra throughout the Roman Catholic
world; and it is then that by common consent, and with common
sympathy, all Vienna rushes to the only spot where lights still
blaze, and there take leave of the gay season by wandering, with
a sort of saturnalian freedom, in a mixed mass of masks, dominos,
and lookers-on, till six o'clock in the morning.

In this strange medley it is probable that many a princess may
find herself face to face with her femme de chambre, or even with
her footmen, for the florin paid at entering is by no means a tax
sufficiently heavy to keep out any Austrian bent on amusing
himself. Wherever else a want of money may show itself, it never
appears in matters of amusement; which all will, must, and do
find means to procure in a degree perfectly astonishing to
foreigners. . . .

To avoid the disgrace of leaving Vienna without having seen

what all the world told us we ought to see, we quitted the brilliant
party at Count Nacko's; and, having returned home to refresh
ourselves by a quiet half-hour, proceeded to this redoubtable
Redoute, in time to hear the last strains of the music from its
ample orchestra.

To those who are familiar with the scenes presented by the bals
de l'Opera, I presume this assemblage would have nothing very
remarkable except the magnificent size of the room, and the
greatness of the multitude collected there, which upon this
evening, I am told, exceeded four thousand. To me, however, it
had all the effect of novelty; I never saw masks before, and, to
confess the truth, I do not feel much wish ever to see them again.
The press was almost intolerable, and the dust raised by it such as
quite to destroy the beauty and effect of this very magnificent
room, or rather rooms, for there are two, upon both of which you
can look at once from a gallery that is common to both. . . . But, as
they are at present, there is not much to admire in them. The
masks were numerous; and many of them, as well as the dresses,
exceedingly grotesque: but wit that speaks only by pasteboard,
wigs, and funny trappings, is not very entertaining; so, after
walking through the closely-wedged throng, mounting to the
gallery, and looking down upon them for nearly an hour, we
returned home between one and two, after the longest day of
dissipation that I ever remember to have passed.

[23] The ceremony of Washing the Feet on Maundy
Thursday, still taken very seriously in Catholic Europe, is
described by an eye-witness in the Hofburg during the
Easter festivities in 1820; from *More Letters . . . Impressions of
Vienna 1819–1829* by Martha Wilmot.

I don't think I have any stories to tell you now, and yet let me
think. I certainly have never yet mentioned a most curious
ceremony which we saw just before Easter, which was the
Emperor and Empress washing the feet of 12 old men and 12 old
women, in imitation of our Saviour's act to his disciples. About
half past eight o'Clock in the Morn^g of Holy Thursday M^r
Bradford and I went to the Palace and as belonging to the
Embassy got into a place railed off for *illustrious* Strangers, in
consequence of which we saw everything. It was near an hour

before the Imperial family arrived and in the mean time the Apartment became crowded to excess. Lady Stewart made a great effort, and to my surprise arrived also. Two long tables had been previously spread, one on the right and one on the left side of the Saloon, at which the 12 guests were already seated, dressed out for the occasion. The Emperor and Empress came in together, and separated each to their respective table followed by their State attendants. I attended to the Empress so I will describe her side, and you may fancy the Emperor doing exactly the same. The Ladies in Waiting took from the hands of the servants large dishes of meat, which they presented in succession to the Empress, and she with her own hands placed them on the table before the old Women who eat most earnestly, and drank the same. This lasted a considerable time during which the Empress stood, helping some with her own hands, removing dishes, replacing them by others, and in good earnest doing the service of the table. When their dinner and dessert were ended, the tables were removed, the grande Maitress tied a cambrick Apron round the Empresses waist, the Grand Maitre presented a Golden Ewer and Basin of water and a towel, she took the towel, kneeled down, and bona fide washed and wiped the feet of each old Woman (no doubt they had been well scrubbed beforehand), after which the Grande Maitresse took off the Apron, and presented 12 little bags of money with long strings, one of which she placed with unaffected good nature and good humour round each of their necks, allowing each to kiss her hand, patting the forehead of the oldest and most infirm, and seeming personally acquainted with all. She then listened to the short prayer which a Priest pronounced and all retired. The Imperial family is remarkable for an unaffected goodnature, which it is impossible not to love as well as admire; it seems to distinguish them all but I don't well know whether to consider this ceremony as humiliating or its reverse, for tis so true that extremes meet. But certain it is that tis a most popular one, and everybody retires full of the praises of Imperial condescension tho' nothing *less* great than Imperial rank, or the Pope, or the first dignitaries in the Greek Church *can* perform it.

[24] The installation of eleven Knights of the Golden Fleece in the Hofburg on 30 November 1836; from *Vienna and the Austrians 1836–7* by Frances Trollope.

(The order of the Golden Fleece was the highest decoration a Habsburg monarch could bestow on his subjects. Founded in medieval times when the Habsburgs ruled the Netherlands, its motif is Flemish in origin.)

We have this morning witnessed by far the most splendid pageant I ever saw, – namely, the installation of eleven knights of the order of the Golden Fleece. The Archduke Albert, and his brother the Archduke Charles, sons of the renowned Archduke Charles, who is uncle to the Emperor, were among them; and the ceremony being altogether one of great dignity and parade, the demand for tickets was very urgent: but, by the kindness of Prince Metternich and Sir Frederic Lamb, we all obtained places.

We were directed to repair to the palace at ten o'clock, as the press in all the rooms leading to the Salles des Cérémonies was expected to be great, and there might have been difficulty in reaching our places at a later hour. On ascending the principal stairs of the palace, we found that, early as we were, a multitude of others were earlier still, for the throng was already such as to make the progress to the great hall a work of some labour. . . .

Having at length safely reached our places, which were in a temporary gallery commanding an excellent view of the whole room, we found ample occupation for the time, before the ceremonies began, in contemplating the varied and brilliant groups of gentlemen that already occupied the floor of the hall. Through this glittering phalanx a stream of ladies were already pressing forward to the different tribunes allotted to them. There were seats in none, except those prepared for the Empress and her ladies, and a few more placed in the tribune set apart for the foreign ministers.

Though not in general a very good stander, an innate love of finery, common I suppose to all my sex, made me endure it upon this occasion better than I ever remember to have done before. The costumes displayed upon this occasion among the gentlemen surpass, both in elegance of outline and richness of decoration, all I had expected to see; though I had heard much before-hand of the great splendour of the Hungarian nobles.

I really know nothing at once so gorgeous and picturesque as the uniform of the Hungarian noble body-guard, with their splendid silver accoutrements, their spotted furs, uncut, hanging at their backs, and their yellow morocco boots. The rich and beautiful skins which they all carry, apparently in the very shape in which they came off the animal, give a most striking air of primitive and almost barbarous magnificence. . . .

The hall itself, as I think I have told you before, is a very fine room, lofty and well-proportioned, with a row of stately columns on each side of it, and decorated with abundance of mirrors and chandeliers. On this occasion the upper end of the chamber was decorated by a magnificent throne, placed on an ample richly-carpeted dais. The draperies of the canopy were of crimson velvet, heavily embroidered with gold, and terminating at each corner with enormous plumes of white feathers; so that, large and lofty as was the apartment, this splendid erection was majestically conspicuous from every corner of it. . . .

It was just half-past nine in the morning when we reached our places, and it was well-known that the ceremonies were not to begin till eleven; nevertheless . . . the movement and the splendour of the gay crowd that occupied the floor, furnished very sufficient amusement till the solemnities began.

At length, a flourish of trumpets announced the approach of the court, and sent all the sabred, starred, and cordoned loiterers back in thick ranks against the galleries, leaving more space than a moment before seemed possible, for the entrance of those to look upon whom we were all assembled there.

The first person who stepped forward into the space thus cleared was the Empress of Austria, her tall and elegant figure shown to great advantage by a dress of black velvet, very richly ornamented about the front and shoulders by diamonds. A white hat and feathers, with a brilliant bandeau of diamonds under it, formed her head-dress; and a rich blond scarf, thrown over her very graceful shoulders, prevented her dress from having so completely the air of an evening toilet as it would have had without it. She walked up the room quite alone, bowing very graciously to the tribunes, and to the throng of courtiers marshalled on both sides of her below them. . . . Then followed the tall and majestic Archduchess Sophia, consort of the Archduke Francis, leading her two little boys, – the eldest of them being presumptively 'the hope of the fair state.' Next to her came the Archduchess Clementina, Princess of Salerno, leading her fair little girl; and then the very pretty young Archduchess Maria Theresa, who in a few weeks is to become Queen of Naples.

The Prince of Salerno, and three young archdukes, followed, completing the party admitted to the tribune of the Empress. A white-plumed host of fair ladies followed, all I think in black velvet dresses. Soon after they had taken their places, another flourish of trumpets was heard from the music gallery, and three very significant taps on the floor from some official baton again cleared the way, making the crowd, which appeared quite sufficient to fill the whole, shrink into about half the space.

Then entered the Emperor [*Ferdinand*], in his robes as grand master of the order, and his cortège, consisting upon this occasion wholly of knights of the Golden Fleece, each followed by an elegant young page to bear his train; and a more splendid line it would be impossible to look upon. The whole procession, including the eleven new knights, were all attired in the rich robes of the order; while their collars and caps, radiant with jewels, formed altogether as imposing a spectacle as it is possible for draperies and decorations to produce.

We had been told that the robes worn at this solemnity were the identical dresses made for the investiture of the knights at the first chapter, held by Philippe le Bon at Bruges, in the year 1429. But this high antiquity does not belong to the dresses we saw this morning. We have, nevertheless, had the opportunity of passing judgment on these same original robes, as they make part of the curious museum of relics preserved in the Ritterbourg at Lachsenbourg. The robes now worn are comparatively modern, being, in fact, only one hundred and twenty-five years old; they were made when Charles the Sixth on arriving from Spain, on the death of his brother Joseph the First, in 1711, restored to the house of Austria the exclusive privilege of bestowing this order.

[25] Mass in the Hofburgkapelle in 1829; from *A Mozart Pilgrimage, being the travel diaries of Vincent and Mary Novello* . . . transcribed and compiled by Nerina Medici di Marignano, and edited by Rosemary Hughes.

(Sunday mass in the Chapel Royal is still an essential part of any visitor's itinerary. The celebrated Vienna choirboys have their origins in the choristers Novello describes here as 'most musicianlike'. Other mention of these choirboys on pages 133 and 135.)

11 o'clock attended the High Mass at the Chapel Royal . . . Mozart in D No. 6 . . . Service conducted by Eybler . . . most musicianlike performance I have yet heard. There were not many performers but all *efficient*.

Gothic chapel small and like the Portuguese rather higher; quite plain. A bronze crucifix. Not a bit of gold except at tabernacle, and round a statue with a niche. Four soldiers with fixed bayonets and their cocked hats on at the altar . . . Lowest gallery for choir, two above for the attendants of the Imperial Family, for whom there are private tribunes overlooking the Altar and Sanctuary and which connect with the interior of the palace. Vaulted roof – nine sculptured Gothic figures half way up the walls in niches, over the [*illegible*] in stone. Chaste and solemn effect. Pity no painted glass in the windows at the Altar.

Good taste of the Emperor in not having any crown or other trappings and insignia of Royalty ostentatiously displayed in his chapel.

Eybler made no fuss or clatter but beat the time steadily and calmly like a sterling and accomplished musician himself who knew that he was surrounded by others who knew their business without much interference from him . . .

[26] The young Empress Elizabeth, wife of Franz-Josef and one of the most dazzling beauties of Europe, is remembered as she was during the 1850s – her high spirits later gave way to melancholy but she kept her looks and (through vigorous exercise) her figure; from *The Austrian Court in the Nineteenth Century* by Sir Horace Rumbold.

(Sir Horace Rumbold, Bart, GCB, GCMG, (1829–1913) was a scion of one of Britain's most distinguished diplomatic families, and doyen of ambassadors in Vienna during the *Kaiserzeit*. He retired in 1909, but his memories went back to the 1830s.)

Certain it is that the sunny grace and charm of the Empress soon completely transformed and brightened a Court which, under the regime of the weakly Ferdinand and his pious consort, may well have been supremely dull and lifeless. The reaction, too, which inevitably followed upon the dismal revolutionary period promptly made itself felt. The city of the Danube became its old cheery *insouciant* self again. It was the age of Lanner and of the younger Johann Strauss, and to their strangely bewitching strains, at the splendid balls given in the great *Ceremoniensaal*, one willingly imagines the girl-Empress gaily dancing to her heart's content. Few only are now left who can recall the gleaming vision of the sovereign lady in those first unclouded years of her happy married life, but with them that vision remains unique, ineffaceable.

At any rate it is pleasant to think of this charming Princess unaffectedly enjoying the pleasures and diversions of her age, like any ordinary mortal, before she entered upon her weary pilgrimage of sorrows. But balls and other amusements – even Vienna balls – and still less the daily routine of Court duties, could be but of little real interest to one so full as she was of mental and physical activities. Without any *pose* or pretension she sincerely aimed at the simple, strenuous life of which we hear so much and see so little. She read a great deal and judiciously; being bent, as she herself would say, on repairing the deficiencies of her education in early youth, when she had not been kept strictly to her lessons, and was allowed, so to speak, to run wild in her happy country home. Although, from the first, she made it a rule scrupulously to abstain from any encroachment on the domain of public affairs, she nevertheless kept herself fully informed of all that went on around her; while her influence with her husband, which never waned up to the last day of her life, was always to be found on the side of progress and enlightenment, and of toleration in matters both temporal and spiritual. . .

From early childhood she had been accustomed to an open-air country life. She roamed freely among the Bavarian Alps with her brothers – a very 'child of the woods,' as she is aptly termed by one of her biographers – and shared all their sports and pastimes. She rode and boated and swam with them, and vied with them in pluck and endurance. Besides becoming, as is well known, a most accomplished horsewoman, her feats in mountain-climbing and as a pedestrian were quite remarkable, and even when she had long passed middle age, the slight, almost too girlish, figure she preserved to the very end enabled her to walk

Empress Elizabeth in a lace-trimmed dress;
by an unknown artist in 1860

long distances which her much younger attendants compassed with difficulty. But in all this there was the same trait of feverish, almost morbid, need of excitement. Of a morning she would ride in turn several horses – the more unmanageable the better – in the great Imperial riding-school at Vienna – the scene of many a splendid pageant – or in the long, shady avenues of the Prater. As a young girl she had amused herself learning what she herself called 'circus tricks' in the *manège* at Munich, but she now went through a complete course of the *haute école*, under the tuition of the able staff of the celebrated Spanische Hofreitschule in the Michaeler platz. She also, it was said, took lessons from one of the best-known female equestrians of the Circus Renz, and became quite proficient in some of the most daring feats that can be attempted on horseback.

It speaks but ill for the good feeling and charity of a certain set in Vienna society at that time that these peculiar whims and fancies of the young sovereign, which were but the outcome of her exuberant vitality and superabundant nervous energy, were allowed to tell against her and to give rise to unkind comments. Far too much stress has been laid on this short and transient period of the Empress's early married days, but there is unfortunately good reason to believe that the unfriendly criticisms, which could not fail eventually to reach her ears, cut her to the quick, and, together with the irksome exigencies of Court etiquette and formality, soon made life at Vienna distasteful to her. All this no doubt contributed to make her avoid any lengthy sojourns in the gay capital, which in after years was to become for her a city of grief and mourning.

[27] The sorrows of the austere and ageing Emperor Franz-Josef who by the first years of the twentieth century had experienced bitter losses that included the suicide of his son, Crown Prince Rudolf (see pages 98 and 206) and the assassination of his wife, Elizabeth; from *At the Gates of the East* . . . by Lieutenant-Colonel J.P. Barry.

There is one presence that pervades the entire feeling of life here that is singularly impressive even to the least emotional traveller. It is the figure of the Emperor, the loyalty to whose dynasty is eclipsed by a universal personal love. Whether in other ages it had a parallel may be matter of opinion, but in our days of the enthronement of individualism, it is phenomenal and unique. At the simple mention of his name, the Viennese eye seems to light up with a tender lambent ray that only burns beside the inner sanctuary, where men enshrine whatever is most precious to them. In the various national Diets of this distracted empire, where the decencies of Parliament seem flung so lightly to the outer winds, the thought of that lonely figure in the Burg hushes on the lip many a bitter gibe, many a maddening taunt; and even after the worst scenes, there is at least one note of sincere contrition from the unruly that any new pang should have been added to the sorrows of the emperor. Everybody, however lowly, remembers his great age, the cataclysms of his reign, the overwhelming tragedies of his home life, his simple tastes, the devotion with which from dawn till dusk he labours at his trade of ruler. Having witnessed the shipwreck of his hopes, and followed the remains of his murdered son to the Crypt of the Capuchins, they saw him go back to his desk, not to weep but to work, as if he grudged any time for private grief from the service of his country. And then when the murdered empress was laid beside her son, and all the palsying numbness of the double tragedy seemed too much even for spectators to bear, the brave old spirit met all the blows of destiny with no other armour but his manhood, and, taking up his load, he again went back to work to give to Austria what service such sorrow still enabled him to render. Looking up towards the apartments in the Hof-Burg, where this veritable king of men, without rancour and without pose, still pursues his daily task, one almost stands in awe of such heroic self-effacement. No traveller can cross this courtyard without the heart for a moment standing still at the salute; for behind yonder windows lives the man who, as husband, father, emperor, presents to the world the noblest instance of a modern martyrdom.

Kapuzinergruft

[28] Maria Theresa's daily devotions in the crypt of the Capuchin Church; from *De L'Allemagne* by Madame de Staël.

(Germaine de Staël (1766–1817) was one of the first independent political women to make her influence felt through her intelligence, personality, books and her salon, rather than from the bedroom of a king. Daughter of Jacques Necker, the Swiss banker who was twice called on to disentangle Louis XVI's finances, she is best known for her passionate and unfaltering opposition to Napoleon.)

It was here, in the crypt of the Capuchins, that Maria Theresa for thirty years heard Mass in the presence of the very tomb that she had prepared for herself beside her husband. This celebrated Maria Theresa suffered so greatly in the early days of her youth that the pious consciousness of the impermanence of life never left her, even in the midst of her magnificence. There are many examples of a deep and constant devotion among the world's sovereigns; as they must obey only death, its irresistible power strikes them the more. Life's difficulties block our way to the tomb; all is made level for kings until the last boundary, and that alone makes it more visible to their eyes.

[29] A visit in 1815 to the Crypt of the Capuchin Church, founded by the Emperor Mathias in 1619, where the remains of most of the Habsburgs are interred; from *Anecdotal Reminiscences of the Congress of Vienna* by the Comte Auguste de la Garde-Chambonas.

(Comte Auguste-Louis-Charles de la Garde-Chambonas was born in Paris in 1783, served briefly as a soldier and even more briefly as a minister of foreign affairs for Louis XVI before fleeing Paris ahead of the Reign of Terror. His estates being confiscated, he attached himself to various great personages of the day, the most important of whom was the Prince de Ligne. Chambonas settled near him in Vienna and delightedly participated in the social whirl accompanying the Congress of Vienna (see pages 120–132). He dearly loved a lord, as his gossipy *Recollections* so entertainingly reveal.)

When we got to the chapel, a monk, after having lighted a large torch, preceded us to the crypts. There were nine tombs of emperors, thirteen of empresses, and in all about eighty of the members of the imperial race. 'It was in this subterranean chapel,' said our guide, 'that every day during thirty years Maria-Theresa heard Mass before the sepulchre she had erected for herself by the side of that of her husband.'

'This trait of Maria-Theresa,' said Tettenborn, 'reminds me of one of the clever answers of Joseph II. When he had granted the public admission to the Augarten, a lady complained that she could no longer stroll about there among her equals. "If everybody were restricted to the society of his equals," replied the emperor, "I should be reduced for a bit of air to the crypt of the Capuchins, inasmuch as it is only there that I should find mine."'

[30] The Kapuzinergruft in 1836, and the devotion felt by the Viennese to their dead Emperor; from *Vienna and the Austrians 1836–7* by Frances Trollope.

This morning we have witnessed another exhibition, and of a different kind. This day is the one known in the Romish calendar as that of '*La fête des Morts*,' or, as the Germans call it, 'Poor Souls' Day.' The churches are all hung with black; no music is heard within them, but masses for the dead are solemnly murmured before every altar throughout the city. It is in vain that innumerable waxen tapers, of all sizes, colours, and shapes, expend their votive light around a hundred shrines; the gloomy hangings seem too mighty for them, and the air of dark and solemn sadness is universal. Every shop is shut, and the entire population appear to have given up their spirits to mourning. The churches in all parts of the city have been crowded during the whole day; yet, nevertheless, multitudes have wandered to the cemeteries without the town, to visit the graves of friends recently lost.

The great point of general interest, however, is the crypt of the church belonging to the convent of the Capucins, for there lie interred the imperial family of Austria. The vaults are on this day open to the public; and we have spent a considerable time within their gloomy recesses, both for the purpose of looking ourselves at this receptacle of the royal dead, and for that of watching the use made of this annual privilege by the people.

Seventy-three bronze coffins are ranged in solemn array around the walls. Some of these are extremely simple, and others in the highest style of magnificence. That of the Emperor Francis the First of Germany, and his consort, Maria Theresa, (for one sarcophagus contains them both,) was erected by the illustrious woman whose bones rest within it, and is, I think, the most splendid of the collection. But the crowd of pilgrims who came, upon this day, to gaze upon the coffin that contains their idol the late Emperor, Francis the First of Austria, was too numerous to permit any very accurate examination of them.

Were I simply and fully to describe to you the strong emotion manifested by the throng, still passing on, but still renewed, when at length they had won their way across the imperial sepulchre to the grating which gave them a sight of the Emperor Francis' coffin, you would hardly give credence to the truth of my tale. You would not think it false, but you would suspect that it was exaggerated; and as, on the other hand, I feel sure of falling short of the truth from mere want of power to do justice to a scene so singular and so affecting, I think I must leave you without any description of it at all.

And yet, perhaps, of all the spectacles I have ever witnessed it was the most striking! . . . The old and the young, the rich and the poor, pressed on together to the tomb of their common father; neither sex, age, nor condition were observed in this unparalleled mêlée of general emotion; and I believe truly, that of all the multitude who thronged that dismal vault, we alone profited by the light of the torches which made its gloom visible, for the purpose of looking on as mere spectators of the scene. We watched tears stealing down many a manly cheek from eyes that seemed little used to weeping, and listened to sobs that spoke of hearts bursting with sorrow and remembered love, beside the tomb of one who had already lain there above two years – and that one an Emperor! . . . Between him and the people that thus freshly weep for him, there must have been a tie more closely drawn than we, in our land of freedom, can easily understand.

[31] The funeral of Crown Prince Rudolf in the Capuchin Church on 6 February 1889; from *The Times*.

(The funeral of the Crown Prince was a sombre occasion overshadowed by the tragic and still mysterious circumstances of his death (see page 206). The events of that winter's night at the hunting-lodge at Mayerling in the Vienna Woods still give rise to controversy as well as a powerful mythology which has inspired ballets and novels depicting Rudolf's supposed 'suicide pact' with the young Marie Vetsera.)

The funeral of the late Archduke Rudolph, Crown Prince of Austria-Hungary, was solemnized at 4 pm today at the Capuchin's Church on the Neue Market, in presence of the Emperor, the Archdukes, the King of the Belgians, Prince Baudouin of Flanders, and the principal members of the Diplomatic Body.

   Inside the church the sight was one of gloom. The Capuchins Church, in the vault of which 11 Emperors are buried, is a small, unpretending edifice, into which not much light penetrates even at noon. The Crown Prince's coffin was set on a catafalque surrounded by large tapers, and these candles rather punctuated the darkness than gave light. In the deep shadows of the chancel one could perceive from the organ gallery several tiers of seats crowded with officers and ladies in mourning. Conspicuous in this assemblage was the Emperor of Austria, in the black uniform of an infantry colonel.

   Beside His Majesty stood the King and Queen of the Belgians, and all the other places of the *estrade* were occupied by Archdukes and Archduchesses. The empress, the Crown Prince Stephanie, and the Archduchess Marie Valeria were absent.

   Cardinal Ganglbauer, Archbishop of Vienna, performed the short funeral service. The organ was silent, and the choristers chanted their responses without accompaniament. During the service the Emperor stood perfectly calm, looking about him with quick movements of the head, as his custom is. After the chanting of the *Libera*, however, His Majesty stepped out from his place, walked up along to his son's coffin, knelt down beside it, and with clasped hands remained for a moment or two in prayer. This was a minute of poignant emotion for all present. Not a sound was heard. Nobody coughed, not a dress rustled, not a sword scabbard clanked on the flagstones. An entire stillness prevailed till the Emperor rose from his knees and walked back calmly to his place.

The vaults are under the care of Capuchin monks of the brown-robed Franciscan Order, and they may be visited by anybody . . . Crown Prince Rudolph will lie henceforth in the crowd of his illustrious departed kinsmen, and from to-day one of these brown Capuchin friars will be trying daily to evade giving direct answers to the question as to how he died. . . .

The official admission of the suicide has had this result – that in some places the ecclesiastical authorities, in accordance with the rules of the Roman Catholic Church, refuse to hold Divine services for the late Crown Prince. On receiving the first news, ascribing the sudden death of his Imperial Highness to apoplexy, the Franciscan Monastery of Linz hoisted a black flag which, however, was at once removed when the truth became known. At Meran, the well-known Tyrolese winter resort, the Canon absolutely refused to celebrate mass in the parish church without special licence from his bishop, and the authorities had to content themselves with a military service, conducted in the open air. On the other hand, the Archbishop of Prague has instructed the Bohemian clergy to pray for the soul of the Emperor's son, who, according to indisputable medical evidence, was in a state of unsound mind when he laid hands upon himself; and there is no doubt that the entire Austrian and Hungarian clergy will receive instructions from Rome to assume the same attitude.

[32] The burial of Franz-Josef, penultimate Habsburg emperor and the man whose sixty-eight-year rule symbolized the Austrian empire, in the Kapuzinergruft in 1916; from *The Fall of the House of Habsburg* by Edward Crankshaw.

If the Monarchy had no war aims, it also had no guide. The old Emperor had held it together for sixty-six years, conducting it in effect from the eighteenth to the twentieth century, and bringing it, more or less united, into Armageddon. Having done that, for all practical purposes he abdicated his authority: in a sense his singing of the mobilization order had been an abdication. He was eight-four, and he had two years and four months to live. He persisted, heroically, in his routine; but he was no longer an effective ruler. His presence was more necessary than ever before as the living symbol of the reality of the Dual State; but he no longer acted as a guide. Guidance, such as it was, was left to the politicians and the generals. But Parliament did not exist. It had not been called since its proroguing in the spring of 1914, and it was not to meet again until after Franz Josef's death. . . .

He died on 21 November 1916, two years short of the seventieth anniversary of his accession. For some time he had been having trouble with his chest. Now, quite suddenly, he was worn out. On the evening of his last day they got him to bed two hours before his regular bedtime. He was too weak to kneel at his *prie-dieu*, so he said his prayers sitting. Everyone knew that he was dying, and an imposing uniformed assembly had gathered in the anterooms at Schönbrunn. But he himself gave instructions that he was to be wakened at half past three next morning; he had so much to do. Within an hour he was dead, and Katherina Schratt [*his mistress for more than twenty years*], led forward by the new Emperor, Karl, laid two white roses on his breast.

By now Vienna was feeling with great severity the strain of war. The real hunger had not yet set in, but the people were weary, apathetic and dispirited. It was too late for the death of the wonderful old man to strike them as a cataclysm; it was not even the last straw. It was to be expected, and it made no difference: a movement was in train which no Habsburg, not even Franz Josef, could withstand. For three days the Viennese filed past the corpse of their Emperor, of their history, as it lay in state at Schönbrunn; but the impact of his death was muffled. And when the final moment came and the coffin was taken to rest in the Capuchin church in the Neuermarkt, its small, plain façade concealing the tomb of so many Emperors, the last theatrical gesture offered posthumously in the traditional Habsburg way seemed more than just a repetition of Habsburg arrogance formally humbling itself at the gates of heaven. When the Court Chamberlain (still Prince Montenuovo) knocked with his golden staff on the closed door with its heavy sable hangings, demanding admission for 'His Apostolic Majesty the Emperor Franz'; when the monk behind the door replied that he knew nothing about His Apostolic Majesty; when the performance was repeated, and, finally, the haughty Montenuovo craved

Emperor Franz Josef I as a young man: he was to rule for 68 years.
By an unknown artist

admission for 'Your brother Franz, a miserable sinner' – when the solemn ritual, as so often before, had been played out and the coffin received at last into the impersonal care of Capuchin Friars, it seemed that at last the symbol had become the truth itself.

Ballhausplatz

[33] Prince von Kaunitz, Austria's First Minister, and his relationship with the Emperor Josef; from *Memoirs of the Courts of Berlin, Dresden, Warsaw and Vienna in the years 1777, 1778 and 1779* by N. William Wraxall.

(Prince Kaunitz (Imperial Chancellor 1753–92) was the most spectacular example of Empress Maria Theresa's talent for finding brilliant individuals to support her threatened throne. To Prince Kaunitz falls the singular achievement of reversing the traditional pattern of European alliances, so that Austria, allied with France and Russia, could attempt to destroy Frederick the Great. His arrival at the Ballhausplatz turned this modest home of diplomacy into a power-house with which every European country had to reckon.)

The Austrian first Minister rises very late, usually at or nearly about noon; but he transacts public business in bed during the whole morning, where his secretaries attend for that purpose. At one o'clock he takes chocolate. His hour of dinner is uncertain, varying capriciously from four o'clock to five, six, and seven in the evening; in consequence of which want of punctuality, all who are able, have running footmen stationed in the Prince's antichamber, to bring them intimation when he is about to appear. If he accepts an invitation to dine with any person, however high his rank, it is only on condition that the wine, bread, and even the water be sent from his own house, and the principal dishes dressed by his cook. A stipulation, which, however humiliating, is never refused by those who aspire to the honor of entertaining him. No crowned head in Europe, I believe, exacts similar marks of deference from his Courtiers; nor could Louis the Fourteenth have experienced greater proofs of servile respect, when he condescended to visit his favorite Ministers or subjects. Naturally chearful, and disposed to the pleasures of society, Prince Kaunitz nevertheless unbends at table. He converses well on almost all topics, reasons with accuracy, and has a vast command of expression. Italian, French, and German, he speaks with no less ease than fluency;

but, French is the language which he usually talks in company, as being most generally understood. It is indeed rare to hear him utter a word in German; for which, like his Prussian Majesty, he does not seem to entertain any predilection. To Italians, of whom there are always many in the Court of Vienna, he never fails to address himself in Italian, if they do not possess French in perfection.

His favorite topics of debate or of conversation, are horses, mechanics, and carriages. It is scarcely possible to be a greater Connoisseur than he is on these subjects; and whenever any of them are mentioned, he harangues with no less perspicuity than information. On politics he rarely or never touches; but, on historical points he is easily led out, and displays, without affectation, a very extensive acquaintance with all the great events of modern Europe. If not a man of shining talents, he is unquestionably possessed of great enlargement of mind, much application, and sound judgment, matured by the most perfect acquaintance with all the financial and military resources of the House of Austria. . . .

His pleasures, at an age so advanced, can neither be very numerous nor extremely varied. He is fond of Music, and likes theatrical entertainments, though he seldom attends them. I have seen him delighted with the 'Ombres Chinoises,' when exhibited in a private room, before a select company. At cards he never plays; but, during the greater part of every evening, he amuses himself at billiards, in his own drawing-room. One of his passions through life, has been architecture, practical as well as theoretical; and it is pretended, that he has not a little impaired his fortune by indulging this propensity. Certainly he has thrown away immense sums, I am told, near a million of florins, or full a hundred thousand pounds, between his house in the suburbs of Vienna, and his seat at Austerlitz in Moravia. Neither of them are yet completed, and he is perpetually pulling down, altering, and repairing. If there is not great exaggeration in these assertions, they will explain the reason, why, after such a long possession of power, he has amassed little for his family. Indeed, it would be difficult otherwise to account for it, since he is not generous; at least not from constitution, though he knows how to affect liberality on proper occasions.

Prince Kaunitz is a good Catholic, but has not any tincture of bigotry or superstition. I believe he rarely, if ever confesses: I know that he never attends, nor hears mass performed, except on Sundays; and then only for ten minutes, not publickly, but in his own house. Superior to the temptation or love of gold, he is not less exempt from any spirit of vengeance. The natural elevation of his mind raises him above Court-cabal, and little ministerial intrigue. An enemy to every species of constraint, the freedom which he exercises himself, he extends to those about him: yet, his dignity never forsakes him for a moment. I have seen him in his own drawing-room, as unconcerned, and as attentive to his game at billiards, while the Emperor stood on one side of him, and the Archduke Maximilian on the other, as if they had both been private individuals of no consequence. He never appeared to me so great as on those occasions. Towards men of genius, artists, and persons distinguished in every line of letters or of science, he is nevertheless condescending and polite to a high degree. Gluck not only dines frequently at his table; but, I have known the Prince address his discourse to him during the whole repast, in a manner the most flattering, while he has not noticed the first nobility of Vienna seated near him. In this part of his character, he stands widely opposed to the Austrian men of rank, who retain many of the prejudices of their ancestors, and rarely open their houses to men of merit or talents, unconnected with the advantages of birth. . . .

Nothing is better known than his dislike, I might almost say his aversion, for the present Emperor [*Josef II*], when he was Archduke and King of the Romans, before his father's death. The Prince never mentioned his character, conduct, or understanding, except with marks of disapprobation. Even after Joseph's accession to the Imperial dignity, he did not alter his language. 'The Emperor,' said he more than once, 'fears me, and I dislike him.' . . . At that time, his Imperial Majesty never visited, nor conversed with him: on the contrary, he held Prince Kaunitz in detestation.

Insensibly, however, their mutual alienation has not only ceased, but has been succeeded by attachment, esteem, and confidence. Those sentiments can scarcely be carried to a higher pitch of reciprocal deference and respect, than at the present moment. How far policy, or views of interest on either side, may have conduced to operate so total a change, it is impossible to assert. Joseph, who is unquestionably a master of dissimulation, may only wait for the proper moment to manifest his real sentiments. But, people here are universally convinced, that no reconciliation was ever more complete. He seems never satisfied with giving the Prince the most flattering testimonies of consideration and personal regard. . . . On the anniversary of his birth, it is customary for Prince Kaunitz always to dine with his eldest son, Count Ernest, and a select party. Upon the second of February, last year, which was the day alluded to, the first Minister went to his son's house, about half past four o'clock. Candles had not been brought in, though it was already dusk; and the company expecting every minute to be summoned to table, were conversing in the drawing-room, when the door opened very gently. A person entered, and on his advancing towards the Countess Ernest Kaunitz, they perceived that it was the Emperor. 'I am come, Madam,' said he, 'unasked, to eat a part of your dinner. I hope you will permit me on this day to shew my respect, and to pay my compliments to Prince Kaunitz.' He accordingly stayed; but, at table he sat on the Minister's right hand, and did not allow of the smallest distinction, considering himself only as a guest. It was difficult for a Sovereign to shew a more delicate mark of attention. I received these particulars from one of the company.

[34] Prince Metternich, another First Minister, as he appeared to an observer of the Congress of Vienna in 1814; from *Anecdotal Reminiscences of the Congress of Vienna* by Comte Auguste de la Garde-Chambonas.

(Prince Klemens von Metternich (Chancellor 1810–48) was the most gifted and powerful diplomat of his day, and at the Congress of Vienna he ensured that the map of Europe was returned to that existing before the arrival of Napoleon. His diplomatic system controlled inter-European relations for thirty years, his aim being to maintain aristocratic government in Europe, and to keep the rising radical middle-class from acquiring power. The tumultuous upheaval of 1848 finally swept him from power.)

Two days before, the Prince de Metternich had also given a great ball at which the majority of the guests of the Austrian Court had been present. It has just struck me that I am nearing the end of my course, and that as yet I have not spoken of one of the most conspicuous personages of our epoch. Almost everybody has tried to portray M. de Metternich. Like M. de Talleyrand, he has had all the honours of history bestowed upon him during his lifetime, but although his portrait has been traced more than once by more skilful hands than mine, I cannot resist the desire to show him as I was enabled to judge him – behind the glamour of power and political reserve in which he has lived since his youth. At that period M. de Metternich might still pass muster as a young man. His features were perfectly regular and handsome, his smile was full of graciousness, his face expressed both benevolence and the most delicate intelligence. He was of average height, and of elegant proportions. Both his gait and demeanour were marked by much nobleness. . . . At the first glance, one felt delighted at seeing one of those men to whom nature had vouchsafed her most seductive gifts, and whom nature, as a rule, seems to take a delight in calling only to the frivolous successes of a society life. It was when attentively scanning his physiognomy, at once supple and firm, and carefully scrutinising Metternich's looks, that the superiority of his political genius at once became manifest to even the superficial observer. 'The society man' disappeared, and there remained nothing but the statesman, accustomed to rule men and to decide important affairs. Mixed up for twenty-five years with the gigantic commotions that disturbed Europe, M. de Metternich showed the lofty aptitude of his mind, and that rare penetration and sagacity which can foresee and direct events. His decision, the result of long meditation, was immovable. His words were incisive, as they ought to be from the lips of a statesman sure of the drift of everything he says. I may add to this that M. de Metternich is one of the most charming storytellers of our epoch.

[35] A darker view of Prince Metternich and his system of repression; from *Life of Prince Metternich* by Colonel G.B. Malleson.

Metternich had had, at Teplitz, an interview with the King of Prussia (July, 1819). He found that monarch hesitating as to whether he should, or should not, grant his people a Constitution. Nothing could be more frank than the language used by Metternich on this point. He told the King, in so many words, that Prussia was the *focus* of revolution; that help to him would be forthcoming only on the condition that he did not introduce representation of the people into his kingdom, 'which,' he added, 'is less fitted for it than any other,' and he succeeded in bringing Frederick William to his views. In a conversation a few days later

Caricature of Metternich in flight, 1848

with the Prussian ministers, he convinced them likewise of the necessity for the repression of free thought and free opinion. And, in agreement with them, he summoned a Conference, in which the several Germanic States should be represented, to meet at Carlsbad, to formulate the action which should be necessary to carry out his views.

The mode in which Metternich proposed to combat the revolutionary feeling is thus formulated by him in a memorandum drawn up for the Emperor Francis, and dated the 1st of August. In this, he states that the measures to be adopted at the coming Conference must be (1) the suspension of the licence of the press; (2) the appointment of commissions for the investigation of the German Universities, and the removal of notoriously bad professors; (3) the formation of a special judicial commission acting in the name of the whole Bund, to investigate the conspiracy discovered against the Bund.

The Conference met the same month, carried out the views of Metternich under his own personal auspices, and nominated a Central Investigation Commission 'for the protection of social order and the calming of all the well-disposed in Germany.'

There remained but one thing necessary to complete the work; to give the death-blow to aspirations for constitutional government. When the allied sovereigns were still under the influence of the gratitude engendered by the exertions which had recovered for them freedom and power, they had inserted a clause in the Treaty of Vienna which suggested the granting of Constitutions by the several rulers of Germany. The existence of this clause had now become a danger. . . .

To understand a man thoroughly it is necessary to dive into his inmost thoughts. This is not always possible even when a man writes his own memoirs, because memoirs may be subsequently altered to suit circumstances. When, however, a conceited and successful man praises himself, such an understanding may be arrived at; for then, we know, he does not lie. The passage I am about to quote will give a better and clearer idea of the opinion of Metternich regarding himself, and of his absolute supremacy in Germany, at this period, than it would be possible to draw from official correspondence. When he had mastered the initial difficulties at the Conference, and had seen clearly that he was about to have an easy victory, he made this entry in his journal:

I have found a moment's quiet. The business of the Conference proceeds very well. I have gone to the root of this matter – a rare thing in moral and political discussions. I told my five-and-twenty friends in an upright and decided manner what we want and what we do not want. On this avowal there was a general declaration of approval, and each one asserted that he had never wanted more or less, or, indeed, hardly anything different. Now, I am surrounded by people who are quite enchanted with their own force of will, and yet there is not one amongst them who a few days ago knew what he wants or will want. This is the universal fate of such an assembly. It has been evident to me for a long time that among a certain number of persons only one is ever found who has clearly made out for himself what is the question in hand. I shall be victorious here as at Carlsbad: that is to say, all will wish what I wish, and since I only wish what is just, I believe I shall gain my victory. But what is most remarkable is that these men will go home with the firm persuasion that they have left Vienna with the same views with which they came.

Can we wonder that with the conviction of his own superiority expressed in the words I have quoted; carrying with him the whole strength of Austria; having moulded Frederick William to his will, and secure in the support of the Czar, Metternich should be supreme in Germany? The words he himself recorded prove that he was not only supreme, but that he felt that he, and he alone, possessed the genius necessary to direct the course of all the rulers of the States composing Germany. It is melancholy to have to record that, disposing of this absolute power, he wielded it in a manner which gained for him the hatred of the races over whom he ruled: he used it to repress liberty, to crush thought, opinion, action; he used it, in a word, to enslave the people to whose valour and patriotism Germany owed her deliverance from Napoleon.

(*See also page 264*)

[36] Fanny Trollope is entertained by Prince and Princess Metternich in 1836 and 1837, first at a Christmas Eve celebration, then at a ball in the New Year; from *Vienna and the Austrians 1836–7* by Frances Trollope.

It is little more than a week since I last wrote to you, and in that interval I have been initiated into many of the quaint devices by which the Austrian Christmas is solemnized. The day after the Turkish ambassador's party we were engaged to dine at Prince Metternich's, for the purpose of seeing the illumination of *the tree*, which was to take place at an early hour, expressly for the amusement of the children; but greatly to our disappointment we received notice, during the morning, that the fête could not have place in consequence of the sudden illness of Prince Metternich's sister, the Dutchess of Wurtemberg. A few hours afterwards, however, we were summoned to the illumination of the tree, as the seizure which had so alarmed the family had passed off without dangerous consequences.

One of the perfections of the Viennese parties is, that they are very punctual to the hour named for them; this is a good habit that I fear we did not bring with us, for we have very frequently found ourselves too late upon occasions when the being so has brought with it real loss. So it was on Christmas-eve. By fearing to arrive too early, we missed seeing the first happy rush of the children when the signal was given that *the tree was lighted*. We reached the scene of action, however, at the moment when everything connected with the pretty ceremony was in full activity.

The large round dining-table was placed in the centre of the great saloon, and on it stood a firtree reaching almost to the lofty ceiling, on the branches of which were fastened a multitude of little waxen lights, such as the devout decorate their favourite shrines withal. Above, around, and underneath this sparkling galaxy of little stars, hung, suspended by dainty knots of various-coloured ribbons, an innumerable quantity of bon-bons and other pretty things which glittered in their rays. To disentangle these, and distribute them to the company, was to be the concluding ceremony; but, meanwhile, a beautiful circle of young faces, radiant with delight, stood round the ample table, one moment gazing at the twinkling brightness of the rich tree, and the next called upon to receive, with rapture greater still, each one a present from the abounding collection of toys that either covered the table or were ranged round it.

The moment after, the animation of the scene became greater still. Here, a huge rocking-horse was put into violent motion by its happy new possessor; there, a game of rolling balls and tumbling nine-pins was set in action. On one side, a princely little coachman, in full Jehu costume, made his whip crack over the heads of his wooden steeds; and, on the other, a lovely little girl was making acquaintance with a splendid doll. Tiny tea-things, and tiny dinner-trays, – miniature cabinets, and minia-ture libraries, – and a world of things besides, more than I have wit to remember or rehearse, were speedily distributed, and

appropriated among as happy a set of pretty creatures as ever
bloomed and sparkled on a Christmas-eve.

Nor was the beautiful mistress of the fête the least charming
object among them. There are some people who, when they give
pleasure, seem to find themselves in the element that is native to
them, and to awaken within it to a keener feeling of life and
enjoyment than in any other. The Princess Metternich is one of
these, and I know from excellent authority that it is not only on a
jour de fête that she shows it. . . . After presents had been
distributed to all the children, I perceived that the tree threw its
light upon other testimonies of affection and kindness. Many
very elegant gifts were presented by the princess to those around
her. No one present was forgotten . . .

15th Jan. 1837
Yesterday, at the mansion of Prince Metternich, we were at the
first grand carnival ball of the season, and a very splendid
entertainment it was. The suite of rooms is a fine one; and the
salle de bal, which, like many other fine receiving-rooms in
Vienna, has walls wearing the appearance of white marble, was
rendered radiant by some hundreds of wax lights, and by the
presence of a very splendid assemblage of company.

Though no country can excel the taste and finish of a Parisian
toilet, the palm of splendour must unquestionably be accorded
to that of Vienna. This surpassing costliness of attire does not
arise solely from the general use among all the married women of
the very finest diamonds in the world, though undoubtedly this
contributes much to it; but, in truth, every article of dress worn
by people of fashion at a Vienna ball is as perfect in costly
elegance as the most lavish expenditure can make it. I will not
attempt to indite a magazin de modes for your instruction, or
venture to enter much into particulars upon this recondite
subject; only one trifling article will I mention as a sample of the
minor finishing required by these *élégantes*. The dainty little
transparencies that are seen depending from between the finger
and the thumb of every fair waltzer by way of a pocket
handkerchief cost at least five hundred francs.

[37] The shooting of Dollfuss in the Ballhausplatz; from *Farewell Austria* by Kurt von Schuschnigg, translated by John Segrue and others.

(In 1934 the Nazis attempted a *putsch* in Vienna. Armed guards broke into the Chancellery and shot Engelbert Dollfuss, Austria's diminutive Chancellor, who bled to death before the Austrian police collected their forces. The Nazis panicked, though, and the *putsch* failed. Four years later there was no mistake and the Anschluss united Austria with the German Reich. By that time the Chancellor was Kurt von Schuschnigg, an ardent patriot who – isolated abroad and outmanoeuvred at home – was powerless to resist the tide.)

Chief Superintendent Johann Greifender, interrogated on July 31, 1934, made the following statement:

'I had received orders to stand by, and at 10 a.m. took up my post near to the accounts department, on the fourth floor of the Federal Chancellery, No. 2 Ballhausplatz, where I was to be on duty until one o'clock. A little before one I heard a noise on the stairs and, opening the door giving on to the staircase, I was confronted by five or six men in uniform, who told me to put up my hands. Looking down to the third floor, I saw two more uniformed men levelling their pistols at my colleague Messinger and disarming him. It occurred to me that I must be among the last to be disarmed; I could not therefore resist. I was taken down to the third floor, where I had to wait on the landing in the company of eight or nine "soldiers" with pointed pistols. Meanwhile, other soldiers had fetched the officials from the rooms on the fourth floor and brought them downstairs, their hands held above their heads. They had to stand there till all were assembled. I pointed out that it was wrong to keep so many people crowded together on the stairs. Whereupon one of the men said: "You keep your mouth shut, we're in command here." An "officer" then came and ordered a general move to the courtyard. The civilians were now separated off, while we were left in the first courtyard close to the main door. I calculate that it took ten to twelve minutes to clear the whole Chancellery.

'Between one-thirty and one-forty-five a rebel came up to us in the yard and asked my colleague, District Inspector Jellinek, whether we were aware that the Chancellor had been wounded.

When we replied in the negative, he asked if we would like to see him, and we, of course, said we would. He then took Jellinek and myself upstairs, where we found the Chancellor in what is known as the Corner Room, lying on the floor in the window nearest the Conference Room. He was lying on his back with his hands stretched out. My colleague and I at once said that a doctor must be sent for, and we were directed to the "Major", who was in the yard outside. We went up to him and asked for the services of a doctor, but he refused, saying that no one was to leave the building. Jellinek then went into the back yard and asked whether there was no doctor among the interned occupants of the building. Finding that there was not, he asked for bandages. While he was still in the back yard, a rebel entered the front courtyard with bandaging material and asked if anyone had any first-aid knowledge. My colleague Messinger and myself volunteered to help and were escorted upstairs, where we found the Chancellor still in the position in which we had left him. He was unconscious. One of the rebels cut open his coat and shirt, handed us the bandages and went away. There were still a few Putschists in the room, and one sat at a desk smoking a cigarette. I held the wounded Chancellor's head and raised him, while Messinger applied the bandage. I then told Messinger that we must get the Chancellor on to some kind of bed, so we dragged up a red sofa and laid him on it. A few of the Putschists helped us. We then washed the Chancellor and bathed his forehead with eau-de-Cologne. One Putschist clumsily sprinkled lysoform over his face, which we wiped away with cotton wool. The Chancellor then regained consciousness. His first question was: "What has happened to the other ministers?" to which I answered: "As far as I know, they are safe." The Chancellor then told us that a major, a captain and a number of soldiers had come in and shot at him. He then inquired whether he could not speak with a minister, and asked in the first place for Dr Schuschnigg. One of the rebels directed us, on inquiry, to the Major. One of them, the Captain I think it was, went out and fetched the Major, who came and said: "You have sent for me, Chancellor, What do you want? If you had not resisted, you would have been all right," to which the Chancellor answered: "I had to, I too was a soldier." The Chancellor repeated his wish to speak with Dr Schuschnigg, but the Major said: "Schuschnigg is not here." The Chancellor then asked for Karwinsky, but the Major made no reply. He then got up and, after some time, returned with Minister Fey. Meanwhile the Chancellor asked if he could be taken to a sanatorium or have a doctor, and also asked for a priest. We appealed in vain to the same effect and I tried to comfort the Chancellor by telling him that the wound was only a flesh wound and needed no doctor. The Chancellor, however, seemed to realize the gravity of his injuries, for he asked us to lift his arms and feet and, when we did so, said: "I can feel nothing. I'm paralysed." He then added: "How good you fellows are to me. Why weren't the others, too? All I wanted was peace. It was we who were attacked; we had to defend ourselves. May God forgive the others." Minister Fey then arrived under escort and, sitting on the arm of the sofa, I heard all that was said. I also renewed the compresses. The Chancellor greeted Fey affectionately and asked how he was, to which Fey replied: "As you see, quite all right." The Chancellor next asked after the other members of the cabinet, and was told that they too were safe and sound. He then asked Fey to request Mussolini, the Italian Premier, to take charge of his wife and children. Fey promised. The Chancellor then said that he wished Dr Schuschnigg to take over the government, or, in the event of his death, Skubl, Vice-President of Police. At this point one of the rebels came up and, leaning across the Major, said: "Chancellor, come to business, we're not interested in that. Give orders to the authorities to refrain from taking any action against the Federal Chancellery until Rintelen has taken over the government." The Chancellor then expressed the hope that all unnecessary bloodshed would be avoided. Lastly, he said to Fey: "Take care of my wife and children." The Putschists then pulled Minister Fey away and took him out on to the balcony. What happened there, I do not know. The Chancellor again complained at being allowed no doctor, fearing that his phlegm was choking him. It was not, however, phlegm that caused this choking feeling, but blood, which we had constantly to wipe away from his mouth. The death-rattle now became more and more audible, and the Chancellor gradually lapsed into unconsciousness. His last words were: "Give my love to my wife and children." Then, after a few gasps, one or two convulsive twitches, his eyes now glassy, he breathed his last. That was at about a quarter to four in the afternoon. The death agony lasted at most five minutes.'

Questioned further on August 4, 1934, Police Superintendent

Johann Greifender added the following statement:

'Supplementing my signed statement of July 31, 1934, I have only the following remarks to make: The Chancellor definitely did not give his consent to the formation of a government by Rintelen. . . .'

[38] Chancellor von Schuschnigg is relieved of his office and Seyss-Inquart appointed by the Nazis in his place; from *Austrian Requiem* by Kurt von Schuschnigg, translated by Franz von Hildebrand.

(With the Nazi entry into Austria, von Schuschnigg's fate, like that of his country, was sealed. Replaced by the Austrian Nazi Seyss-Inquart, he was imprisoned in a concentration camp, from which he was released by the Allies in 1945.)

In the meantime, evening had come. The grey outlines merged in a dusky uniformity. Vienna's buildings lost their individuality, as did Vienna's population. At this hour danger lurks in every large city. Unrest spreads easily, and the unreasoning crowds are prone to rash impulses and precipitate action.

I looked around me. In the Chancellery I saw the offices of Austrian statesmen of the past: Schwarzenberg, Beust, and Andrássy, Kalnoky, Berchthold, and Aehrenthal. These men had occupied the office where now burned a perpetual lamp before a carved wood Madonna. It was the spot where four years ago Engelbert Dollfuss bled to death. And next door – my own office.

I walked a few steps through the large hall where more than a century ago the statesmen of Europe had held the great Congress of Vienna. Slowly, painfully, I said good-bye to these historic rooms, good-bye also to my country, my Austria.

Suddenly I noticed a number of young people in the hall again with that close-cropped haircut. One young man brushed past me without an apology. He turned round and looked me up and down with a purposely offensive, superior smile. Then he went on and slammed the door as if he were at home. I stared after him, and suddenly I realized: Invasion! Not at the borders as yet, but here, in the Chancellery: the Gestapo.

I tried to find Seyss-Inquart. On my way over to the President

I heard the undefinable but unmistakable noise of mass demonstrations in the streets. I heard the tramp of marching feet, shouts, songs. I entered the President's office. President Miklas was adamant. He would not appoint a Nazi as Austrian Chancellor. On my insistence to appoint Seyss-Inquart he said again: 'You desert me now, all of you.' But I saw no other possibility than Seyss-Inquart. With the little hope I had left I clung to all the promises he had made me, I clung to his personal reputation as a practising Catholic and an honest man. I suggested to the President that I should speak immediately over the radio to the Austrian people. He agreed.

The broadcasting facilities in the Chancellery were still intact, and the necessary preparations were made at once. Secretaries, officials, and functionaries crowded into the room. I entered after the President and looked around me. Many friends were there, and also Seyss-Inquart.

The microphone was in the middle of the room – about five paces from where Dollfuss was shot to death. The announcer stepped forward. 'Ladies and gentlemen, the Chancellor of Austria.'

I spoke for about ten minutes. I told the Austrian people how this situation had developed and that we called all the world to witness that we had acted in strict accordance with our political commitments, our treaties, and to the best of our knowledge and ability. That we solemnly protested against the threatened violation of our country's sovereignty, which was as uncalled-for as it was unjustifiable. That Austria yielded to force because even in this hour we were determined to avoid bloodshed in a fratricidal war. That, in accordance with this determination, the order had been given not to oppose the German armies. I ended my speech with a few personal words of farewell.

[39] The announcement of the Nazi annexation of Austria on 13 March 1938; from *Fallen Bastions* by G.E.R. Gedye.

(G.E.R. Gedye, the most perceptive of the inter-war correspondents in Vienna, witnessed the rise of Nazism in Austria and, frustrated by the British policy of appeasement, ended his contract with the *Daily Telegraph* to write *Fallen Bastions*. It was a bestseller.)

Less than twenty-four hours before Hitler's entry [*See page 161*], the annexation of Austria had been made known with cynical abruptness. We of the foreign press were invited to attend at the Austrian Chancellery at 7.30 p.m. on Sunday, March 13th. All the Press Department officials, with one single exception, had been arrested – the Austrian civil servants with whom we had been accustomed to work for years. In their place was a glib gentleman with a monocle, of anything but 'Aryan' appearance, who had formerly been correspondent of a Vienna newspaper in Bucharest, where he was a well-known boulevard figure. M. Lazar first informed us that the Head of State, President Miklas, had been ordered by Chancellor Seyss-Inquart (from whom he had only just taken the oath of loyalty) to resign. Miklas had obeyed, and Seyss-Inquart had become in consequence Chancellor and President at the same time. Consulting his watch, he asked us not to go, as on the stroke of eight he had another very important announcement to make. In between he entertained us with tales of how he had never expected to become Press Chief of Austria until twenty-four hours before, when the Nazis had offered him the job as he sat 'drinking a whisky-and-soda in a Berlin bar'. As the last stroke of eight sounded, Lazar, who was in a state of nervousness which suggested that another whisky-and-soda might have been welcome, announced the annexation. Telling us that the post he had just assumed had at that instant ceased to exist, he read out what he called a 'Federal and Constitutional Law'.

The return of the last guard at the Federal Chancellery, 3 April 1938

The Congress of Vienna

[40] The purpose, and the style, of the Congress of Vienna; from *The Austrian Court in the Nineteenth Century* by Sir Horace Rumbold.

The autumn of 1814 saw the opening at Vienna of the memorable Congress where the map of Europe – which a quarter of a century of warfare and the stupendous Napoleonic conquests had rendered unrecognisable – had to be made afresh, and the destinies of countless populations determined for good or evil. No meeting in more recent times can be compared to it. The concourse of sovereigns, princes, and statesmen, together with celebrities of every kind who flocked to it from all quarters, was quite unprecedented. But although the work got through by this high council of the nations was prodigious – some of its traces being still visible at the present day – the really distinctive trait of the Congress was its outward gaiety, not to say frivolity. So apprehensive was the Austrian Court lest anything should mar the lustre of the great gathering that, on the death of Queen Caroline of Naples, which took place three weeks before the opening of the Congress, no official mourning was ordered for this last surviving daughter of the Empress Maria Theresa, who was not only the Emperor's aunt, but the mother of his second wife, the Empress Theresa.[1] The hospitality dispensed by the Emperor Francis was of the most lavish character. The vast, rambling Hofburg was filled with royal guests who, with such of their suites and attendants as were lodged outside the precincts of the palace, were all provided for from the Imperial kitchens; the daily cost of their entertainment being put by one authority at 50,000 florins (£5,000). . . . During fully six months – from October 1814 till March 1815 – there was an unbroken round of balls, banquets, concerts, masquerades, dramatic performances, amateur theatricals, *tableaux vivants*, and *carrousels*. Half the aristocracy of Europe had been drawn to the Congress, and, if we are to trust narrators such as Varnhagen von Ense and de la

---

[1] One of the motives assigned for this was the difficulty of officially notifying the decease, there being another Queen Caroline of Naples, the wife of Murat, whose dethronement had not yet been finally decided upon.

Garde Chambonas, the number of beautiful women who were present, and took part in the *tableaux* and other scenic representations, must have been surprising.

Meanwhile the great conclave sat all through the autumn and winter, and the chief questions in debate still remained unsolved. *Le congrès danse, mais il ne marche pas*, was one of the last witticisms of that veteran observer, the Prince de Ligne, who died full of years amidst his old haunts in December 1814.

[41] The deliberations and the cost of the Congress; from Richard Bright's *Travels from Vienna . . . in the year 1814*.

I shall certainly be excused for not attempting any detailed account of those proceedings, the general results of which are now known to all. The grand subjects in discussion were the future conditions of Poland, Saxony, and the Italian States, – in fact, all those points in which political expediency appeared to be in opposition to justice. It was the difficulties arising on these subjects which caused the proceedings of the Congress to be so long and tedious, – so many different interests to be consulted, so many scruples to be overcome, and so many just and honest men to be perverted from their ways; – what wonder that some months should have elapsed in consulting, in protesting, and in recanting. Of what notes and memorials, – of what representations and concessions – did we not daily hear: of sturdy ministers who faltered, and of faltering ministers who grew firm. In the midst of all these rumours, it was ever the anxious inquiry, whether England was the steady champion of justice? – whether she boldly asserted and strenuously maintained that character which the boasted freedom of her principles led Europe to expect, and which her preeminence, both in arms and finance, seemed to have placed her in a condition to retain? . . .

All the imperial and royal guests were lodged in the Bourg. Each sovereign had a complete suite of rooms in the lower part of this extensive building; while their attendants, secretaries, physicians, and other officers, occupied the upper stories of the same edifice. For all these, establishments were regularly provided by the Austrian court. Every royal person had a separate equipage, with six or eight horses, and equerries, and a crowd of servants, as well appointed as those which attended immediately on the person of the Emperor. Neither were the potentates, the Emperor of Russia, and King of Prussia, the King of Bavaria, or the King of Wirtemberg, alone thus provided for, but the Empress of Russia also, the Queens and the Duchess of Oldenburg, were splendidly attended, and even each of their principal officers had a pair or four horses, according to his dignity, constantly at command. I have heard it asserted, that between two and three hundred imperial carriages were in daily use, a very large proportion of which had, of course, been prepared for this occasion. They were all painted green, and adorned with either silver or gold. Many of them approached, though none of them equalled, either in elegance or workmanship, the best English carriages.

In the grand square of the palace, four distinct royal guards were constantly mounted, each consisting of about fifty grenadiers; they were stationed near the apartments of the respective sovereigns, upon whom they attended; and whenever the approach of a monarch or general officer was discovered by the sentinels on duty, the intelligence was passed in a yell more hideous than ever issued from the mouth of a Cherokee Indian.

[42] Mingling with the crowned heads of Europe at a redoute during the Congress; from *Travels from Vienna . . . in the year 1814* by Richard Bright.

Not having yet delivered my letters, I accompanied a gentleman of Vienna, with whom I had made an accidental acquaintance. We entered the room about nine o'clock in the evening. It is a magnificent saloon, finely lighted, surrounded by a gallery, and forming a part of the large pile of building called the Bourg or Imperial Palace. Never was an assembly less ceremonious; every one wore his hat; many, till the room became heated, their greatcoats; and no one pretended to appear in an evening dress, except a few Englishmen, who, from the habits of our country, and some little vanity, generally attempt to distinguish themselves by an attention to outward appearance. Around the whole circumference of the room were four or five rows of benches, occupied, for the most part, by well-dressed females; while the other parts presented a moving multitude, many of whom were in masks, or in dominos, and were busily engaged in talking and

The crowned heads of Europe seated around Prince Metternich
(centre) at the Congress of Vienna, 1815

laughing, or dancing to the music of a powerful orchestra. My
companion squeezed my arm, as we passed a thin figure with
sallow shrunken features, of mild expression, with a neck, stiff,
bending a little forwards, and walking badly. 'That is our
Emperor.' I shook my head and smiled. He was alone, and
dressed like the rest. 'Pray allow me to doubt a little till I have
some farther proof.' – 'There, do you see that little man with
white hair, a pale face, and aquiline nose? He was almost pushed
down as he passed the corner; – that is the King of Denmark.'
Again I shook my head in disbelief. 'Here the Emperor of Russia
approaches.' I looked up, and found the information true. His
fine manly form, his round and smiling countenance, and his
neat morning dress, were not to be mistaken; they were the same
which, some months before, I had seen enter the church at
Harlem, to the thundering peals of the grand organ. I soon

recognised the tall form, the solemn and grave features, of the King of Prussia; and afterwards seeing these two in familiar conversation with the two monarchs, whose pretensions I had disputed, was satisfied their claims were just. 'That short, thick, old gentleman, is the Grand Duke of Saxe Weimar. That young man near him, the Crown Prince of Wirtemberg. Here, turn your eyes to that seat. The large elderly man, with a full face, – he looks like an Englishman, – he is the King of Bavaria.' – '*Pardon,*' I exclaimed, stepping quickly aside. 'That was the Grand Duke of Baaden,' said my monitor, 'whose toe you trod upon; he was talking to Prince William of Prussia. Here, fall back a little to let these gentlemen pass, they seem very anxious to go on. One, two, three, four, five; – these are all Archdukes of Austria. – There seems a little press towards that end of the room. – See, three women in masks have beset the King of Prussia; he seems not a little puzzled what he shall do with them. – Now a party of waltzers draws the attention of the crowd, and the King is left to dispose of his fair assailants as he thinks fit. – Do you see that stout tall man, who looks at the dance? – he is the Duke of Saxe Coburg; and by his side, not so stout as himself, is his brother the Prince Leopold.' – 'Who is this young man next to us, marked with the small-pox, who is speaking broken English?' 'It is the Crown Prince of Bavaria; he is said to be very fond of your nation. And here,' giving me another hearty squeeze with his elbow, 'is an English milord.' He had upon his head a remarkably flat cocked hat, – two ladies in dominos leaned upon his arm. The hat, unique of its kind, rather excited a smile in my companion. After a little more pushing, for the room was now become very full, we encountered a fine dark military looking man, not in uniform of course, but with mustachoes. 'This was Beauharnois, viceroy of Italy.' In this way, for two or three hours, did we continue meeting and pushing amongst hundreds of men, each of whom, had he but made his appearance singly at a fashionable rout in London, would have furnished a paragraph to our newspapers, prints to our shops, titles to our bazaars, distinctive appellations to every article of our dress, and themes, if not ideas, to our poets.

As the night advanced, refreshments were provided for those who paid for them, in apartments fitted for the purpose, and several rooms were opened, adjoining to the gallery, where the company might order suppers; and the whole did not break up

till a late hour in the morning. Such was my first introduction to
some of the members of the Congress.

[43] The star-struck Comte de la Garde-Chambonas (see
page 95 for biographical details) and his patron, the
Prince de Ligne, attend a redoute, and the Comte describes
the general conduct of the sovereigns during the Congress;
from his *Anecdotal Reminiscences of the Congress of Vienna*.

It was nine o'clock when we reached the imperial palace, better
known as the Hofburg.

That ancient residence had been specially chosen for those
ingenious *momons*, character-masques in which the incognito of
the domino often lent itself to political combinations in themselves masterpieces of intrigue and conception. The principal
hall was magnificently lighted up, and running around it, there
was a circular gallery giving access to huge rooms arranged for
supper. On seats, disposed like an amphitheatre, there were
crowds of ladies, some of whom merely wore dominos, while the
majority represented this or that character. It would be difficult
to imagine a scene more dazzling than this gathering of women,
all young and beautiful, and each attired in a style most
becoming to her beauty. All the centuries of the past, all the
regions of the inhabited globe seemed to have appointed to meet
in that graceful circle.

Several orchestras executed at regular intervals valses and
polonaises: in adjoining galleries or rooms minuets were danced
with particularly Teutonic gravity, which feature did not
constitute the least comic part of the picture.

The prince had spoken the truth. Vienna at that time
presented an abridged panorama of Europe, and the rout was an
abridged panorama of Vienna. There could be no more curious
spectacle than those masked or non-masked people, among
whom, absolutely lost in the crowd, and practically defying
identification, circulated all the sovereigns at that moment
participating in the Congress.

The prince had a story or anecdote about each. 'There goes
Emperor Alexander. The man on whose arm he is leaning is
Prince Eugène Beauharnais, for whom he has a sincere affection.
When Eugène arrived here with his father-in-law, the King of

Bavaria, the Court hesitated about the rank to be accorded to him. The emperor spoke so positively on the subject as to secure for Eugène all the honours due to his generous character. Alexander, as you are aware, is worthy of inspiring and of extending the deepest friendship.

'Do you know the tall and noble-looking personage whom that beautiful Neapolitan girl is holding round the waist? It is the King of Prussia, whose gravity appears in no wise disturbed by the fact. For all that the clever mask may be an empress, on the other hand it is quite on the cards that she is merely a grisette who has been smuggled in.

'That colossus in the black domino, which neither disguises nor decreases his stature, is the King of Würtemberg. The man close to him is his son, the Crown Prince. His love for the Duchesse d'Oldenbourg, Emperor Alexander's sister, is the cause of his stay at the Congress, rather than a concern for the grave interests which one day will be his. It is a romantic story, the *dénouement* of which we may witness before long.

'The two young fellows who just brushed past us are the Crown Prince of Bavaria and his brother, Prince Charles. The latter's face would dispute the palm with that of Antinous. The crowd of people of different kind and garb who are disporting themselves, in every sense of the word, are, some, reigning princes, others archdukes, others again grand dignitaries of this or that empire. For, except a few Englishmen, easily picked out by their careful dress, I do not think there is single personage here without a "handle" to his name.

'This room in particular only represents a picture of pleasure, my dear boy. . . .'

The intercourse of the sovereigns was marked by a condition of unparalleled intimacy. They vied in showing reciprocal friendliness, attentions, and in anticipating each other's wishes. Not a day went by without interviews conducted with a cordial frankness worthy of the age of chivalry. Were they bent upon disproving all that had been said about the want of mutual understanding, the ambitious views, the motives of personal interest which generally distinguish a congress of crowned heads? Or did they yield to the novelty and charm of a mode of living and a feeling of brotherhood contrasting so forcibly with the frigid etiquette of their Courts?

In order to avoid the restraint of a rigorous ceremonial and of questions of precedence, it had been arranged between them that age alone should decide points of priority in everything, at their entering and leaving apartments, at the promenades on horseback, and in their carriage drives. The decision, it was said, was due to the initiative of Emperor Alexander. The following are the ranks as they were settled according to age.–

1. The King of Würtemberg, born in 1754.
2. The King of Bavaria, born in 1756.
3. The King of Denmark, born in 1768.
4. The Emperor of Austria, born in 1768.
5. The King of Prussia, born in 1770.
6. The Emperor of Russia, born in 1777.

This precedence was, however, only observed in the pleasure parties. As for the official deliberations of the Congress, the sovereigns did not attend any.

One of their first acts of courtesy was the reciprocal bestowal of the badges and stars of their Orders. Those various decorations of all shapes and denominations became a positive puzzle, for besides a long list of the saints of the calendar, there were some of the strangest names, like *the Elephant, the Phœnix, the Black, Red, and White Eagles, the Sword, the Star, the Lion, the Fleece, the Bath*, etc. This exchange was the prelude to others somewhat more important, such as the presents of kingdoms, provinces, or a certain number of inhabitants. One of the ceremonies of that kind most frequently referred to was the investment by Lord Castlereagh, on behalf of his sovereign, of the Emperor of Austria with the Order of the Garter. The Prince de Ligne, who was one of the eyewitnesses, told me that this solemnity was conducted with much pomp and circumstance. Sir Isaac Heard, Garter Principal King of Arms, came expressly from London. It was he who invested the Emperor with the dress of the Order, and attached that much coveted insignia; after which Lord Castlereagh presented the latest recipient with the statutes of the Order. As a fit acknowledgment of the courtesy, the Emperor conferred on the Prince Regent and the Duke of York, his brother, the rank of field-marshal. . . .

The habits of the sovereigns were those of private individuals. It was evident that they were only too pleased to shake off the burden of etiquette. Very often the Emperor of Austria and the

King of Prussia were to be seen strolling about the streets arm-in-arm and dressed in mufti. Emperor Alexander similarly often took walks with Prince Eugène.

They paid each other visits and prepared surprises for one another like cordial friends of old standing; in a word, royal good-fellowship reigned throughout. On Emperor Franz's fête-day Emperor Alexander and the King of Prussia bethought themselves of surprising him as he left his bed, and made him a present, the one of a dressing-gown lined with Russian sable, the other of a handsome silver basin and ewer of exquisite workmanship and made in Berlin. The accounts of those cordially intimate scenes found their way to the public and formed the subject of general conversation. . . .

Meanwhile the sovereigns generally spent their mornings in reviewing the troops at parades, and at shooting-parties, either at the Prater or at this or that royal demesne. On the other hand, they forgathered every day for an hour before dinner, and were supposed to discuss the subjects that had occupied the attention of their plenipotentiaries. The carping outside world maintained, however, that politics were the thing least talked of in that august Olympian assembly, and that the announcement of a forthcoming pleasure party more often than not monopolised the conversation. Business was ousted and the gods became simple mortals.

[44] The Imperial Carrousel takes place in the Spanish Riding School in the Hofburg during the Congress; from *Anecdotal Reminiscences of the Congress of Vienna* by Comte Auguste de la Garde-Chambonas.

The imperial riding-school, constructed by Charles v., and ever since called the 'Hall of the Carrousel,' had been set apart for the function. The structure, the vast interior of which is as spacious as an ordinary church, has the form of a long parallelogram. All around it there runs a circular gallery communicating with the apartments of the palace. Seats for twelve hundred spectators rose in a magnificent sweep of tiers. The gallery was divided into four-and-twenty sections by as many Corinthian columns, against which were hung the scutcheons of the knights with their arms and mottoes.

At each end of the vast arena two stands, occupying the whole length of the building, had been erected. They were draped with the most gorgeous textile stuffs; the one set apart for the sovereigns, empresses, queens, and reigning princes; the other, exactly facing it, intended for the ladies of the twenty-four paladins about to prove that they were the fairest among the fair. Above these stands were the orchestras, in which forgathered all that Vienna could boast in the way of distinguished musicians.

One of the lateral galleries was reserved for the ambassadors, the ministers, and the plenipotentiaries of Europe, for the military celebrities, and for the illustrious foreign families. The Austrian, Hungarian, and Polish nobles occupied the other gallery. Immediately under the imperial stand was the row of rings to be carried away by the competitors at full tilt. Ranged round the arena on pillars were Turkish and Moorish heads with the traditional turban, equally intended to serve as targets for the combatants. No doubt the hatred of the Teuton warriors for their invaders and implacable foes was kept up in days of yore by similar devices. Finally, in order to prevent accidents, the floor of the riding-school was hidden beneath a layer of fine sand, half-a-foot deep. At the door of the hall there was a barrier, marking the entrance to the lists. Behind that door were posted the heralds-of-arms with their trumpets and in gorgeous costumes. Numberless lustres and candelabra holding wax candles shed through this huge interior a light scarcely inferior to that of day. . . .

At eight to the minute a blast of trumpets by the heralds announced the arrival of the twenty-four ladies, escorted by their valiant champions. They took their seats in the first row of their stand.

All, in virtue of their grace and beauty, deserved the name of 'belles d'amour' that had been given to them. They were the Princesses Paul Esterhazy, Marie de Metternich, the Comtesses de Périgord, Rzewuska, Marassi, Sophie Zichy, etc. It is impossible to imagine a more gorgeous and at the same time graceful spectacle. These ladies were divided into four quadrilles, each distinguished by the colour of their dresses, namely, emerald green, crimson, blue, and black. All their dresses were made of velvet, trimmed with priceless lace and sparkling with precious stones. . . . A second blast of trumpets announced the arrival of the sovereigns. At their entrance every body rose, the four-and-twenty ladies flung back their veils, stood forth revealed in all their beauty, and were greeted with unanimous applause, mingled with the acclamations due to the presence of the monarchs. . . . The sovereigns and the spectators being seated, the building immediately rang with stirring military music, and the twenty-four champions appeared at the barrier. They were the pick of the nobility of Europe . . . The pages and squires drew up in line on each side of the arena. The four-and-twenty knights, two abreast, rode up first to the stand of the sovereigns, and lowered their lances in sign of salutation and obedience before the queens and empresses; the latter graciously responded with a wave of their hands. Retracing their steps, the knights direct their horses to the other stand, and offer similar homage to their ladies, who, however, rise in response, and thus give the spectators an opportunity of judging the beauty of their features, the elegance of their figures, and the richness of their dresses. After riding twice round the arena, all the paladins retire, awaiting a new signal.

The heralds soon sound a joyous blast, which is answered by the musicians in the orchestras. The lists are open, and the different games intended to show the skill and strength of the competitors begin. Six knights, followed by their pages and squires, appear. They begin with the *pas de lance* (tilting at the ring); the horses are put to the gallop, and each knight, rapidly borne along, removes at the point of his lance one of the rings suspended before the imperial stand. Each quadrille repeats the same movement three times, until the rings have mostly disappeared, and the dexterity of the competitors has been put to a severe test. At the end of this first exercise the lances with the rings carried by each upon them are handed to the squires, and the second game begins. Each champion, armed with a short dart, flings it with consummate skill at the Saracens' heads, and without slackening his pace picks from the ground, by means of a second curved javelin, the dart he has just flung. After that, drawing their swords, and bent on the necks of their cattle, the knights gallop towards their motionless adversaries, and strike them, endeavouring, however, to cut them down altogether.

Half-a-dozen different games followed, and the whole was wound up by a cleverly simulated combat between the knights – so cleverly simulated that the Prince de Lichtenstein bit the dust, and was carried away unconscious.

[45] Napoleon's escape from Elba and his arrival to ecstatic support in France bring the merrymaking of the Congress to an abrupt halt; from *Anecdotal Reminiscences of the Congress of Vienna* by Comte Auguste de la Garde-Chambonas.

The news of Napoleon's landing at Cannes came while the ball at M. de Metternich's was at its height. The tidings had the effect of the stroke of the wand or the whistle of the stage-carpenter, which transforms the gardens of Armida into a wilderness. In fact, the thousands of candles seemed to have gone out simultaneously. The news spread with the rapidity of an electric current. In vain did the orchestra continue the strains of a waltz just begun; the dancers stopped of their own accord, looking at and interrogating each other; the four words, 'He is in France,' were like the shield of Ubaldo which, presented to the gaze of Rinaldo, suddenly destroyed all the charms of Armida.

Emperor Alexander took a few steps towards the Prince de Talleyrand. 'I told you that it would not last,' he said. The French plenipotentiary did not move a muscle of his face, and simply bowed without replying. The King of Prussia gave a sign to the Duke of Wellington, and both left the ballroom together, followed almost immediately by Emperors Alexander and Francis and M. de Metternich. The majority of the guests seemed bent upon disappearing unnoticed, so that finally the place became deserted save for a few apparently terror-stricken talkers. . . .

It would be impossible to depict the aspect of the Austrian capital from that moment. Vienna was like an individual who, lulled to sleep by dreams of love and ambition, suddenly found himself violently awakened by the rattle of the watchman or the clanging of the belfry warning him that his house was on fire. The various guests from all parts of Europe could not recall without dread the phases of the period that had just gone by. The constantly renewed disasters of a quarter of a century war; the invaded capitals; the battlefields bestrewn with the dead; commerce and industry paralysed; whole families, nay, whole nations, in mourning – all this presented itself simultaneously to their minds; and the recollection of the lurid flames of Moscow lent additional terror to the picture. . . .

'The Congress is dissolved,' Napoleon had said, on setting his foot on French soil at Cannes. Meanwhile, on the 11th March, in the midst of the general consternation, a company of amateurs still played in the Redotto hall *Le Calife de Bagdad* and *Les Rivaux d'eux-mêmes*, and, strange though it may appear, there was a larger audience than might have been expected. It was, however, the final flicker of the expiring lamp; the last feeble sound of the broken instrument. Pleasure took flight. 'The Congress is dissolved.'

Stefansdom

[46] A Turkish visitor is impressed by the Stefansdom in the seventeenth century; from *In the Empire of the Golden Apple* by Evliya Celebi. Translated by Richard Bassett.

All Vienna's churches stand in the shadow of St Stephen's which lies at the very centre of the city. Nowhere in Turkey, Arabia or Persia or in the rest of the Christian world, or indeed anywhere else in the seven zones of our earth, has such an impressive building been erected, or indeed can one ever be constructed again.

Each traveller to this land believes that this church is unique and that is true. I have been to the land of the Poles, to the coast of the Ocean and in the city of Kassa [now Kosice] in Hungary [now Slovakia]. All these places have great churches but the cathedral here is of an extravagant age and splendour. And only Allah knows the value of all the treasures and precious stones which lie within her walls.

When one sees the church from afar, one is blinded by the bright polish of its roofs and its windows made of crystal and painted glass. The entire cathedral glitters and shines like Mount Ararat in Kurdistan. It blinds the human eye. It is like a mountain of light, this Christian church – if only our mosques could be as well appointed.

Inside the calm is only broken because the German believers bring their boys to sing with the organ – ten on each side. They sing sweet melodies and old psalms which in their tremulations seduce the hearts of any listener and bring tears to the eye.

The organ itself has a heart-rending sound like the voice of the anti Christ. It must be good if a blind man hears the organ – he must imagine that it is the voice of the Prophet himself. But this organ has nothing to do with such strength for it is nothing more than a collection of pipes, although brought together with such magical talent that to hear it leaves the senses spinning.

The Stefansdom

[47] Music in the Stefansdom in the eighteenth century; from *Musical Tours in Europe, 1772* by Dr Charles Burney.

(Dr Charles Burney (1726–1814), musician and travel writer, was the father of the novelist Fanny Burney.)

The first time I went to the cathedral of St Stephen, I heard an excellent mass, in the true church style, very well performed; there were violins and violoncellos though it was not a festival. The great organ at the west end of this church has not been fit for use these forty years; there are three or four more organs of a smaller size in different parts of the church, which are used occasionally. That which I heard in the choir this morning is but a poor one and as usual, was much out of tune; it was played, however, in a very masterly, though not a modern style. All the responses in this service, are chanted in four parts, which is much more pleasing, especially where there is so little melody, than the mere naked *canto fermo* used in most other catholic churches; the treble part was sung by the boys, and very well; particularly, by two of them, whose voices, though not powerful, had been well cultivated.

[48] A French Protestant in the Stefansdom in 1808; from *De L'Allemagne* by Madame de Staël.

Vienna is an old town, fairly small but surrounded by very spacious suburbs: they claim that the town enclosed within the fortifications is no larger than it was when Richard Coeur de Lion was imprisoned not far from its gates. The streets in that part are as narrow as those in Italy; the palaces are a little reminiscent of those in Florence; in fact, nothing there resembles the rest of Germany except some Gothic buildings that call to mind the Middle Ages.

    First among these buildings is the tower of St Stephen: it rears above all the churches in Vienna and majestically dominates the good and peaceful town, whose generations and whose glories it has seen pass. They say it took two centuries to build this tower, starting in 1100: the whole history of Austria is connected with it in some way. No other building can be as patriotic as a church: it is the only one in which all classes of the nation can gather together, the only one which recalls not only public events but private thoughts, the inmost feelings, which rulers and citizens have brought within its precincts. . . .

The tomb of Prince Eugène [*of Savoy*] is the only one for a long time to have been erected in this church: it awaits other heroes. As I approached it, I saw attached to one of the columns surrounding it a small piece of paper on which it was written *that a young woman asked us to pray for her during her illness*. The name of this woman was in no way indicated; an unhappy being was appealing to strangers, not for succour but for prayers; and this was happening beside the lifeless body of a celebrity who perhaps also has pity on the suffering of the living. A pious custom of Catholics, and one which we ought to copy, is that of leaving churches always open; there are so many moments when one feels the need of their sanctuary! And one never enters there without re-experiencing an emotion which benefits the soul and which as if by some holy ablution, returns strength and purity to it.

[49] Good Friday and Easter Day in the Stefansdom, 1814; from Richard Bright's *Travels from Vienna . . . in the year 1814*.

On Good Friday, the burial of our Saviour was commemorated in all the churches. I saw it in St Stephen's. Service was first performed at the grand altar, where the archbishop, bishop, and several of the clergy, officiated. During that time, the crucifix stood upon the altar, concealed from public view. But the veil was at length gradually drawn up, and the body of our Saviour exposed to the adoration of the people; after which the priests, about twenty in number, clad in the most splendid habits of their order, formed themselves in procession; and in the midst stood the archbishop with robes of purple lined with ermine, with a mitre of white silk embroidered with gold; he was accompanied by the bishop, likewise in his full robes. The reverend archbishop, bending with age, bore the crucifix. They moved solemnly down the middle aisle, pausing from time to time to pay homage to the sacred emblem. They passed up the right aisle to an altar, where the archbishop placed the crucifix upon a bench covered with velvet; and the priests and many attendants advancing in turn, prostrated themselves and kissed the body of our Saviour. Another service being performed, the whole proceeded as before, but accompanied by persons bearing torches, to a chapel in a remote part of the church, where they deposited the crucifix with the utmost solemnity of prayer. Then, returning to the grand altar, they again employed themselves in prayer and chaunting, and at length arrived at the left aisle, which was completely darkened. The light of the torches here illuminated a monumental group of angels in white marble, and a black cross hung with white drapery. Here they repeated similar ceremonies; and soon after, having made another circuit through the church, the procession concluded. There was something in this solemnity more striking than is usual on such occasions. The effect was magnificent. The groups of adoring priests, – the fine Gothic architecture, – and the gloom which pervaded the church, – and the solemn music, were admirably suited to recall a lively remembrance of the events it was intended to commemorate. . . .

In the [*Saturday*] evening the Imperial family, with all the members of the ecclesiastical establishment, made another solemn and splendid procession round St Stephen's church, in the presence of a vast concourse of people. The following day was Easter Sunday, and, as my landlady, or her servant, had been early at the church with a fine white loaf, some eggs, ham, and horse-radish, folded in a napkin, to receive the blessing of the priest, I was favoured with some of this bread to my coffee, and, after attending the high mass, was invited by my landlord to partake of their family dinner, the first dishes of which were composed of those viands, which the priest had rendered holy in the morning.

[50] The Stefansdom – exterior, interior and its colouring; from *Vienna and the Austrians 1836–7* by Frances Trollope.

St Stephen's, as a metropolitan archiepiscopal church, is small; but the beauty of many parts of it, and the graceful, solemn, and harmonious effect of the whole, place it decidedly in the very first class of churches. Like a multitude of other noble cathedrals, it was intended to have two spires; but at the end of between four and five hundred years it still stands unfinished with one.

The nave of the Stefansdom

And that one ... I hardly know whether it would be more just to say, that its exceeding beauty is sufficient to atone for every imaginable deficiency in every other part of the edifice, or that its light and elegant form leads one to regret the more bitterly that the rich structure is not rendered perfect by having another and a similar graceful pinnacle piercing the heavens on the other side of it. There is one peculiarity in this lovely spire, that, as far as my memory goes, renders it unique. Instead of being placed, as at Antwerp, Strasburg, Salisbury, etcetera, on a tower, it rises, fine by degrees and beautifully less, from the ground.

This church of St Stephen's is so very beautiful, with its dark mellow tone of colouring, its rich carvings, its graceful proportions, and the indescribable air of dim religious sanctity which seems to envelope every part of it, that I suspect it is not easy to form a fair unprejudiced opinion on the merits of this deviation from common usage. I think it probable that a spire of ordinary beauty thus placed beside an ordinary building, would not have a good effect; but I can scarcely imagine it possible that any one could be found, while standing in the Stephensplatz, and looking at this delicately-wrought pyramid, who could be capable of saying, 'That spire would be better were it other than it is.'

This master-piece, which rises to the majestic height of five hundred feet, is towards its top very visibly out of the perpendicular. A gentleman who, if I mistake not, is entirely to be depended on, told me that this was the effect of the bombardment by the Turks at their second visit to Vienna, in 1683: another has told me that the injury was done at the bombardment of the town, on the 11th May 1809, by the French: and another still, who accidentally stood near us while we were looking at it, assured me that the obliquity had been occasioned by an earthquake. Whatever were the cause, the injury has been very considerable; and this enormous height of delicately perforated stone is now sustained by a frame-work of iron within, which is supposed to render it as secure as if it had never been shaken.

The interior of this beautiful church is as fine as the exterior. The pillars which support the nave are the most richly ornamented that I remember; and the extraordinary profusion of stone carving in pillars, pulpit, altars, and monuments, gives to the whole building the air of a holy museum, to which every pious worker in stone of the middle ages made a point of contributing something.

But not all this richness in the detail could have sufficed to produce that exquisite effect of harmonious gloom which strikes so forcibly upon the feelings on entering the St Stephen's of Vienna, were it not for the strangely uniform and universal tint that pervades every part of it. The shade of colour differs a little between the walls and the various richly-wrought objects seen against them; but, like the 'Brown Girl' of Murillo, the whole offers nothing to the eye to cut that soothing series of dark, soft, clear-obscure tones which it is so delightful to look upon.

I had gazed long and steadily at these fine grey walls, and, I may say, *enjoyed* their harmony of tint, without being at all able to understand why it was that there was such a dark richness in their colour, as made even the unscathed and holy solemnity of Westminster Abbey seem pale in my remembrance; when, at last, Mr H— exclaimed, 'The walls are painted!'

There appeared something almost profane in the assertion, and it was most strongly controverted by more voices than one. On close examination, however, the fact was fully established: not only is the native stone coated with some species of dark colouring, but in many places, though in general they are nearly effaced, we traced the coloured lines intended to indicate the neat layers of cement by which the blocks are joined.

Whatever might have been the reason for laying on this artificial surface, whether it were to cover some previous profanation of whitewash, or for the purpose of protecting the crumbling material, I have at present no means of knowing; but, whatever the motive, the operation has been performed with such successful attention to general effect, that it is impossible not to admire it.

[51] Vincent Novello attends Mass in the Stefansdom in 1829; from *A Mozart Pilgrimage, being the Travel Diaries of Vincent and Mary Novello* . . . transcribed and compiled by Nerina Medici di Marignano, and edited by Rosemary Hughes.

Sunday, Vienna, St Stephen's Cathedral, 8 o'clock, Chorale in G and sermon, at 9 o'clock High Mass . . .

Introit in C quite in Palestrina's solemn and churchified style . . . the service began with a procession round the church by the priests who sprinkled the people with Holy water as they proceeded . . .

The Mass was in a poor commonplace old style like what might have been written by Hasse or Vinci; all the movements were short and unsatisfactory. The best voices were the trebles. The orchestral performers were of the mediocre kind.

The resonance is much less than what might have [been] expected in so large a building, probably on account of there being no *transepts* but only a small recess under the large towers.

Beautiful Altar piece of sculpture at the Cathedral; two fine stained glass windows close to the Altar. Pity the rest were destroyed except the first one on the left of choir and the beautiful little chapel – with 'dim, religious light' – under the South-west Tower near the great door, which seemed to be seldom or never used. Exquisitely fine painting of a single head at the Altar in the side Chapel to the left of the High Altar, worthy of Guido – as much force and energy of expression as I ever saw.

[52] A mid-nineteenth-century ascent of the spire of the Stefansdom; from *Austria . . .* by J.G. Kohl.

My best friend in Vienna was named Stephen, and when I heard he had become a widower lately, I went to pay him my visit of condolence. At first I did not very well understand the expression 'become a widower,' as, to the best of my knowledge, my friend Stephen, who was above four hundred feet high, and five hundred years old (being no other than the renowned steeple dedicated to that abovenamed saint) had never been married, although he had many brothers, as the double steeple in Rheims, the sister steeples in Munich, Lubeck, and other places. I asked, therefore, with some reason, 'how he could have become a widower,' and was answered 'Because it has pleased the fates, and the safety police to relieve him of his *cross*.' So this was a piece of Vienna wit, which will not be taken amiss by any married lady in the world, I think, for the compliment implied is far greater than the discourtesy at first apparent. If it be maintained that every married man bears his wife enthroned in honour far above himself, as Stephen's Tower bore his cross, it must be admitted that the matrimonial burden cannot but be a light one to so great and portly a gentleman. This cross was also united with a double eagle, spreading its lordly pinions over the Tower, even as married ladies sometimes extend another pretty little instrument authoritatively over the heads of their wedded lords, or wedded servants as they should rather be called.

Stephen, as he is sometimes laconically styled in Vienna, is in general fanned by the pinions of more peaceful birds, or by the harmless, though, from its great height, sometimes outrageous god of wind; but nearly every hundred years this tower has had visiters of another description, lowering, black, hard-headed fellows, who cared little how they ruffled his carefully arranged toilet. Between the different bombardments, which Vienna and St Stephen's Tower, in particular, have suffered from the Hungarians, Turks, – a second time from the Turks, and lastly from the French; exactly a hundred years have each time elapsed. Since the last shooting match, forty years have nearly flown away; from what direction the bombs of 1907 or 1909 are to whistle, it is not difficult to guess; for every traveller who visits Austria must ask himself why all the windows and loopholes, looking to the north-east, are not a little better fastened up. Perhaps Stephen may weather the bombardment of 1907, and, perhaps, a sixth or a seventh, but at last his courage may sink under these repeated attacks, till one day the old, crazy, useless Stephen, out of regard to the heads of the worthy citizens, will be ordered to be removed altogether. God be thanked, the hands by which, and the heads for whose sake this will have to be done, lie still in the darkness of the future. At present the good people of Vienna are busied in removing the old wornout bones, and substituting new ones. I examined the work closely. The permission is obtained in the office of the church-master, where a printed passport for this little journey to the clouds is issued. . . .

St Stephen's Tower is inhabited from top to bottom by very different kinds of men and animals. At the bottom, strangers are under the guidance of two young ecclesiastics. Further up, as far as the roof, the church servants bear sway; we then enter the territory of the bell-ringers, and at the very top of the tower watchmen keep watch and ward. All, according to their own fashion, do the honours of the place, and levy a contribution on travellers. On all sides one is called upon to look and admire; here is the hole through which, some years ago, a man, weary of life, flung his hat down into the church, and then flung himself after it – there are the bells, cast by order of the emperor Joseph I, from the captured Turkish cannon – here is the great crescent, which the Vienna people fastened to their tower to induce the Turks to spare the splendid edifice – there are the twelve engines and thirty cisterns for the protection of the building against fire. In March they are filled with water strongly impregnated with salt, which is thus preserved throughout the summer. Admiration is also challenged for the great ugly double eagle lying with outspread pinions on the roof, probably the largest figure of a bird in the world. If it could rise into the air it might pass for the offspring of the far-famed roc; from the extremity of one wing to that of the other the measurement is one hundred and eighty feet. Each eye is formed of four gilded tiles, and each beak contains not less than thirty such scales.

People who are fond of taking exceptions against modern times, may find abundance of opportunity on the roof of this cathedral. In 1830 it was found necessary to repair a portion; the new tiles were shaped and coloured after the model of the old; but after the lapse of only ten years they are worn out. The glazing and colour is worn off the greater part, the white glaze turning quite red, and displaying the native hue of the clay, while the old tiles, the work of the middle ages, retain all their original tints and freshness. It is feared that the roof itself may suffer from the badness of the tiling, and a renewal of the work is already talked of. . . .

The length of the piece latterly removed from the tower, from apprehension of insecurity, is about eleven fathoms; that is, as the whole tower contains about seventy-two fathoms, nearly a sixth of the whole. This piece had long swayed from the right line, in consequence of an earthquake, it was said, but at first with an inclination of only three feet from the highest point of the cross. At last, however, it was asserted that the highest point was a whole fathom out of the perpendicular. Many smaller parts had also been much injured, partly by time and natural causes, partly by the different bombardments. The [*repair*] work was begun on the twenty-fourth of September, 1838; it was hoped that in three years it would have been finished, but it will certainly require three more to restore the noble building to its former magnificence and perfection. What a day of joy will that be for the people of Vienna!

The very solid manner in which the scaffoldings are erected, must have offered no small difficulty; from below, all this joinery cannot be looked at without a slight sensation of fear, lest some tremendous hurricane might in its sport scatter these beams like matches, and hurl them down upon the roofs and heads below. Whenever the wind is very high, the work must be discontinued, and the workmen retire . . . The difficulties experienced in the execution of the building may be estimated from this one circumstance, that half a day is required to raise the stones . . .

In order that the new stones used in the repairs may not be too conspicuous by the side of the old, they have invented a new colour, wherewith to stain them, but the right shade has not been caught, and the places repaired are easily recognizable from below. We pointed this out to the people about, but they assured us, that after many attempts no better colour could be found. It struck us at first as very extraordinary that it should be so very difficult to hit the colour of a mass of old gray stones, and began to examine them more minutely. We found such a variety of shades on every side and every stone, that it was clearly impossible that one and the same colour should suffice to blend old and new harmoniously together. The tints, moreover, depend partly on the vegetation, – the mosses which cover nearly the whole surface of the tower. In some places these mosses are withered and decayed; the stones are then covered with a dark gray coating that can be rubbed to dust between the fingers. Here and there occur patches of young moss, producing a grayish green tint; then come whitish grays, bluish and yellowish colourings. To give the right effect it would be necessary to lay on all these tints and blend them softly together; and even this would scarcely suffice, as the appearance of the whole changes with the weather. In rain and damp weather not only the bare stones change their colour, but also those covered with moss. The mosses attract the moisture, and many that look withered in dry weather seem to gain new life after rain. In a wet season the verdure of the tower on one side becomes extremely vivid, and it is impossible to follow all these changes with any artificial colour. It is a question whether it would not have been better to leave the new stones of their natural colour, trusting to time to assimilate them. Be this as it may, it is certain that the chosen colour is much too palpably blue, and ought to have been blended to a yellowish gray. . . .

From the wooden galleries erected for the repairs, the panorama of the city of Vienna can now be enjoyed more conveniently than ever. I wished to look on this spectacle from the summit of one of the side towers. This summit is formed like the leaves of a rose flattened at the top and affording just space enough for two human feet. We ascended accordingly, and perched like squirrels on the topmost branch of a tree. The beautiful city of Vienna lay at our feet. It was a most beautiful, calm, clear day. We heard and saw all that was passing in the city; even the songs of the canary birds in the windows of some houses ascended to us and we could see the butterflies fluttering over the house-tops in search of some green spot in this (for them) dreary waste. We could have told a gentleman we saw walking below, where the brother was of whom he was in search; for we saw him at the same time driving at his leisure on the glacis. This glacis, which surrounds the inmost core of the city, with its broad green ring, lends the panorama its principal ornament; it causes the whole picture to fall into picturesque parts, and permits the fine rows of houses in the suburbs to be seen to full advantage. They lie round the outer edge of the glacis like white flowers in a wreath of green leaves. The tower keeper named to us all the market-places, streets, houses, and palaces we saw beneath, showed us the Danube, the first range of the Carpathian mountains, the Styrian Alps, and the roads that led to Germany, Moravia, Bohemia, and Italy, and 'that is,' added he, 'the high road to Hungary.' Here was matter for a prophetic homily, but I did not preach it, for it would have been a voice calling in the desert.

The walls, the Glacis and the Ringstrasse

[53] A description in 1665, by a Turkish envoy, of the fortifications of Vienna, which had defied the first siege of Sultan Suleiman the Magnificent; from *In the Empire of the Golden Apple* by Evliya Celebi. Translated by Richard Bassett.

The fortifications of Vienna have altogether eight principal gates with several others along the banks of the Danube. Where the land is low, the ramparts are almond-shaped and with some twenty-seven bastions are a formidable piece of construction, a powerful defence with high walls and extensive cover: a menacing fortress and a veritable temple of paganism. May Allah allow it to fall into our hands.

The shells which the Sultan Suleiman fired at the western fortifications [*in 1529*] still lie buried in the walls. Each year, though, monks come from other provinces and rebuild the damaged walls in accordance with their evil beliefs, and make them as strong as the castles of Alexander.

[54] The defences of Vienna before the Turkish siege of 1683; from *Vienna in the Age of Metternich* by Stella Musulin.

Vienna was now standing on the brink of major ordeal. Until now the sounds of battle had been remote, all the more so for the lack of news and the air of studied unconcern under which those in authority concealed their profound anxiety over the future. Seen from the Kahlenberg, or if it had been possible, from the air, the town looked very much as it had for well over a century and as it would continue to look until 1857. Vienna lay like a great starfish, its arrowhead-shaped bastions pointing out into the surrounding Glacis, the defensive ring, 1,900 feet across, as wide as the range of a late seventeenth-century cannon.

Now, when so few of those palaces are left which the great architects of the late seventeenth and early eighteenth centuries, Fischer von Erlach the elder and younger, Lukas von Hilde-

The siege of Vienna by the Turks in 1683;
engraving by Johann Martin Lache

brandt and others, built along the outer rim of the Glacis, it is not
easy to visualize the splendour in which the capital of the Empire
lay, surrounded, as was the person of the monarch, by names
which were the jewels in his crown: Schwarzenberg, Schönborn-
Batthyány Trautsohn, Auersperg, Harrach, Kinsky, Liechtenstein. And the patch of grass which the survivors may still possess,
what consolation is this for the gardens on which speculative
building so soon encroached? The greater part of this defensive
belt upon which nothing was allowed to be built consisted of
meadows, lanes and poplar-lined avenues, while the noxious
River Wien flowed between the Karlskirche and the city walls.
Further down to the south-east a 'flea market' offered the poorest
sector of the population all sorts of second-hand goods, particu-

larly clothes, and the lowest prostitutes were to be found after sundown near the walls, but well clear of the gates. The impression given by contemporary artists, who, of course, always exaggerated distances, is of a kind of vast no-man's-land separating the walled city from the encircling palaces, and all the villages at their backs. The scene is often shown relatively empty of people, apart from a picturesque hay wagon or two. The truth must have been quite otherwise, and the traffic on the main roads – through the Kärntnertor (Carinthian Gate) and along the present Wiedner Hauptstrasse, or through Mariahilf to Schönbrunn, will have been heavy. Mostly on foot, there were thousands whose business brought them daily into the city; not only the hewers of wood and drawers of water – rising rents were consistently pushing people with fixed incomes out into the suburbs.

[55] Colonel Hoffman, liaison officer between the defenders on the walls and the Imperial relief force under Prince Sobieski (see also page 214) comments on the barbarity and tenaciousness of the Turkish besiegers; from *Eye-witness Accounts of the Siege of Vienna* collected by Karl Rach. Translated by Richard Bassett.

Today (1 September, 1683) we sowed mines in front of the Burg as the enemy has already reached the inner wall. Starhemberg sorties out with 400 men to destroy the enemy here, but though the troops drive the Turks to the escarpment – the enemy is strongly reinforced and our attack comes to a sudden standstill. We experience heavy losses and must withdraw. The Turks who follow kill all our wounded. Following us into the gates, they continue the fight and only the arrival of Counts Serenyi and Scherffenberg with a detachment of officers finally drives them back.

One of our men trapped outside is wounded by a Janissary who is about to kill his victim until we shoot him, but though mortally wounded he falls on our man, stabbing until his last breath. (We eventually under cover of darkness but with great difficulty manage to retrieve our wounded man.)

Field Marshal Count Starhemberg during the defence of Vienna
against the Turks in 1683; design for a fresco by Karl von Blaas

[56] The orders given by Count Kaplir on 7 September 1683, preparing the city to face a final all-out attack by the Turks; from *Eye-witness Accounts of the Siege of Vienna* collected by Karl Rach. Translated by Richard Bassett.

Chains are to be erected across all streets near the walls to form a last line of defence in the event of the enemy penetrating the walls. Because a general attack is to be expected any day, all inflammable roof materials are to be removed forthwith. All troops to be on day and night alert. All priests are asked to rally the population in the city's churches so that as many prayers as possible can be lifted up so as to help the day come when the city will be relieved.

In the the evenings it is true that the Turks have not set off any salvoes but there is much music and a great deal of shouting to be heard from his lines. BE VIGILANT!

[57] After the battle which lifted the Siege of Vienna in 1683, the young Irish Count Taaffe writes in triumph to his brother, the Earl of Carlingford; from *Eye-witness Accounts of the Siege of Vienna*, collected by Karl Rach. Translated by Richard Bassett.

(Taaffe, like many Irishmen, served the Habsburgs with distinction; one of his descendants was Prime Minister under Emperor Franz-Josef in the nineteenth century.)

We have freed Vienna! If the victory is not as great as we might have hoped, this is due to the cowardice of the enemy whom we have driven from the field in great disorder. The enemy has enormous losses. He has left us all his artillery, most of his tents and all his baggage. I have just heard that the entire treasure of the Vizier has fallen into our hands . . .

The Poles have captured the great flag of Mohammed which the Sultan gave to the Vizier. Our cavalry has found thousands of gold ducats.

[58] The walls and Glacis as they appeared in 1836; and a May Day review of troops on the Glacis by Emperor Franz I; from *Vienna and the Austrians 1836–7* by Frances Trollope.

Vienna properly, or rather literally, so called, is, to use a phrase of Horace, 'the least part of herself.' The Stadt, or centre of this elegant city, is surrounded by fortifications which form, prob- ably, the most beautiful town promenade in the world. The elevation of the wall which supports this glorious terrace is from fifty to seventy feet, following the inequalities of the ground; and the walk is varied by many bastions, several plantations of ornamental trees, and in one or two points by public gardens, through which the passage is never impeded. Some of the pleasantest mansions in the town have their principal windows looking upon the Bastey, as this beautiful promenade is generally called, and their entrance in the streets; while others have their entrance from the Bastey; at which points a carriage approach is arranged from the street below, but always in such a manner as not to interfere either with the beauty or convenience to the gravelled terrace.

Outside this magnificent wall, the masonry of which is worthy of all admiration, runs a fosse, now converted into drives and walks of great beauty and enjoyment, and ever affording on one side or other of the town the most perfect shelter from the winds with which its neighbour mountains are apt to visit it.

Rising on the exterior circle of the fosse is the Glacis, also devoted to the health and pleasure of the population, planted in many parts with trees, and everywhere intersected with well- kept walks and drives.

Then comes the Vorstadten, or, as I should describe it, the outer town, forming, excepting where the Danube cuts through it, a complete circle of faubourg round the city. When I tell you that the dwelling-houses of the faubourgs amount to five times the number of those in the city, you will understand what I mean when I say that Vienna is the least part of herself. One reason why the singular arrangement of this town is so delightful is, that the view from many points of the walks and drives is highly beautiful; having the fine range of the Kalenberg mountains on one side as a back-ground, and a multitude of objects, full of interest and beauty, presenting themselves in succession near the eye, as you make your circular progress. But there is another reason still, and that of infinitely greater importance to its enjoyment, which is the perfect freedom from filth, or external annoyance of any kind. How the thing is managed passes my comprehension; but neither in the streets of the city, on its noble and widely-spreading ramparts, beneath its lofty walls, in its deep wide fosse, or its extended Glacis, is any sight or scent to be met that can either offend the senses or shock the feelings in any way. . . . .

Yesterday was the May-day we have been looking forward to as the occasion that was to show us Vienna out of doors. Nor were we disappointed; for, though we had neither May-pole nor chimney-sweepers, it was by far the gayest May-day I remember. . . . .

The spectacle next in order was a review of all the troops in the garrison by the Emperor. The pretty Glacis was the scene of this gay military display, and nowhere can a spectacle of the kind be seen to greater advantage than from the lofty ramparts which overlook it. The Archduke Albert told me of this review at the birthday ball at the French ambassador's, or we should have missed altogether the only thing of the kind that has been within our reach since we entered Austria. Like everything else that Vienna has shown us, it was *bien monté* brilliant, and of the *highest finish*, but not on a very extensive scale. For the uniforms and trappings, it was quite a little 'champ du drap d'or;' and few men look so well on horseback as the nobles of this most picturesque and chivalric empire. The young archduke rides in the field as the son of his father should ride, and in short the whole thing made a beautiful picture.

[59] Radetsky's funeral on the Glacis in 1858; from *Recollections of a Diplomatist* by Sir Horace Rumbold.

(Field Marshal Radetsky, immortalized by Johann Strauss in his celebrated march, was a remarkable man. Schooled in the old ways of Austrian military incompetence during the Napoleonic Wars, he nonetheless proved forty years later (and aged well over eighty) that when well led the Austrians could match the Italians with ease. Though he was outnumbered and outgunned, his strategy brought dazzling successes at Custozza and Novara, and saved Franz-Josef's Italian provinces.)

Emperor Franz I in procession through the Kärntnertor, 1814

These Italian occurrences remind me of one of the grandest and
most impressive military pageants I ever witnessed. Radetzky
died in Italy in January 1858, and his body was brought home
for interment. The Emperor resolved to receive the remains with
exceptional honours. On the day of the funeral the garrison of
Vienna, strengthened by the troops quartered in the neighbourhood, some 40,000 men in all, were drawn up in massive columns
on the Burg Glacis to receive the funeral car which had been
deposited in a neighbouring church. When all was ready and the
procession duly marshalled the Emperor rode out of the Burg,
attended by a single aide-de-camp, and took command of the
entire force. I watched the *cortège* from the windows of an
apartment in the Leopoldstadt. It was a cold, dark day and light
flakes of snow were whirled about by the bitter gusts of wind. For

The funeral procession of Field Marshal Radetsky, on the Glacis in 1858

hours the troops went past; horse, foot, and artillery; Hungarians, Italians, and Croats; renowned regiments like *Deutchmeister Infanterie* or the veteran Marshal's own Hussars; Dragoons and Lancers, Jägers and Cuirassiers – all in winter campaigning dress, with no gold and no glitter, but the absolute perfection of military trim and equipment. Dead silence in the crowd that thronged the pavements on the line of march, and no sound but the rumble of the artillery waggons, the tread of the battalions, the clatter of horses' hoofs, the clanking of spur and scabbard, the roll of the muffled drums, and – most striking to me of all – the music of the bands playing a solemn strain which seemed strangely familiar and yet had a new and unaccustomed rhythm. Some clever Capellmeister had had the simple, but ingenious, thought of adapting old Strauss's brilliant Radetzky march to a minor key and a dirge-like measure, and, as regiment after regiment filed by, there came up through the frosty air a fresh wail of this famous melody, with just enough of its old original fierceness and wildness left in it to carry the mind back to the days when they had hoisted the octogenarian into his saddle at Custozza or Novara, the troops as they passed him cheering like mad for 'Vater Radetzky,' and pressing onwards with such irresistible *élan*, to the sound of diabolical *Sturmmarsch*, as to drive their gallant foe from position after position till all was over and the Kaiser held his own again in Italy.

Thus they bore him in sternest military pomp to the Northern Railway station, whence he was to be taken to his ancestral vault in Moravia, and surely never were honours better bestowed. Radetzky and the 40,000 faithful men whom he kept to their standards saved the Monarchy at its darkest hour, when all around was crumbling to pieces, when Vienna and Prague were at the mercy of the mob, when Hungary was in flames, and the Emperor a fugitive at Olmütz. It is no exaggeration to say, in the words of Grillparzer, that the Empire was for a time in [Radetzky's] camp alone, and that in reconquering Italy he remade Austria.

[60] The building of the Ringstrasse on the Glacis in the 1850s; from *The Fall of the House of Habsburg* by Edward Crankshaw.

Nineteenth-century Vienna suffered, like every other city, from the galloping blight of tenement housing, as the fields were put down to slums. But the compact centre of the city remained intact; and, at the height of the industrial expansion, this living heart, with its steep-roofed Gothic cathedral reared high above the Baroque palaces and churches of Fischer von Erlach and Hildebrandt, was encircled by the finest street in Europe. The Ringstrasse was built on the old open glacis left by the Emperor Josef when he pulled down the city walls late in the eighteenth century. Planted with multiple rows of limes and plane trees, it took in the palace of the Habsburgs and raised a new skyline composed of massive buildings which might have been put up to celebrate the founding of an empire rather than its end: the Opera, which had first call on the finest native singers from a dozen lands; the Burg Theatre, the shrine of a great tradition expressed in the brilliances of Sonnenthal and Kainz; the Parliament building, to replace Schmerling's wooden 'circus'; the monumental twin museums of art and science; the great new university; the City Hall; the Palace of Justice; the Ministry of War – all splendid among gardens, parks and trees. This feverish institutional building in the grandest manner must have filled the city with a sense of power and purpose, although it did not get into its stride until after the loss of Italy. It was designed as the crown of Empire; but it turned out to be a tomb.

[61] The Ringstrasse in the late nineteenth century; from *Austria: her people and their homelands* by James Baker.

The other centre of Vienna is in the beautiful garden space on the Ring, where rises up yet another tall spire over the handsome Rathaus; and not far off is the classical building wherein sits the Reichstag. From these two centres Vienna and Austria are ruled; but from Schönbrunn, on the outskirts of Vienna, comes the mighty influencing power of the Imperial Crown, for some sixty years borne by Francis Joseph I, who ever wields the highest controlling power, and moulds and bends the authorities for the welfare of the State. . . .

From this modern centre of the capital, where we halted before the Rathaus, to get a glimpse at her history, the picturesque tree and garden-planted Ring encircles the city, and by electric tram, or in a droshky, we can visit all the historic spots, the great ecclesiastical and lay monuments, that so richly embellish Vienna.

A statue of Pallas Athenae rises before the Greek portico of the Parliament House, a statue that has given opportunity to the wits of Vienna to say that they have placed all the learning outside the building, but the *coup d'œil* from this statue of all the great and handsome buildings around, with the lovely well-kept gardens surrounding them, is one difficult to surpass for beauty.

The Rathaus, the Hofburg Theatre, the University, the delicate gothic of the Votive Church, and stretching away to the right the long line of trees, and the vast handsome buildings of the Imperial Museum, with its superb collections of industrial art, and the famous picture gallery [*now in the*

Kunsthistorischesmuseum], that holds the collections once housed in the Belvedere, and very much more of inestimable value, all these handsome and interesting buildings are in view. Many and many a day can be spent on this Ring, amidst the art treasures, and in the museums housed in the Rathaus and elsewhere; in the Volksgarten, that is on the other side of the Ring, is music, such as the Viennese love; whilst not far off is the luxurious and artistic opera house. On the other side of the Ring, round about the Schiller Platz, are many of the public official offices of the Empire. As throughout Austria, music is every-where in Vienna; the Austrian military bands are certainly the finest in Europe for delicacy and expressiveness of execution, and the various orchestras, under enthusiastic directors, give excel-lent renderings of the best music; of course never forgetting the light joyous music the Viennese love. The museums, picture galleries, and educational establishments of Vienna are exces-sively numerous, and if Vienna has no such mighty High Technical school of such colossal proportions as Charlottenburg, Austria's system, as we have seen, of this type of education, and the Polytechnic and textile and technical schools here, and spread everywhere through the Empire, have perhaps done more for the artisan of Austria and the artistic trades of the Empire than has the system of Germany.

[62] A fond reminiscence of Sacher's Hotel and Restau-rant at the turn of the century; from *At the Gates of the East . . .* by Lieutenant-Colonel J.P. Barry.

There is a restaurant in Vienna that enjoys a more than Austrian renown. What the Café Anglais on the Grand Boulevard was in its hey-day in the long ago, that with its own special cachet is Sacher's Hotel and Restaurant facing the Opera. It is more like a private palazzo than a hostelry, where the head-waiter might easily be mistaken for the Grand Duke. It has a reputation for expensiveness, but measured by London standards that reputa-tion is not particularly deserved. I am sure you would not get such a 12 or 14 franc dinner *à la carte*, including wine – and such wine – in any house of similar standing in London. If you are weary from a long railway journey, go to Sacher's to be resuscitated. If you are in the glooms, you will be divested of your doldrums by the waiter as if they only sat owlishly on the shoulder of your topcoat. If you have a liver, coddle it with kindness; give it the delicious fat of the land, a bounteous satiety. Tickle it with a salade *à la* Sacher, and follow up your conquest with a simple little sweet, say, a Baba à l'Allemande or a Mousse aux fraises. And, Kellner, if you please, some Vöslauer à la Bourgogne – yes, a generous bottle. If your heart is soused in those bitter waters that Oriental poets in sarcastic frenzy call the Ocean of Love, ah! then hie thee at the double to one of Sacher's little tables, and you will come away with the conviction that a generous benevolence is the daintier passion, and that all mankind, including woman, are quite lovable in their way. Then as you sit back over your coffee – a Capucin or a small Schwarz – blowing hoops of Yenitje into the empyrean, you will fall into a reverie of wonder whether there was ever so much balm in Gilead in the brave days of old. See Naples and die, quoth'a! What a lugubrious philosophy! Better a thousand thousand times to dine at Sacher's and – Live!

[63] Vienna in general and Sacher's in particular, just after the First World War; from *Europe in Zigzags* by Sisley Huddleston.

Yet what a proud show Vienna makes! – its Burg Theatre with its view over the Ring, formerly the old walls of Vienna, and now its boulevards; its beautiful Volksgarten, its Rathaus Tower, its Belvedere, its picture gallery, its palace dating from the Thirteenth Century, into whose courtyard the populace was permitted to enter and watch the sovereigns through the windows. . . . And the Prater Park with its chestnut trees, its café tables, its orchestras playing Strauss waltzes, Hungarian melodies, and Wagnerian operas! And the Stadt Park, into which poured students, laughing girls, and comfortable-looking bourgeois.

We went of course to Sacher's. There the Viennese were dancing light-heartedly, while a man, carrying an instrument like a garden hose, went round and round the room, spraying a somewhat unpleasant perfume into the air. . . .

I looked round Sacher's. Its famous mistress was still in charge, though she was shortly afterwards to relinquish the establishment which has been known to European travellers for I know not how many years. Frau Sacher was the friend of princes and students alike. Everybody in Vienna will tell you of the black cigars which she smoked and of the autographed photographs of celebrities which she possessed. Everybody will tell you how she permitted the *nouveaux pauvres* to dine without paying when Vienna was passing through its most severe tribulations; and how her property was respected during the period of rioting when nothing else was spared. . . . Well, Sacher's has certainly no aristocratic air to-day; its habitués are of the student and bourgeois classes, with the inevitable sprinkling of gay girls. . . . Perhaps there never were so many Grand Dukes as is pretended at Sacher's; any more than there were at Montmartre. Every European capital has this kind of legend; it did no harm, and you could persuade yourself that your neighbour was a Balkanic potentate, while he could persuade himself that you were one of the numerous Germanic Kinglets. . . . Dining out and dancing was thus thrilling in its possible encounters. They have all of them, Archdukes and Counts, been to Sacher's, and have tasted Frau Sacher's own *torte* – layer upon layer of cake – and her Fürstpückler – the best ice-cream in the world. . . . Now Archdukes and Counts are rare, and Frau Sacher has retired.

[64] Early storm-warnings on the Ringstrasse in the 1930s; from *With an Eye to the Future* by Osbert Lancaster.

During all this extensive wandering only one sight had in any way suggested that the prevailing tranquillity and cheerfulness of the European scene might possibly prove illusory – that of the freshly blackened ruins of the Justizpalast in Vienna. Only a week or so before our arrival a quite unexpected and seemingly purposeless riot had broken out on the Ringstrasse developing into a savage uprising in which many policemen had been massacred, public buildings set on fire and which it had soon become obvious was far too well organised to have been wholly spontaneous. This deplorable outbreak of mob violence, of which lurid photographs were still being sold on the streets, coming at a time when the stockmarkets were booming and the Credit Anstalt solvent, when faith in the League of Nations was still high and it was generally assumed that every day and in every way everything was getting better and better and better, had left public opinion profoundly shocked. Finally, in default of any rational explanation, it was optimistically decided that it was an isolated phenomenon to which no sequel would be attached and one best forgotten as quickly as possible: nevertheless the postcards and the gaunt ruins on the Ring remained productive of a certain unease which even the sight of Frau Sacher, encased in black satin and pearls, with her French bulldog on her lap, still reassuringly installed outside her hotel puffing away at a long black cigar, could only partially dispel.

[65] Intimations on the Ringstrasse of the violence that brought an end to Social-Democracy in Austria, in 1934; from *Down River* by John Lehmann.

(The establishment of a Socialist government in Vienna after the fall of the monarchy in 1919 soon resulted in a vast programme of welfare-state activity. The flagship of this, admired throughout Europe in the 1920s, was the building of workers' flats, often to a striking design, in the outlying suburbs. During the brief but bloody civil war in 1934, they formed the bastion of Socialist defence against the Clerico-Fascist forces.)

The first six or seven weeks of the year can be bitterly cold in Vienna. Snow often lies piled and half-frozen in the streets from December until March; on the top of the old snow new snow falls, or rain that turns to ice in the following night, and heaps obstructions in side alleys and small squares that only a far richer city could afford to keep clear. Under grey skies the days hardly seem to be born before they have died.

The first days of February 1934 were particularly cold and cheerless. To the oppression of the Winter was added a continually increasing political despair, and the Social-Democratic government of Vienna, whose coffers had been drained by the general crisis and the financial offensive the Federal Government, headed by Dollfuss, was waging so ruthlessly against them, had very little to spare to keep the city spick and span.

At eleven forty-six, on the morning of February 12th, a foreign student, coming out of a Viennese library, was surprised to find the trams on the Ringstrasse at a standstill, with little groups of puzzled passengers stamping their feet around them. He asked a policeman, who surprised him by his nervous manner, what had happened, and received the answer: 'A cable's broken. But it won't take long to mend it.'

But the minutes went by and the hands of the electric clocks at the big crossings still continued to point at eleven forty-six. And in the little cafés of the narrow back streets, where the light has to burn all day, the billiard players waited to finish their games, plunged in darkness.

The afternoon crept on: darkness continued. It began to be clear to the foreign student that only a big strike, not a broken cable, could be responsible for this stoppage. And as the sun went down, the unpleasantness of the complete night that was swallowing up the city was enhanced by the wild rumours that were now flying from mouth to mouth, and the noise of firing from the outer districts of factories and working-class homes. The firing grew in intensity, began to envelop all districts except the central core of the Old Town, the chief stronghold of the bourgeoisie and the Executive, and down some of the main streets armoured cars of the Police and their auxiliaries roared their way, firing recklessly at any one who dared to show himself abroad.

The truth was known in the newspaper offices of London, Prague and Paris before it was known to many Viennese citizens who had no direct contact with the political organizations: the long awaited trial of strength between the armed proletariat and the forces of reaction had begun, the battle that was to end a few days later in the utter collapse of the once powerful Social-Democratic Party in Austria, amid the corpse-strewn ruins of tenement houses and workers' clubs, and the crocodile tears of a 'pocket Chancellor'.

[66] Hitler drives along the Ringstrasse, in 1938; from *Fallen Bastions* by G.E.R. Gedye.

Little did the wildly cheering masses dream of the Führer's real mood as he drove into Vienna on the greatest day of his amazing career. For the Nazis this was the culmination of their five-years' struggle, and to say that the crowds which greeted him along the Ringstrasse were delirious with joy is an understatement.

Despite the brutalities and horrors which his entry foreshadowed, I found something pathetic about the frenzied conviction of these small middle-class people, roused by fanaticism out of their normal stolidity, that for them the millennium had come to Vienna with the little man in the brown uniform standing in the enormous army car, whom I watched moving rapidly past the Hofburg to the Hotel Imperial, which had been cleared of its guests to make room for him. His car was closely preceded and followed by thirteen police cars, in which stood the keen-eyed SS of the Gestapo in their black uniforms, with the sinister skull and crossbones on the cap, sternly scanning the crowds for any trace of danger. A triple row of Berlin police in their pale-green uniforms and shakos *faced* the packed masses for the same purpose. The roaring of the great crowds – the greatest I have ever seen in Vienna – must have been plainly audible to Schuschnigg [*see p. 116*] and the many thousands of less distinguished Nazi prisoners in their cells as the triumph reached its culmination. The SS heaved a sigh of relief as the Dictator reached the Imperial unharmed. The crowds could not understand – knowing nothing of the pictures of disorganised columns which filled Hitler's mind – why their god did not come out and speak to them. For once the 'leadership principle' failed – the crowds refused to go home despite warnings from the loudspeakers that the Fuhrer was 'too tired' to speak to them. Finally the conqueror of the city whose dosshouses he had left many years before, an obscure and embittered failure, came on to the balcony. One Austrian General was willing to grace his triumph that day – the aged Nazi General Alfred Kraus, who more than a year before had promised Goering that the invaders would not be resisted. Hitler spoke only a few sentences to gain peace from the crowds, saying that Germans from Konigsberg to Cologne and from Hamburg to Vienna, 74,000,000 of them, swore that day an oath to be united forever. Actually, of course, the oath was sworn only by Herr Hitler himself and the crowd, but let that pass. The 'leadership principle' had reasserted itself.

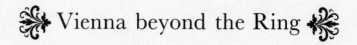 Vienna beyond the Ring

Leopoldstadt

[67] An account of the vast mixture of races living in the capital of the polyglot empire, which added greatly to the exoticism of the city's poorer districts, especially the Leopoldstadt; from *Austria . . .* by J.G. Kohl.

The Turks, the Hungarians, and all the nations beyond, far into Asia, call that Betsch which we christen Vienna, and signify by Nyemzestan, the whole of our German fatherland, of which they suppose his majesty of Austria to be sovereign lord. It is true, that the emperor Francis renounced this title, and the glory of the *German empire* has long since passed away; but it is long before the setting of a star is observed in distant regions, as its rays, once transmitted, still conjure up its image before us. Brandenburg is corrupted by the Turks into Trandebog. Betsch or Vienna is, to them, next to Trieste, the most distinguished place of traffic in Germany.

Two great water-roads connect Germany with the east: the Adriatic Sea and the Danube. At the head of the one lies Trieste, and of the other Vienna; and from these two places branches out the whole commerce of the east to the interior of Germany, as it develops itself from Constantinople to Trebisond and Smyrna. Vienna is the last westerly point before which a hostile Turkish army encamped, and the most western seat of an eastern commercial colony or factory.

The people who are the great agents of this commerce, through their own trade and their river navigation, are the Servians – the Rascians, as they are called in Vienna and Hungary. . . .

The Rascians have their colonies in Pesth, Vienna, and other cities on the Danube, where they are mingled with the other inhabitants, as the Armenians, Bucharians, and Greeks, are in southern and western Russia, and as the Jews are in other countries; and are the principal masters of vessels on the middle and lower Danube. They are to be met with their wives in all the public places in Vienna, habited in a strange mixture of European and Oriental costume. After the Rascians, the Turco-Spanish Jews play the principal part in the commercial world of

Vienna. This remarkable branch of a remarkable nation, was scattered over the whole Turkish empire after the most catholic kings of Spain had driven them from their dominions. They have commercial establishments in all the Turkish states of Africa and in Asia; and, as agents between the east and west, they have also fixed themselves at Vienna, where their houses are very considerable. Like the Servians, though in fewer numbers, they have extended their branches as far as Pesth, Semlin, Belgrade, and are more especially important in the relations of the Danube countries with Thessalonica.

These Spanish or Turkish Jews have adopted the eastern costume, probably because it was a *sine qua non* of their admission into the Turkish dominions, but they retain the Spanish language. They converse and correspond with each other from Belgrade to Salonica, and from Neusatz to Vienna in Spanish; probably it is found convenient here as a language very little known. They enjoy many privileges in Vienna, among others, that of being reckoned Turkish subjects, although established in Austria, and are consequently, under the protection of the Turkish ambassador, as independent of the native authorities as the Franks are under that of their consuls in the Turkish dominions. . . . The whole number of Orientals in Vienna, is generally reckoned at about a thousand souls.

[68] The role of the Jews in Vienna, one of considerable importance in the city's history, was often one of success in business, inevitably resulting in an anti-Semitic backlash; from *The Polyglot Empire* by Wolf von Schierbrand.

(Wolf von Schierbrand was an American journalist stationed in Vienna.)

In the Leopoldstadt quarter of Vienna, where the humbler Jews mostly congregate, there was suddenly an endless concourse of new, strange figures – men in long gabardines, tiny circular caps of silk or velvet on their heads, and corkscrew curls meandering down the sides of the face; women with wigs and ancient finery, blooming young Esthers and Susannahs ambling along with downcast eyes. Along the quays of the Danube Canal there was an endless procession of these – a new edition of Hebrew fugitives mourning by the waters. Rabbis in every costume and of every degree of holiness were scattered amongst them all.

But the Hebrew pilgrim in this vale of tears bears aye the reputation of being irrepressible. From among this conglomerate collection of distressed humanity there soon came forth the men of business. It was instructive and interesting to watch their methods. As against the non-Jewish world they were a unit. They aided and supported each other. They clubbed their means of ready money together and jointly not only tried but accomplished neat strokes of business, netting them perhaps $10,000, $20,000, $50,000, and then dividing it pro rata. Some of them, ay, many, did big business on no capital at all, just on credit. I recall a few sample cases of that description. Mendel Weixelbaum and Abraham Schweissfuss vouched for each other at the bank. Neither had a penny, but their cousin in Vienna, Ike Meisel, had some credit *and* a few dollars, and Ike vouched for *them*. So they there bought on credit three carloads of soap, raisins, apples, lubricating oil, and sold it the same day with a joint profit of about $4,500. Now they had money all three of them. Within a fortnight they were numbered among the 'war usurers.' A bunch of ten of these penniless capitalists made such clever use of their eloquence, sagacity and knowledge of the produce market that, in October, 1914, they cornered all the lentils in Vienna and made a fortune out of the deal. Within the winter of 1914–15 these fugitive gentry from Galicia cornered some of the foodstuffs most in demand – such as macaroni, dried peas and beans. These completely disappeared from view. But meanwhile these legumes, after being withdrawn from the open market, went from hand to hand, netting big profits at each deal and turning a score of the dealers into 'war millionaires.' Speculation in indispensable commodities became the specialty of the Jewish refugees from Galicia that had found a haven in Vienna. Of course, they did not have it all their own way. The Austrian government began to interfere, but against this pressure there were always invented new and successful dodges and ruses. The courts took a hand and sent a score or more to jail. But that did not stop it. The thing paid too well. Neither did the imposition of heavy fines stop it. There was, for example, this case: A wholesale dealer in wine, with branches in Vienna and Prague, by contract secured from a number of vintners in the Tyrol some 90,000 gallons of Tyrolese wines, both red and white, at an average price of K. 4.80 (or about $1.00) per gallon. With the aid of some of the financial geniuses recently arrived from Galicia he sold the wine at K. 13.60 per gallon, netting 300 per cent. of profit. The court deciding under the war decrees that this constituted usury, not legitimate speculation, fined the defendants K. 10,000. But that left them still a net profit of about $160,000. It was similar in most cases. But not this alone. Speculation in this field induced speculation in other fields. And the enormous and easy profits bred corruption all round.

The Prater

[69] Josef II gives the Prater to the people of Vienna on the death of Maria Theresa; from *Memoirs of the Courts of Berlin, Dresden, Warsaw and Vienna in the years 1777, 1778 and 1779* by N. William Wraxall.

This act of disinterestedness was immediately succeeded by another, calculated to acquire universal popularity, and to conciliate in a peculiar manner the affections of the lower ranks. On the north of Vienna are situated two very extensive parks, or gardens; one called the 'Prater,' the other the 'Hof Garten,' almost adjoining the city itself. They were the immediate property of the Empress Queen, and none except persons of quality ever entered them; even they enjoyed that privilege only during particular months of the year. Joseph instantly after his accession, threw open both these pleasure gardens, and gave the most ample permission to every person of whatever description, to walk or ride in them, at all seasons.

[70] Michael Kelly visits the Prater in the 1780s, with the composer Salieri; from *Reminiscences* by Michael Kelly.

(Michael Kelly (1764(?)–1826) was a celebrated singer and actor. According to Stephen Storace, he made singing history by being the first tenor not to sing his high notes falsetto. Born in Dublin, he studied singing in Naples in 1779, and after singing in several European cities was engaged as principal tenor in Italian and comic opera in Vienna, where he was a great success. He was a friend and great admirer of Mozart.)

The Prater, as I said before, I consider the finest public promenade in Europe, far surpassing in variety our own beautiful Hyde Park. It is about four miles in length; on each side of the road are fine chesnut trees, and a number of avenues and retired drives. These roads, on spring and summer evenings, are thronged with carriages. On all sides, as in our Hyde Park and Bushy Park, deer are seen quietly grazing, and gazing at the passing crowds. At the end of the principal avenue is an excellent tavern, besides which, in many other parts of this enchanting spot, there are innumerable cabarets, frequented by people of all ranks in the evening, who *immediately after dinner* proceed thither to regale themselves with their favourite dish, fried chickens, cold ham, and sausages; white beer, and Hoffner wines, by way of dessert; and stay there until a late hour: dancing, music, and every description of merriment prevail; and every evening, when not professionally engaged, I was sure to be in the midst of it.

The Danube runs through part of this charming retreat. One evening, Salieri proposed to me to accompany him to the Prater. At this time he was composing his opera of Tarrare, for the Grand Opera House at Paris. At the back of the cabaret where we had been taking refreshments, near the banks of the Danube, we seated ourselves by the river side; he took from his pocket a sketch of that subsequently popular air which he had that morning composed. *Ah! povero Calpigi*. While he was singing it to me with great earnestness and gesticulation, I cast my eyes towards the river, and spied a large wild boar crossing it, near the place where we were seated. I took to my heels, and the composer followed me, leaving '*Povero Calpigi*', and (what was worse) a flagon of excellent Rhenish wine behind us, which was to me a greater bore than the bristly animal, whose visit seemed intended for us. The story was food for much laughter, when we were out of danger. Salieri, indeed, would make a joke of anything, for he was a very pleasant man, and much esteemed at Vienna; and I considered myself in high luck to be noticed by him.

[71] Beethoven, writing to his friend the Baron Ignatz von Gleichenstein, makes a rendezvous in the Prater; from *The Letters of Ludwig von Beethoven*, edited by Dr A.C. Kalischer, translated by J.S. Shedlock.

(The Wild Man is a common name for an inn in Austria, although this one in the Prater is no more.)

Vienna, 1807

As I shall not have sufficient time this morning, I will come about midday to the Wild Man in the Prater; I presume I shall not meet with any wild men there, but beautiful Graces, and for that I must first of all put myself into harness. I know that if I come just on the stroke of twelve, you will not consider me a glutton, and so I will be punctual. If I still find you at home, well and good; if not I will hasten to the Prater in order to embrace you.

Your friend,

BEETHOVEN

[72] The Prater in 1814; from Richard Bright's *Travels from Vienna . . . in the year 1814.*

The Prater has already been mentioned as a place to which the people resort for amusement. It is situated on a large island formed by the Danube, and is a very magnificent ornament to the city, and a delightful place of recreation for its inhabitants.

The principal drive is between double rows of horse-chesnut trees, and is above two miles long in a straight line. Many other drives and walks intersect the woods, but all the intervening space of turf and grove, with the exception of some preserves for game, is open to the pedestrian. The grand avenue terminates at one end, in extensive public walks, called the Augarten, where a large building is constructed with rooms for entertainments, and saloons for public balls and concerts; while the garden, which affords a variety of arbours and recesses for tables in the open air, is laid out in avenues formed by cut hedges and magnificent trees, and occupies a space equal to half the city of Vienna.

Near to the grand drive of the Prater are several houses for refreshments, and some buildings for public amusement; – a circus for exhibitions of horsemanship, – a panorama, – several houses for what are called in Germany Carrousels, from their resemblance to horsemen in a tournament; or, as we should term them, merry-go-rounds, – and a very high and extensive scaffolding for the display of fire-works, near to which is erected a kind of open theatre for the spectators. The whole island is adorned with elms of large and beautiful growth; but, as it is flat and low, there are, near the banks of the river, many alders and willows, the latter of which have attained a most unusual size. To this delightful place the people flock in crowds, even during the winter, if a bright day invite them; but, as the spring advances, and the trees begin to cover themselves with leaves, and the days

to lengthen, these visits are more general, and the hour of retiring
becomes later. At this season it is not unusual to see a double
unbroken row of carriages extending for at least a mile, each
preserving the exact line, to which it is strictly kept both by
custom, and by the interference of men in the livery of the police,
who are stationed at regular distances.

[73] The size of the Prater impresses Fanny Trollope in
1836; from her *Vienna and the Austrians 1836–7.*

To-day we have made our third visit to the Prater, yet I suspect
that I have omitted to tell you anything about it; which is the
more sinful, because it is one of the few things in Vienna to which
report has done justice, and the not offering my tribute of
admiration to its beauty may be enough to lead you into the
great blunder of doubting if all you have heard in its praise be
true. Doubt no longer, then, if my testimony can content you, –
for as I have driven and walked, and driven again, through the
whole of its wide extent, I am qualified to pass judgment, and I
certainly believe that no city in the world has an area of such
extent and beauty attached to it, devoted freely and without
reserve to the use and enjoyment of the people.

This noble park possesses, in truth, every possible advantage
to render it a source of enjoyment to all ranks. In size it is so
magnificent, that our three Parks, and Kensington Gardens to
boot, might be placed within it, and leave space enough between
them to prevent quarrelling for room. A branch of the Danube
passes through it; – the innumerable drives in all directions are
excellent; the trees abundant, and many of them peculiarly
magnificent in growth, – and the numerous herds of deer which
seek shelter beneath them are so tame, that every sentimental
Jacques may enjoy the pleasure of gazing at a group of fifty
together without fearing that his step or his voice should startle
them. In addition to all this, may be found for the seeking,
abundance of agreeable cafés, restaurants, and guinguettes,
where all sorts of refreshments may be obtained at the same
prices as in the town, and whence every evening during the fine
season those strains of music may be heard which seem to form as
necessary a part of the existence of an Austrian as the air he
breathes, or the bread he eats.

Pleasure gardens in the Prater

[74] Horse-racing in the Prater in the 1880s; from *My Youth in Vienna* by Arthur Schnitzler.

(Arthur Schnitzler (1862–1931), the turn-of-the-century Austrian dramatist and novelist, satirized the immorality of Viennese life beneath its veneer of baroque courtesy in a number of plays. Along with the works of the brilliant satirist Karl Kraus and the writer Peter Altenberg, his writing sums up the frivolity and unpredictability of Viennese social life:)

During this year [1882] I became a steady visitor at the races. Actually it was not so much a sporting interest that drew me to the Freudenau, nor were the results on the board the only or even the main attraction. That lay far more in the whole marvelous atmosphere of elegance, amusement and grace which appealed to my senses. The landscape and how it was peopled held their especial charms for me; the track with its hurdles and ditches, a white fence all around it, circumscribed in the distance by woods; the lean jockeys seated on their noble horses with the flaring nostrils, their shiny bright-silk blouses puffed by the wind; their red, blue and gold sashes; the crowds – a dark mass thinning out and lost on the outskirts of the raceway; and above all this whirring, murmuring, fluttering, surging – a pale blue sky with its little white clouds spread out above the crowns of the Prater trees all the way to the Hungarian flatlands; and added to all this, a peculiar almost intoxicating *mélange* of hay, stall and meadow smells mixed with every variation of exotic perfumes. No wonder that from one time to the next one would long for the magic of this scene and these smells, and for the cool damp air that even on more humid days blew from the invisible Danube flowing nearby, through this field of gaiety. More often than not I would find myself, with my friends, in the so-called 'gulden' seats, with other bourgeois citizens, students, salesmen, bank clerks and their ladies – for the most part harmless folk for whom the races were a Sunday pleasure and sport, much like any other; or with habitual second or third rate bettors. But sometimes, when money was scarce, I could be found in the twenty-kreuzer section, amid the lower classes, if that's the way one wants to put it; among which, however, the more well-to-do elements were also quite numerous. Sometimes, for instance if one had won the last time round and arrived, not by train but in a *fiacre*, galloping down the Hauptallee, one could be seen strolling in the enclosure, wearing a yellow top coat – until Derby Day of course with a top hat – binoculars slung around one's neck, among counts, bankers, bookies, cavalry officers, crooks and ardent followers of the sport, to say nothing of their hybrid varieties, feeling as if one belonged, and slightly overcome by snobbishness, one would look with a measure of contempt, as if at a strange far-off world, at those pitiful or comic creatures who had to make do with the cheaper seats, or, *sans* necessity, were perfectly satisfied with them. But wherever one happened to be, whether in the enclosure or in the 'gulden' seats or among the common people, one felt united with those who belonged there. One knew the colors of the stables, the pedigrees of the horses, had one's favourites among the owners, the riders, the racers, knew all about their chances for the day and placed one's bets, a dilettantish and insouciant gambler, on the outsider rather than the favourite, always in the hope that this was the race that would make one a rich man.

[75] Amusement parks in the Prater in the 1930s; from *Down River* by John Lehmann.

I had two favourite ways of approaching the Prater, and both, for preference, on a clear night in early Summer. The first was direct from the bustling traffic-centre of the Praterstern, where you found yourself already plunged in the raucous din of the steam-organs, the switchbacks and circuses, with the lights of the Riesenrad, the Giant Wheel, above the nearest cinemas and cafés. Down the Ausstellungsstrasse the crowds moved slowly and densely before the various booths and their shouting impresarios – The Dragon's Cave, The Flying Railway, the Chamber of Tortures, a shooting gallery, a circus with the Tallest Man in the World on show, and a dozen others. A lane branching to the right took you straight into the rowdy, blazing heart of the Wurstlprater – the Clown's Prater – past the cinemas and open-air restaurants with their military bands playing to the little orange-lit tables behind the leaves. There the three great attractions of the Prater were waiting for you. First, and most imposing, the Riesenrad. As one of the illuminated observation cars slowly swung you up, you could see all Vienna twinkling below, from the street-lamps of the suburb of Floridsdorf and the winking lights of Aspern's aerodrome beyond the Danube in the east, to the concentrated glow from Hietzing and Schönbrunn on the other side. Then the Hochschaubahn, or Switchback-with-a-view, with its yelling carloads plunging into the grottos and roaring out again, catching a glimpse as they flew of the masses below them among the flowering chestnut-trees; and next to that the miniature Lilliput Railway, that went puffing and hooting in and out of the meadows while the delighted children it carried beamed to right and to left like Royalty in a pageant, and a bored signalman remembered just in time to wave his red flag by the crossing. Beyond these were scattered innumerable other entertainments, the Spectre Railway with its balcony open to the alley along which the couple in the electrically-driven chair suddenly found they were rolling – a short and surprising interlude between dark tunnels and dancing skeletons and opening tombs – to be caught by the laughing crowd in an embrace of mixed horror and affection, and beside the Spectre Railway the Autodromes, Waterdromes, Merry-go-rounds, Swinging Boats, Mysterious Houses, Alpine Toboggans, and Palaces of Performing Fleas. If your pocket was full, you could spend hours in the Wurstlprater and still not have exhausted its possibilities. Its special charm, in contrast to other established fun-fairs, lay, I think, in its situation, with the meadows and chestnut-trees mingling into it; this made it possible for the dozens of restaurants and cafés, big and small, which were scattered round it, to pretend to be right in the country, planting themselves under groups of ancient trees and putting up leafy trellises as a screen to make the music, the lights, the beer and the *gulyas* within all the more seductive to the 'Prater-Bummler'. Some of these restaurants had leather-shorted dancers and musicians imported from the provinces to make the illusion all the more complete; others relied on a gramophone playing jazz and popular songs and a couple of loud-speakers – and seemed just as well patronized. Through this maze of refreshments and entertainments the Viennese masses strolled dreamily and hurried eagerly, tried their strength and their skill at shooting, watched other people risking themselves in fantastical devices for producing thrills for hours on end, laughed and perspired and drank and made love, and went home to bed with their last groschen spent; soldiers in their grey-green Austrian uniforms, sailors from the Danube harbour, portly Fathers and buxom Mothers struggling with too many and too excited children, young workers with open shirts and tilted caps, arms linked in their girls' arms, boys in shorts and the favourite white stockings roving in bands, awkward or hysterical families up from the country, respectably dressed burghers and tradespeople with demure daughters, artists, athletes, scouts, students, unemployed, pickpockets and plain-clothes detectives.

The other way I liked to enter the Prater was across the meadows that lie between the third district and the Hauptallee. There all was quiet, except for an occasional tram, and only faintly in the distance the jangle of the steam-organs. There were indistinguishable figures on the benches among the trees, above whose dark topmost branches and blossoms the fairy lights of the Giant Wheel arched into the deep blue sky. You came into the life of the Wurstlprater suddenly, on reaching the Hauptallee, with its string of expansive café-restaurants. But the Hauptallee itself, where in Spring the Confirmation children were driven in taxis and ancient fiakers loaded with flowers in traditional procession, and the district beyond it were almost deserted at night; the time to visit them was early afternoon. In this part of the Prater the huge Rotunda used to swell above the trees, a hall built for the 1873 World Exhibition and used twice a year during the Viennese Fair right up to 1938, when it was burnt down no one knows how; the Trabrennplatz, where trotting races, a sport the Viennese are particularly fond of, were held; the fine modern Stadium and the open-air baths next door; and further down still, the riding alley, the golf course, and the smart polo ground and race-course, the Freudenau, close to a pretty stretch of water which serves as a sort of Viennese Serpentine. All pockets and all tastes were catered for in the Prater, from those who wanted to pack every moment of a non-stop day's outing from early morning to midnight with every kind of sport and entertainment, to those who wanted to wander off, alone or in twos or threes, under shady trees and over twisting meadows.

But the happiest days of the Prater were already over by the time I came to know it. In impoverished post-war Vienna the crisis of the early 'thirties made a difficult situation almost desperate; reduced wages or no work at all meant no money to spend in the Prater, and rich visitors grew rarer and rarer. New side-shows used often to be closed down in bankruptcy almost as soon as they were opened; old-established restaurants changed hands again and again, cut their prices, altered their signs; a week or two of rain in the season had catastrophic results for the precarious finances of the Prater tradespeople, and the lanes and paths beyond the pale of the lamps were more haunted than they used to be by pickpockets and the desperate victims of unemployment.

The Belvedere

[76] The building of the Belvedere; from *Vienna, legend and reality* by Ilse Barea.

The Belvedere is a terraced garden with an upper and a lower palace. Johann Lucas von Hildebrandt built them, and planned the garden as well, between 1700 and 1724. It was a challenge to the French court, and the counterpart to the Duke of Marlborough's Blenheim Palace. But while Blenheim is the perfect example of exotic Baroque transplanted, fantastically, into an Oxfordshire landscape, the Belvedere fuses contemporary elements of international architectural art in such a manner that it seems to belong to the soil on which it rose. Prince Eugene, the puny, solitary, cantankerous Italian bred at Versailles who never learnt to speak German properly and signed his name in the trilingual version of 'Eugenio von Savoye', was the architect of the regenerated Habsburg empire and therefore of Vienna's rise to the status of a true metropolis. Here he grew roots. He chose as the site for his summer residence a long slope overlooking Vienna from the south-east, so that the ridge of the Kahlenberg, bisected by the spire of St Stephen's, bound the horizon. First the gardens were laid out by a Frenchman imported from the Bavarian court. Then Hildebrandt built at the foot of the hill a long, one-storeyed, outwardly simple edifice in which the Prince set up living quarters decorated with the most lavish extravagance of marble, stucco and gold; this was the Lower Belvedere. Finally the Upper Belvedere Palace on the hill crest was completed for great receptions and festivals.

Articulated by the copper-green roof, the jutting middle part, and four octagonal, domed corner pavilions, it seems an Arab tent out of the Thousand-and-One Nights, hovering weightlessly above the top-most terrace. Long clipped maple hedges lead down from it and meet below, on the level, in miniature mazes. Dark, low yew hedges, and balustrades with small statues along yellow-sanded walks link the two palaces, and on each side of the garden an imposing staircase, with a sloping pavement of huge stone flags set between twin stairs,

marks the cut from incline to level. In the niches of the leafy walls
stand sandstone figures with fluttering draperies. A great basin
with leaping fountains, tritons and nereids breaks up the centre
of the slope, and shallow basins are sunk into squares of lawn.
High up, on the steps to the flagged ceremonial terrace, lie
amiable sphinxes. From there Canaletto's nephew Bernardo
Bellotto (whom likewise the Viennese insist on calling Canaletto) painted a view of the distant city, with the two great
cupolas of St Charles Borromee and the nearby Salesian convent
church to the left and right in the middle distance.

[77] The foundations of the art collection in the Belvedere
by Josef II; from *Memoirs of the Courts of Berlin, Dresden,
Warsaw and Vienna in the years 1777, 1778 and 1779* by N.
William Wraxall.

Joseph appeared to be wholly insensible to the arts, not only
before his father's death, but, for a considerable time afterwards.
So little taste had he for painting, that he usually turned his back
on the finest productions of the great masters, Flemish or Italian.
Though endowed by nature with an excellent ear, he betrayed
no partiality even for musick. For sedentary occupations,
reading, and the improvement that results from the study of
polite letters, he manifested a total disinclination. By degrees,
however, his indifference for works of genius has diminished. He
could not visit Italy, and become familiar with the monuments of
art profusely scattered over that beautiful country, without
catching some portion of enthusiasm. On his return from Rome
and Florence, some years ago, he began to display this change in
his character; as the best proof of which, he caused the finest
pieces of painting to be collected from all the palaces of the
Empress Queen, and brought to the 'Belvedere.' He even
superintended in person, and directed the placing of the most
capital pictures, in the gallery of the above-mentioned palace.
Prince Kaunitz piques himself on having, by his example and
exhortations, awakened, directed, and formed the Emperor's
taste.

The Belveder, 1835

[78] The Belvedere paintings (which today are in the Kunsthistorischesmuseum) admired by a traveller in the early nineteenth century; from Richard Bright's *Travels from Vienna . . . in the year 1814*.

The Imperial collection of Paintings at the palace called the Belvedère, in the suburbs, consists of nearly 1400 pictures, distributed in twenty-three rooms, and arranged under the Italian, German, and Flemish schools. There are in each class many of great excellence. The Titians are numerous. It is particularly rich in the works of Rubens, to which nearly two whole apartments are devoted; and there are several fine pieces by Vandyke. With the works of the German masters it is unusually stored. There are some rich and beautiful productions of Albert Dürer; and, on the whole, both the ancient and modern works of this school place it on a footing with the two well-known collections of Munich and Heidelberg. There is, unfortunately, no correct catalogue of the collection; the only one, which was published in 1781, is now, in consequence of the additions and changes which have taken place, of little use. In each room is hung a list of the pictures, and the masters to whom they are ascribed.

[79] One of the later inhabitants of the Belvedere was Archduke Franz Ferdinand; from *Archduke Francis Ferdinand* by Victor Eisenmenger.

(Dr Victor Eisenmenger was the Archduke's physician, and accompanied the heir to the Habsburg throne on many of his travels inside and outside the empire – until the Archduke's assassination at Sarajevo in 1914.)

The Archduke was accustomed to being overcharged even by the Austrians. I received a characteristic reply from the Austrian photographer who took a group-picture at the base of the Pyramids; when I reproached him because of his exorbitant demands, he said: 'I do not have an Austrian Archduke for a customer every day.'

He had to protect himself against this tendency. His extensive purchases in antique shops did not permit of a noble gesture. Fair-dealing business men had to suffer from the unreliability of their competitors and the former only made matters worse by their foolish attitude. My friend Förster who is one of the most reputable business men in Vienna complained to me: 'Look here, your Archduke is really stingy. He asked me the price of a watch which he liked. Knowing his peculiarities, I mentioned an exceptionally low price: 500 crowns. He replied: "Well, I suppose you'll take 300." That is not a nice thing for such a gentleman to do.'

'Well, what did you do?' I enquired. 'Of course, I had to let him have it. I could not permit him to go to a competitor.' 'And what do you think his opinion of you is now?' I asked him.

The Archduke actually mentioned this incident some time later as proof of the unreliability of Viennese merchants and was convinced only with difficulty of the real facts in the case.

Anyone rendering him the slightest service, be it welcome or unwelcome, expected a big reward. The man who opened the door of his carriage would expect a banknote, the station-master a decoration and if their expectations did not materialize they spoke of ingratitude and niggardliness. . . .

It is true that at times he went too far in his economy and became petty. At a breakfast in Lölling, a plate of strawberries was served and taken away again almost untouched. He summoned the cook and asked what would be done with the strawberries. 'I shall give them away,' said the cook. 'That must not happen again,' said the Archduke and the cook withdrew. When I asked him what he would do with them now, he grumbled: 'I'll throw them into the garbage. For 5 kreuzer the boys will bring me enough fresh ones.'

He was accused of obstinacy and fits of temper and of not being able to brook interference. Obstinacy, the stubborn adherence to an opinion once formed, is a bad quality only, if this opinion be a wrong one. In matters of importance he was nearly always right, as the political events which followed his death proved. Trifles do not matter. Rather, he should be accused of a lack of opportunism, for he always expressed his opinion forcibly and without consideration. It is not correct that he would not brook contradiction. As his physician, I was frequently in a position where I had to contradict him or to deny him a wish. Once he had overcome his initial mistrust of me, I was always able to enforce whatever I deemed necessary without much opposition.

It was different if he met with a stupid or, as was often the case,

Archduke Franz Ferdinand in the uniform of cavalry general

a factious contradiction. On such occasions it could happen that his hot temper led him to the limits of tact and Court etiquette and he was carried away by a fit of anger. To call such fits of passion attacks of raving madness and to draw a conclusion that they are symptoms of incipient paresis, as was done recently by a learned gentleman, is as inadmissible as to conclude that this diagnosis showed symptoms of progressive paresis on the part of the learned gentleman. . . .

The Archduke was mistrustful, like many Hapsburgs. Any thinking person who has a great deal to do with his fellow-man, must become mistrustful. In a ruler, mistrust is not a fault but a virtue.

His good qualities: keen political understanding, energy and insight into human character, were the qualities of a ruler. As in every human being, these were accompanied by weaknesses. I must refer anybody who is inclined to be too harshly critical of them to the quotation from *Götz of Berlichingen*: 'Wherever there is strong light, there is a sharp shadow.'

The Karl Marx Hof

[80] Fighting at the Karl Marx Hof in 1934; from John Lehmann's *Down River*.

(In February 1934, fighting broke out between government troops and supporters of Dollfuss's Clerico-Fascist regime on the one hand and the Socialist workers on the other. For more than a week troops with artillery laid siege to workers' flats. Around the Karl Marx Hof, the fighting was particularly intense.)

In Vienna, the most spectacular events were the continual battles that raged round the great Karl Marx Hof, which was stormed and taken, after savage fighting, by the Government, retaken by the Socialists, re-stormed and bombarded by Major Fey's artillery until some parts of it lay in ruins and dead and dying were strewn all around it, and whose defenders were only on the fourth day entirely and finally driven out; the defence of the Arbeiter Heim in Ottakring, whose smashed and bullet-riddled façade remained for years as a hideous memento of February; the epic of the whole district of Floridsdorf, the battles that raged in its tenements, factories, gas and electricity works, an epic which includes the heroic episode of Georg Weissel and the fire brigade; the seige of the Goethe Hof in Kaisermühlen, where the Schutzbündler defended themselves against all machine-gun and artillery attacks until the last, and in whose cellars long after the fighting had stopped the foreign relief committees found starving women and children, too proud and too despairing to look for help themselves from the surrounding world; and the great retreat to the frontier of a company of Schutzbündler through the snow that now lay deep after the storm of Wednesday, fighting all their way against pursuing police-cars and aeroplanes. But the battles in the proletarian districts of Simmering and Favoriten, where radical influence was stronger, and in the tenements of the Reumann Hof, Matteotti Hof and Indianer Hof (re-christened Fey Hof after that doughty soldier had forced his way in when all resistance was at an end) on the Margareten Gürtel, and in Sandleiten in Hernals, were hardly less moving and terrible.

[81] The Prince of Wales temporarily endears himself to the inhabitants of the Karl Marx Hof by championing them against the Fascists; from *Fallen Bastions* by G.E.R. Gedye.

Right on the heels of this arrived the Prince of Wales – afterwards Edward VIII, now Duke of Windsor – for one of his several pleasure visits to Vienna. On his last day he embarrassed the Clerico-Fascist Government terribly by demanding to be shown the great monument of the Socialists, the model workers' homes which they had put up right round the city and which the Government were trying hard to make everyone forget. Quite without invitation I attached myself to the Prince's suite for this trip, which was the only politically interesting part of his whole visit to Vienna, although, of course, columns had to be written by the correspondents every day about his doings. The Fascist Major Lahr and the Clerical Anti-Semite Herr Kresse, two people nominated Vice-Burgomasters after the Counter-Revolution, called to fetch him from his hotel. . . .

They of course pumped Heimwehr-Fascist propaganda hard into him throughout the morning. The Prince received it all with a glassy stare, and here and there a sudden question which quite put the plausible Major Lahr off his stroke. In the Karl Marx-Hof I heard him drumming into the Prince the usual stuff about 'ferro-concrete fortresses', long-prepared 'machine-gun nests' and Austro-Bolshevists, the only basis for which was that the narrow windows of w.c.'s made excellent loopholes for machine-gunners defending the buildings. The Prince listened politely but apparently coldly, firing off abrupt questions about bathing accommodation and communal laundries. Lahr was only deterred when, in the midst of some of his most blood-curdling stuff about that *méchant animal*, the Austrian worker, who had dared to defend himself with machine-guns against the Fascist attack, the Prince jerked out: 'Yes, yes, I know all about that. But do tell me, Major, where did you put that battery of howitzers which knocked all those holes in the left wing?'

It was not the first time that the Prince had been an *enfant terrible* about this building. It so happened that at the time of the shelling the Austrians had put on a wonderful 'Austrian Exhibition' in London. Baron Frankenstein was taking the Prince round and showing him some beautiful photographs of baroque churches and palaces in Vienna, when the Prince of Wales shot out: 'Hasn't Your Excellency got a photograph of the Karl Marx-Hof put up here?' As the Karl Marx-Hof at that time was in parts a gaping ruin, there was quite an outburst of coughing amongst his Austrian and British escort and a hurried move was made to a different part of the exhibition.

Soon all underground Socialist Vienna was seething with admiration for the Prince because he wore in the buttonhole of his dinner-jacket at night resorts a red carnation, traditional badge of Austrian Socialism. Stories grew up of how the Austrian police had asked him to desist, and he had replied: 'Nonsense – I stand by the workers of Vienna, and I am going to show it'. It was a pretty delusion concerning one of the Prince's dressy little habits. Needless to say, all the sympathy he had won vanished overnight when he made his last appearance in the limelight with his disastrous tour to Germany as guest of those whom the Austrian Socialists recognised as the deadliest enemies of the working classes anywhere to-day, the Nazis.

Schönbrunn

[82] Frederick the Great's special ambassador to Austria, Count Otto Christoph von Podewils, has an audience with Maria Theresa on 29 June 1746; from his *Memoirs*. Translated by Richard Bassett.

Last Sunday at ten o'clock I had my first audience with the Empress at Schönbrunn. As is customary for such occasions, I was shown into her room by the master of the household Count Khevenhuller, who also remained throughout the audience, as did the mistress of the court, Countess Fuchs, who is, however, ill . . .

The Empress's build is a little less than average. Her figure before her marriage was very beautiful but the numerous births have left her considerably aged. Nonetheless, she has a rather easy walk and a majestic bearing. Her appearance is noble even if she undermines this with the clothes she wears.

She has a round and full face with a broad brow. The well defined eyebrows are like her hair, blonde without a hint of red. Her eyes are large and lively, full of feeling and bright blue. Her nose is small and her mouth if a little large rather pretty. Her expression is open and bright, her manner friendly and spirited. One cannot deny that she is a beautiful person.

She attempts, with considerable success to match the character and competence of her generals. She herself served in the last Italian campaign and every one who was there assures me that she was the strongest of her officers. She does not love the King of Prussia.

[83] A young French regimental apothecary watches from Schönbrunn as the Battle of Aspern rages in the distance; from *Papers of an Army Apothecary* by Cadet de Gassicourt. Translated by Richard Bassett.

Napoleon ordered me to remain in Schönbrunn and so I missed the battle, but as soon as I heard the cannonade I climbed the

Empress Maria Theresa, by an unknown artist, 1750

Gloriette to see both armies. The thick smoke prevented this, as well as the flashes of 400 guns and the smoke of burning houses. I recalled how the Duke of Montebello (Marshal Lannes) had felt uneasy about the battle. 'We have hurried too much, gentlemen. I expect no good from this battle, but however it ends, it will be my last.'

A General arrives, wounded. He tells me Lannes is dead. The Viennese spirit is egregious. They curse our wounded even in hospital.

[84] After the Battle of Wagram, Gassicourt, the army apothecary, returns to Schönbrunn which became Napoleon's residence in Vienna; from his *Papers of an Army Apothecary*. Translated by Richard Bassett.

The Austrians have really a splendid character. I am greeted everywhere I go and treated so courteously, as if I were bringing them news of THEIR army's victory.

It is not easy when one lives in Schönbrunn, the Headquarters of an Emperor, to retain a military note. The Prince of Neuchatel and the military staff spend much of the day giving each other decorations to adorn uniforms which have seen little of the battle. None of the soldiers on duty here shows them much respect; not surprisingly, as they have demonstrated so little courage.

[85] A visit to Schönbrunn during the Congress of Vienna, to see the exiled Napoleon's wife and infant son who were living there at the time; from *Travels from Vienna . . . in the year 1814* by Richard Bright.

(Empress Maria Louisa and her son both died in Vienna before Napoleon III, her husband's nephew, briefly restored the family's glory.)

The Empress Maria Louisa was, during all this period, called upon, for the most arduous exercise of resignation, and the most unexampled efforts of patience, amidst the agonies of contending affections, which ever fell to the lot of woman. She suffered with a dignity which did honour to her character. With her infant, to whom but a few months before, the eyes of all Europe had been directed, she lived in quiet seclusion at the palace of Schönbrun, a few miles from Vienna. She took no part in those festivities with which her father's court reechoed, but daily paid a respectful visit to her parents, and returned to her infant charge, awaiting in patience the result of events over which she could exercise no control. Whatever might be the political feeling with which the fallen Emperor was viewed, it was unmixed commiseration alone which could attend the misfortunes of the Empress and her guiltless child. I was one day tempted by curiosity; if the interest

of the object may not deserve a better name; to transgress so far
the limits of propriety, as to call with a friend at the palace of
Schönbrun, and request that we might be indulged with an
introduction to the infant king. We found that all the servants
about the palace were Frenchmen, who still wore the liveries of
Napoleon. When our request had been made known, a female
attendant came to the antichamber and told us, that the child
was at present with its mother; but if we could amuse ourselves
for an hour in the gardens, and would then return, our curiosity
should be gratified. We accordingly came at the appointed time,
and were ushered into a room where the infant was sitting on the
floor amusing himself, amidst a profuse collection of playthings.
We were introduced to Madame Montesquieu, and one or two
other ladies who were present. The infant king of Rome; then
indeed styled the Prince of Parma; was at the moment occupied
with a toy, which imitated a well-furnished kitchen. He was the
sweetest child I ever beheld; his complexion light, with fine white
silky hair falling in curls upon his neck. He was dressed in the
embroidered uniform of an hussar, and seemed to pay little
attention to us as we entered, continuing to arrange the dishes in
his little kitchen. I believe he was the least embarrassed of the
party. He was rather too old to allow of loud praises of his beauty,
and rather too young to enter into conversation. His appearance
was so engaging, that I longed to take him in my arms, yet his
situation forbade such a familiarity. Under these circumstances
we contrived a few trifling questions, to which he gave such arch
and bashful answers as we have all often received from children
of his age, and, after a few minutes conversation with Madame
Montesquieu, we withdrew.

[86] A magnificent sleighing party at Schönbrunn during
the Congress; from *Anecdotal Reminiscences of the Congress of
Vienna* by Comte Auguste de la Garde-Chambonas.

The Empress of Austria, the King and Queen of Bavaria, besides
several other personages in far from robust health, who feared
the cold, had gone to Schönbrunn in closed carriages. A
magnificent fête had been prepared and many invitations issued.
The return was to take place at night and by torchlight. After the
banquet to which all those who made up the sleighing party were

Napoleon's arrival at Schönbrunn: the French cavalry are in the foreground and the Gloriette behind the palace. Aquatint by Francois Aubertin, after T. Martinet, 1822

invited, the principal Viennese actors presented one of the prettiest pieces of the French stage, the *Cendrillon* of M. Étienne, which had been translated into German. A grand ball was to wind up the entertainment. The Prince Koslowski, the Comte de Witt, and I repaired betimes to Schönbrunn.

The sleighs on their arrival formed into a circle around the frozen lake of Schönbrunn, which was like a polished mirror, and was covered by skaters in the most elegant costumes of the various countries of Northern Europe. The scene was very animated, with the various sledges in the shape of swans, gondolas, etc., and reminded one of a Dutch kermesse, especially in respect to the itinerant vendors of fortifying drinks patronised by the energetic performers. The picture was in reality unique in virtue of the various servants in livery, both on foot and on horseback, and the sleighs of the Court itself, not to mention the enormous crowds of spectators who had come all the way from Vienna.

A young man attached to the English embassy, Sir Edward W—, a member of the London skating-club, and accustomed to astonish the promenaders in Hyde Park on the Serpentine, executed some wonderful feats in the way of figures, pirouettes, and single and double curling. Like the Chevalier de St George, who on the pond at Versailles traced the name of Marie-Antoinette, Sir Edward traced the monograms of the queens, the empresses, and other female celebrities, who left their sleighs to admire his skill. Others, less perfect than he, no doubt, but very skilful nevertheless, performed Chinese and European dances, including a waltz. The latter was danced by two Dutch ladies in the picturesque dresses of Saardam milkmaids, to the applause and admiration of everybody.

[87] Schönbrunn's gardens and the Gloriette in the mid-1830s; from *Vienna and the Austrians 1836–7* by Frances Trollope.

Yesterday being another of those bright days which make the autumn of this country so delightful, we took advantage of it to visit the imperial residence of Schönbrunn. It was here that Napoleon, the first and last, fixed his head-quarters while his troops were in possession of the Austrian capital; and it is here that the imperial family of Austria pass the chief part of every summer. The Emperor and Empress are indeed still there, though they seldom fail to drive into town for an hour or two every evening, for the purpose of witnessing the performances either at the Opera or Bourg theatre; but early next month the court becomes established at Vienna until April.

The palace of Schönbrunn is at the distance of one league from Vienna, and the road to it is in excellent order; an advantage not always found in the neighbourhood of this city. But its Mac-Adamish smoothness is all that can be recorded in its favour, for it passes through as ugly a flat as can well be imagined; and, what is infinitely worse to those who take no snuff and smoke no tobacco, it runs for a considerable way beside that most unsavoury of streams, the river Wien.

This black and vilely-smelling ditch is a foul blot upon the beauty and neatness of this lovely city, and must certainly produce a miasma extremely prejudicial to health. Surely this receptacle of abominations could not have existed in its present state during the reign of Maria Theresa. It is impossible to believe that one, whose days may be counted by the noble and beautiful works with which she adorned her empire, could have passed to her imperial creation at Schönbrunn within reach of this black and noxious stream, and suffered its unhallowed waters to flow between the wind and her regality. . . . The palace itself, which is said to be more commodious than superb, is not shown, or at least not without higher authority than we brought with us; but the gardens, which are truly magnificent, are as freely given for the enjoyment of the public, as the air that blows over them.

Such sights, however, are not among those that can be graphically described. It is not easy to talk of mountains and torrents in such a sort as to produce any thing like a true picture on the mind: but alleys, statues, fountains, and parterres are more stubborn still; for, if you do contrive to bring them with tolerable distinctness upon an ideal canvass, they seem as stiff and as hideous as the perspective of a drop-scene in a country theatre. But such a garden as that of Schönbrunn, spite of all that can be said against clipt trees and formal arcades, is a noble, I could almost say, a majestic spectacle. And not a little is its beauty increased by the skilful manner in which each portion of the large enclosure is made to set off and enhance the effect of all the rest. Thus, that part which is laid out with old-fashioned skill, and such scrupulous attention to regularity that it seems as if every leaf took orders from the gardener before it ventured to sprout, is made to soften by degrees, first into turf and shrubbery, and at last into a bit of genuine forest scenery.

At rather less, I should think, than a quarter of a mile from the garden façade of the palace, rises a sudden hill of no great elevation, but which looks more considerable than it really is from its abruptness: up to this point the wide expanse is laid out in the very stiffest style of old German gardening; but here the almost precipitous lawn is flanked by shrubberies and forest-trees, among which I remarked several beautiful oaks, of a species unknown in England, but with which I had become familiar in America.

On the summit of the hill these side plantations become wilder still, and spread away, I know not where, but far beyond our following. In the centre, and exactly opposite to the palace, is erected a very imposing sort of garden summer-house, called La Gloriette, three hundred feet long and sixty high. It is approached by an almost monstrous flight of steps from each side, decorated by colossal trophies, and consists of a fine arcade, with a magnificent saloon in the middle; from the windows of which, as well as from the elegant arches on each side of it, is seen an extremely fine view of Vienna, with its background of mountains. It would make an admirable panorama.

I know not if this building has ever been used for the purpose of giving summer fêtes, but no place could be better adapted for such a purpose. The roof of the whole edifice, saloon, arcades, and all, forms a terrace which of course embraces a view more widely extended still than that below: a stout garde-fou surrounds it, and benches are placed at intervals along the whole extent, so that it forms as delightful a promenade as it is possible to have without shade. I should like to take a midsummer walk there by moonlight.

[88] Exotic animals in the menagerie at Schönbrunn, and exotic plants in its gardens, admired by a mid-nineteenth-century traveller; from *Austria . . .* by J.G. Kohl.

The menagerie of Schönbrunn incloses a part of the imperial garden, near which there passes a miserable, scantily-filled ditch, that in summer smells abominably, and which it is amazing to me does not appear the frightful object it is, to the thousands of Vienna people who daily resort thither. The menagerie occupies a large circular piece of ground, in the centre of which, on a little elevation, stands a many-windowed summerhouse, the abode of the gaily-plumaged parrot kind. If I were a courtier I should use all my influence to get these birds removed from so conspicuous a place, lest it should occur to some to draw odious comparisons between them and the court circle.

From this parrot centre the whole circle is cut by radii into numerous sections. All these sections are divided by walls and hedges, and broad walks. Each section contains the stalls, baths, ponds, pasturages, and pleasure-grounds of a particular species, and since the present emperor has filled up the places that had become vacant, there is a tolerable number of interesting furred and feathered creatures, to whom Asia, Africa, or America has furnished paws or claws, hoofs, horns or antlers, the appetite for bread or for blood.

The bears, tigers, and other carnivorous animals, are daily in view of the public; the prisons of the other must be especially opened to the curious. The brown bears sat, like poor beggars, in their dens, and received thankfully a morsel of bread. If it was thrown on the top, they climbed up the iron grating and thrust their paws through to reach it. One of them, when we took out some more bread, sat up on his hind quarters and moved his fore paws up and down like a petitioner till he got a piece. A tiger or a lion would never learn to do this. The nature of the bear seems to partake of the monkey as well as of the dog. The old bears in Schönbrunn are the grandchildren of bears likewise born in captivity, and have, in their turn, descendants, the fourth generation, therefore, of a tamed race. It would be interesting to learn, if in later generations the character of the animal will undergo any considerable alteration. But, unfortunately, the people here keep no exact account of their charges, which might be useful to the student of natural history.

It was a hot day, and the polar bears, the bloodthirsty animals, who wear on their body the colour of innocence, and cover their necks with the silver locks of venerable age, when all the while they have not an honest hair on the whole body, were splashing about in the water all the time we stayed. They are the only animals who do not require their dwelling to be warmed in the winter. Like their far more amiable brethren, the brown bears, they are fed only on bread and milk, which, it is said, enables them to bear their imprisonment better.

The beautiful royal tiger we found lying on one side with all his legs stretched out, but so that his hind legs rested between the two fore ones. The keeper said this was his ordinary position when at rest. We durst not disturb him, as he takes it very much amiss even if people only touch his den, growls fearfully, and is long before he can be appeased. His lady is of a much gentler character. The cages of the tiger, lions, and other wild cats, are divisible into two parts by means of sliding partitions, that the animals may be driven into one while the other is cleaned. A third division projects like a balcony, in which they can enjoy the sunshine and open air, and show themselves to the public. The bears have their baths in addition. . . .

There is certainly deeply rooted in the human soul a peculiar pleasure in the enjoyment of what is dangerous, and that with the timid as well as the courageous, with this difference, that the former love danger only when they are certain it will not affect them personally. Our companion in Schönbrunn who, if all signs deceived not, was an arrant poltroon, would persist, in spite of the intreaties and prohibitions of the keepers, in teasing the lions and tigers with his riding whip till they got up and showed their teeth. We on our side could not withstand the temptation of creeping into one of the cages to examine its internal arrangements. It was a leopard house; the walls were carefully plated with iron and painted light blue. The arrangements for carrying away all dirt, and the division into front and back dens, appeared to us to be very judicious. The leopards, it must be observed, for whom these apartments had been prepared, had not yet taken possession of them. . . .

The birds are lodged and provided for in a similar way, and there is a fish-pond for the waterfowl. Carp are fattened for the spoon-billed geese, who will sometimes swallow a fish weighing three pounds, and measuring a foot in length, without betraying the least inconvenience. If the lion's capacity for swallowing were of the same relative size, he could dispose at once of a whole lamb. It must be an enchanting sight to see the ostrich run in his native deserts; for even the few light springs that he takes in his poor fields in London, Paris, or Schönbrunn, when the keepers allow him to escape from his narrow cage, afford a pleasing spectacle, in which the lightly fluttering plumage of his back plays a principal part. They have taken much pains at Schönbrunn to obtain young from the ostrich, but have as yet got nothing beyond the eggs. . . .

The gardens of Schönbrunn are yet more distinguished for their plantations and their botanical collections than for the animals they contain. Not that the long avenues of beautiful, large, but most cruelly mutilated lime trees, are entitled to much admiration. There is certainly a method of altering the natural growth and figure of trees to the advantage of garden decoration. . . . In Schönbrunn, however, by cutting one side of the trees and leaving the other in their natural irregularity, they have produced nothing but deformities, resembling high flat walls on one side, and wild forest denizens on the other. They are not even clipped of an equal height, but shoot up here more, there less, so that the image of the wall is not kept up, and nothing is to be seen but the mutilated tree. If any one should turn columns out of marble statues to form a portico with them, he would be cried out upon for his barbarism, but if he only half cut his statues, and then made them do service as walls, we should thank him still less for his pains. They take a great deal of trouble, however, to bring these trees into order, and have, among other machines, one fifty or sixty feet high, consisting of several stages, and rolled about on castors to enable the gardeners to reach the branches the better with their shears and axes.

But we ought not in gardens like those of Schönbrunn, where there is so much that is admirable, to waste much time in finding fault with these lime trees. We willingly abandoned ourselves to the guidance of the obliging attendants of the gardens, and followed them through their vegetable treasury, and if unable to give a satisfactory account of its wealth, we will at least attempt some description of the more distinguished objects.

There are many plants here, not in the greenhouses but in the open garden, which we should seek elsewhere in vain. One of the most splendid specimens is the *Sophora Japonica*, a large magnificent tree, with excessively fine feathery leaves. It stands on a beautiful lawn, and the windings of its boughs, and the whole figure of the tree, are so picturesque, that it has been repeatedly painted, and has its portrait in the emperor's collection of pictures of the plants and trees of Schönbrunn.

Artists are almost constantly employed in these gardens, in drawing either for the emperor, or with scientific objects in view.

The green and hot-houses are all handsome and spacious, and a new temple of the Dryads in right imperial style is now in progress of erection. . . .

For several trees standing in the open air, separate huts are erected in the winter, for example, the *Acaucaria excelsa*; and this must be elevated every year, as the tree grows rapidly. Every plant produces, or attracts, some particular species of insect, and every where we saw the most judicious arrangements for their destruction. From the Brazilian fan palm long threads depend, and every one of these threads is a panegyric on the vigilance of the Schönbrunn gardeners, for they are preserved in their entire length, neither torn nor in any way injured, as we so often find them in other green-houses. The palms in which this garden is richer than either the Jardin des Plantes at Paris, or Kew Gardens near London, have very long, very fragile roots, which require the greatest care in planting, and that that care is here bestowed the healthy slender growth of the palms bear witness. The *Stenia pallida* has a beautiful blossom, which has the appearance of being formed from yellow wax, and is very easily broken off. To avoid this, every blossom is provided with a prop composed of the slenderest splinters; many other plants had the like, with the addition, where the plant was very tender, of a little cushion of some soft material between the prop and the flower. I did not see a single neglected or sickly-looking plant.

❧ The approaches to Vienna ❧

[89] The Hussars' temple in the Vienna Woods; from Richard Bright's *Travels from Vienna . . . in the year 1814.*

(Perched on a dramatic precipice high above the Vienna Woods stands this classical temple erected by Prince Liechtenstein to the memory of the Hussars who died saving his life when he was attacked by French cavalry during the Napoleonic Wars.)

At another time they [*Viennese holidaymakers*] will visit the heights of the Johansberg, and, tracing the divided bed of the Danube, will mark, with regret, the whirlwinds of dust that float over to the city, to which the descending sun bids them again return; or they will roam the day in the delicious mountain bosom of the Brül, look from the surrounding heights on the rough and alpine features of Carinthia, or read the monumental lines engraven on the temple raised by the gratitude of Prince Liechtenstein to the memory of the four soldiers who fell in rescuing him from the enemy of their country.

RUHET SANFT AUF DIESEN HOHEN
EDLE GEBEINE TAPFERER ŒSTERREICHS KRIEGER
RUHM BEDECKT BEY ASPERN UND WAGRAM GEFALLEN
VERMAG EUER FREUND NICHT DIE ENTSEELTEN
LEICHNAME ZU BELEBEN, – SIE STETS ZU EHREN, IST SEINE PFLICHT.

REST SOFTLY ON THESE HEIGHTS,
YE RELICS OF BRAVE AUSTRIAN WARRIORS,
WHO, BEDECKED WITH GLORY, FELL AT ASPERN AND WAGRAM. –
THOUGH IT BE DENIED YOUR FRIEND TO REANIMATE,
IT IS HIS DUTY TO RENDER YOU UNCEASING HONOUR.

[90] The Vienna Woods in the 1930s; from *Down River* by John Lehmann.

Next to the Prater, comes the Wiener Wald as a popular Viennese playground and a place to learn to know the people intimately. There are few cities as fortunate as Vienna in their surroundings; the Wiener Wald is a glorified Summer park, providing all kinds of scenery and opportunities for all kinds of sport in its romantic setting of monasteries and castles and historic villages. Nor do the attractions of the Wiener Wald disappear in Winter; on the contrary, hardly are the last leaves off the branches, when the first snow is falling over the hill-tops and among the tree-trunks, and the young Viennese are getting their skis out, waxing them, rubbing grease into their boots, and packing their rucksacks for a Sunday's expedition.

I used to set out sometimes from the centre of Vienna in late Summer afternoons in a car, and find myself within only half an hour so deep among hills and forests, and able to fill my lungs with so exhilarating an air that it was almost impossible to believe I was not in the depths of Styria or Tirol, instead of a few miles from a capital city of two million inhabitants. On one side we could see wooded ridge after ridge, and scarcely a house breaking the slopes or marking the intervening valleys; on the other a wild irregular landscape descending to the Danube in the remote distance, and then further hills, with perhaps a little village and its baroque church spire perched on one of them. That was on the Hadersfeld side of the Wiener Wald. But sometimes I travelled out in a more southerly direction, through the pretty suburb of Mauer, or Perchtoldsdorf where the tower stands which marks the nearest point to Vienna the Turks ever reached, or of ancient Mödling and Baden, with their baroque elegance and *Kurort* atmosphere; then we might wind in and out for a long time among little colonies of the wooden 'week-end' houses that were built in hundreds after the War, and as we climbed up hillsides covered with the pale purple and white of Autumn crocuses, we looked back to see, far behind us and framed in the cleft of the valley, the last outskirts of Vienna, a blurred white-gleaming complex of tenements and factory chimneys and towers. Strangest of all were the lonely monasteries and castles one came across suddenly round the bend in a road, a tower perhaps perched on a spur among the hills, yet somehow contriving to be invisible up to the last moment. Some of these castles were deserted and in ruins, some had been turned to modern uses, some carefully restored by their owners; one and all made a curious contrast to the gay baroque suburbs among their vineyards, the week-end houses and secluded little 'smart' hotels frequented by actresses and film directors, and the streams of holidaying Viennese that went rowdily by them on motor-bikes on Saturdays and Sundays.

The Wiener Wald can be said to begin in Grinzing. There winter sports are held, though for the average Viennese the slopes beyond Neuwaldegg are more attractive. In the meadows round Rohrerhütte, and further out by Kaltenleutgeben and Sulz and Hochrotherd, if the snow was good, you could meet every day numbers of ski-enthusiasts, mostly children and students on their holidays and unemployed who had not yet had to sell or pawn their oufits; but on Sundays you would hardly see a patch of white snow for the crowds whirling down on their skis, tumbling in the snow, dodging in and out of the trees, and laboriously struggling uphill again. The trams and buses leading out from Vienna were jammed with them early in the morning, and returning trams and buses equally jammed with them in the evening, happily exhausted, dripping snow everywhere, the swollen rucksacks of the morning like deflated balloons. Sunday and snow in the Wiener Wald – particularly if the snow had melted a little and then frozen on top – meant also intense activity in first-aid: from the ambulances hurrying hither and thither you might almost imagine a battle was in progress. The casualties were, however, rarely so bad that they could not be dealt with on the spot, though even fatal accidents sometimes occurred when an inexpert skier crashed full-tilt into a tree.

If Spring was the time for hiking and mountain climbing in the Wiener Wald, and Winter for skiing and tobogganing, Autumn was the ideal season for visiting historic places, when for miles and miles the woods that cover hills and valleys were a slowly smouldering fire of leaves. The two chief meccas of the Wiener Wald were the Monastery of Heiligenkreuz and the village of Mayerling. The majority of those who came to see Mayerling were foreign tourists, but Heiligenkreuz has always been a centre for innumerable expeditions, and I can remember no visit on a Sunday or holiday when it was not swarming with trippers from Vienna – buses, cars, motorbicycles were parked deep outside its gates. Not only is it beautifully placed in a woody valley, and beautiful to look at and rest in, with its surprisingly successful mixture of gothic and baroque, its wide honey-coloured walls, which surround the outer courtyard and the restaurant under the trees, glowing in the sun; but it is also the burial-place of many famous Babenbergs and Habsburgs, including Frederick the Quarrelsome and that Leopold the Virtuous who was responsible for Richard Coeur-de-Lion's imprisonment. Here, too, the Baroness Vetsera is buried, a name more closely connected with Mayerling, where the great

Habsburg tragedy of 1889 took place. In Mayerling the Crown
Prince Rudolf's hunting-box is still standing, but one part of it,
where he and Marie Vetsera were found shot dead, was pulled
down to make way for a chapel when the whole building was
given by the Habsburgs to the Carmelites. I have come across old
inhabitants in the village who told me the strangest stories of that
January night, stories which undoubtedly had grown stranger
with the passage of time. This village, with its convent of
perpetual silence and its memories of disaster I had always found
an unsmiling, almost oppressive place; it must seem even more so
now, since the history of the last Habsburgs has taken on a more
darkly tragic air.

[91] An eye-witness account of the events at Mayerling in
January 1889; from *Rudolf: The Tragedy of Mayerling* by
Count Carl Lonyay.

(Count Hoyos and Prince Coburg visited Mayerling on 29
January and breakfasted with Crown Prince Rudolf, who
complained of a cold and cancelled his day's shooting with them.
Prince Coburg returned to Vienna; Count Hoyos dined with the
Crown Prince that evening, and continues his account of events
below.)

The menu was particularly simple: soup, goose-liver pie, roast
beef, roast venison, and pastry. My august host displayed a good
appetite and drank plenty of wine. He complained of severe
catarrh, but expected that it would soon pass off. When I asked
him if I could lend him some handkerchiefs, he replied that he
had enough to last until the next day.

    We sat smoking until about nine o'clock. Then the Crown
Prince said that he must attend to his cold, got up, shook hands
with his usual cordiality and withdrew, bidding me good night.

    How could I foresee that I had shaken his hand for the last
time? I retired to my apartments, some little distance away, and
went to bed at ten o'clock.

    His Imperial Highness had told me the previous evening that
he had ordered breakfast for the following day, Wednesday, the
30th, to be served for us all immediately upon the arrival of the
Prince of Coburg from Vienna. As I knew that the Prince would

be travelling by the same train we had arrived by the previous day, it was obvious that he would arrive at the same time, namely ten minutes past eight. Therefore, I decided to go to the castle at eight.

It was still a few minutes before this hour, and I was quite ready, when my valet announced the castle guard, Zwerger. When the latter entered he informed me that the Crown Prince's personal servant, Loschek, wished to let me know that he had been unable to wake the Crown Prince. When I said that he must be sleeping very well and soundly, I was informed that the Crown Prince had been up at half-past six, and had gone into the ante-room, fully dressed, and there had ordered Loschek, who slept in an adjoining room, to waken him again at half-past seven, and to order his breakfast, and the hackney-cab driver, Bratfisch, with the carriage for the same time. Then, whistling to himself, he had gone back to his room. Loschek had now been knocking uninterrupted since half-past seven on the bedroom door, first with his knuckles and then with a piece of wood, without evoking a sign of life. The bedroom door leading into the antechamber and the door leading from the spiral staircase from the first floor to the bedroom were both locked and the keys were missing.

There were obvious reasons for suspecting a disaster. I hastened with the guard, Zwerger, to the castle. On the way, Loschek repeated his account. After I myself had knocked and called the Crown Prince loudly, I asked quickly if the place were heated with coal. I was told that it was not. As Loschek would not undertake the responsibility of finally breaking down the doors, I ordered that they should be broken down on my own responsibility. Now Loschek explained for the first time that the Crown Prince was not alone, and added that a Baroness Vecsera [*sic: vere Marie Vetsera, the Crown Prince's mistress*] was with him. This news naturally caused me the greatest embarrassment, all the more as I had neither suspected the presence of the Baroness at Mayerling, nor had I known of her relations with the Crown Prince. Indeed there was not the remotest reason for me to suspect the existence of any such relations. Now the worst was to be feared, on account of the deathlike silence in the bedroom. It was hardly possible to think that one could render effectual assistance, as almost an hour and three quarters had passed since half-past six. The responsibility which I would have to assume

Crown Prince Rudolf;
miniature on ivory by Friedrich Wailand

was overwhelming. By my watch it was nine minutes past eight. Prince Coburg should be arriving at any moment. When I remarked upon this a servant ran out and returned saying that the Prince was just driving up.

In the billiard-room I briefly explained things to the Prince, and after a short deliberation we decided to have the doors burst open on our own responsibility. On account of the exceptionally delicate circumstances, Loschek was to go in alone and see how matters stood. The nomination of other witnesses was to be left – unless such postponement were dangerous – to His August Majesty.

As the door leading to the outer part of the house was locked, Loschek, in the presence of Prince Coburg and myself, tried to break the lock with a hatchet, but the door itself had to be crashed in. Loschek looked into the room and told us that both occupants were dead in bed. Our horror and grief were beyond words. But we had to decide whether a doctor should be called. As there were no signs of life, this was not desirable. The chief thing was to find out whether help would be in vain. Loschek must convince himself of this. When the door had been unlocked from the inside, through the broken panel, Loschek entered the room. He came back a few minutes later, explaining that there was not a sign of life in the bodies. The Crown Prince was lying bent over the edge of the bed, with a great pool of blood in front of him. Death from cyanide of potassium, as was indicated by the hæmorrhage, was presumed. It was only later that death from a bullet wound was proved.

(*See page 98 for Crown Prince Rudolf's funeral*)

[92] The Mayerling cover-up; from Edward Crankshaw's *The Fall of the House of Habsburg*.

The news came to the Hofburg out of a blue sky, shattering the daily routine. The Empress [*Elizabeth*] was having her daily lesson in modern Greek; Stephanie [*Rudolf's wife*] was in the middle of a singing lesson; Franz Josef himself was on the point of knocking off work for the morning to spend his usual hour with Katherina Schratt. In that splintered and arrested moment it took a little time for the truth to be grasped, then digested. Rudolf was dead; he had died side by side with a seventeen-year-

old girl. She must have poisoned him, and then herself. No, it had
been a shooting. Then she must have shot him, and then
herself. No – and here the Court doctor was wonderfully firm,
maintaining his professional integrity in the full blast of the
Emperor's wrath and indignation (neither lasted long) – it was
painfully clear that the Crown Prince had done the shooting; he
could say nothing else in the official death certificate. Franz Josef
bit on this bullet: he knew honesty when he saw it; after the first
short outburst of Imperial rage, he knew how to respect
professional duty. His only son and heir had murdered a
seventeen-year-old débutante, then shot himself: so be it. This
did not mean that he had to waste pity on the Vetsera. It did
mean that Rudolf had to be buried in the Imperial vault, the
Kaisergruft, among his ancestors, below the little church of the
Capuchin Friars, and then mentioned no more. It meant a
furious row with the Cardinal-Archbishop of Vienna and the
Papal Secretary, who frowned on suicide. It meant clearing the
remains of the Vetsera out of the way. It meant turning Rudolf's
favourite hunting-box, hidden in one of the smiling uplands in
the heart of the Wienerwald, into a shrine where nuns should
pray for his soul for ever. It meant carrying on as though nothing
at all had happened, so that nobody, nobody but Elizabeth and

Crown Prince
Rudolf's body is
brought to Vienna at
2 a.m.

Katherina Schratt, and then the few who saw him break down at
the dedication service at the Mayerling chapel, should have the
least idea of the depth of his suffering, or its nature. All this was
enough for one man. The removal of Marie Vetsera's body was
the affair of Taaffe and Baron Krauss the head of the Vienna
police. Rudolf had asked that the unfortunate girl should be
buried with him in the parish church at Alland, the village
nearest to Mayerling. But Taaffe in those first panic-stricken
moments when it still, improbably, seemed that the truth might
be hushed up, knew very well that this dying request could not
even be considered. It was he who was responsible for the swift
train of action which expressed itself in the macabre and cruel
story of Marie Vetsera's transfer, in a coach, in torrential rain, at
dead of night, held upright between her two Baltazzi uncles, to
the swiftly dug grave at the ancient and lovely monastery of
Heiligenkreuz. Taaffe was afraid, above all, of the Press.
Already, before the full news was released, he knew that certain
journalists had been putting two and two together, had been
watching the house in the Salesianergasse close to the palaces of
the Metternichs and the Schwarzenbergs, where Marie had
lived, had been interrogating neighbouring tradesmen about
her movements and about the movements of her mother, who,

alarmed at her disappearance, plunged wildly and appeared
before Elizabeth almost in the moment that the dreadful news
reached the Hofburg. The Press had to be kept away and misled
at all costs. And the Vetseras and Baltazzis must pay for their
fearful indiscretion. They did. The whole weight of the bureau-
cratic machine was summoned up in a moment to suppress the
truth. For this Franz Josef has been blamed. By the time the truth
came out it was too late to compose the affair more elegantly.
The deed remained, exposed for all to see, undefended and
unexplained. The deed was the deed of men harassed beyond
endurance, striking out savagely in defence of a sacred principle,
the principle of the Monarchy. It was not done in cold blood.
And there was, thereafter, no cold-blooded attempt to twist the
facts in mitigation.

[93] The legend of the Spinnerin-am-Kreuz; from *Vienna
Yesterday and Today* by J. Alexander Mahan.

About two miles south of the center of Vienna on Triesterstrasse
and a short distance beyond the Franz Josef-Spital stands a
beautiful Gothic tower dating from the fourteenth or fifteenth
century. Concerning the building of this monument there is but
little that is definitely known. Historians differ by almost twenty-
five years as to the time of its construction, a wide discrepancy in
regard to an event that must have occurred not more than five or
six centuries ago. There is one great mystery in connection with
this tower. According to all historians it was there before the
Turkish invasions of 1529 and 1683, and it stood directly in the
path of the approaching and retreating Mussulmen. Outside of
Stephansdom it was probably the sightliest and most artistic
shaft in existence during those days. Moreover the legend of its
erection connects it directly with the crusades, which were little
else than a warfare for the extermination of Islam. Why was this
tower not destroyed? The Turks had plenty of powder to blast
the great sections out of the Ring-wall and could easily have
wrecked the monument at any moment during their sieges.

At the time of the crusades a knight named Hintberg marched
away to fight the Mohammedans. As far as the Wienerberg he
was accompanied by his beautiful young bride. At that point the
road begins its descent, and just where he had his last view of
Vienna they parted. The separation was a sad one but the bride

promised to meet him at the same place upon his return. One may easily imagine the faithful Frau waving her fond farewells as the warrior disappeared down the long road leading to the mysterious Orient. She marked the spot with a few hastily gathered stones and from that moment the place was to her a hallowed ground. Every day she returned to sit and recall the last moments with her departing husband. As the time for his probable return approached she came at daybreak and remained till darkness veiled the road so that she might not possibly fail in her promise.

Presently she built a cottage on the cherished spot and took up residence to make sure of being there at the important moment. To support herself she spun garments and sold them to the passing soldiers. Weeks stretched into months and months into years and still her husband did not come nor did he send her any message by returning knights. He was given up for dead by all save his faithful wife. Many of her friends tried to persuade her to abandon hope and re-marry and some spoke of her as being unbalanced by the long vigil. But all this only increased her faith. At length the idea entered her head and took possession of her heart to build a monument to celebrate the day of his arrival. The only way to earn money for such an enterprise was to spin and sell more garments. So she spun in wind and weather, and sold to all who came to buy. Hot or cold, rain or shine, she spun and spun and spun. No one in Vienna and perhaps not in the whole wide world ever spun as she did. She was in a certain sense the medieval prototype of all modern spinsters. The longer she waited the stronger grew her love and the more magnificent must be the monument. So the impulse to spin waxed ever more and more compelling.

Finally one day an old man, shriveled, bent and gray, after many long years of imprisonment by the Saracens, stumbled up the road searching for the bride of his youth. There he found her busily spinning. It was a happy reunion and they immediately set about building a memorial which should stand for centuries to remind all women to be faithful to their absent husbands. Thus was built the Spinnerin am Kreuz. . . .

For centuries the Spinnerin am Kreuz was the place of execution for criminals from the city of Vienna. One mentions this with regret in connection with a monument that stands for such a noble sentiment.

The column is a perfect little gem of Gothic architecture,

rising delicate as lace to the height of fifty-two feet. It was
faithfully restored in the year of 1892.

[94] The Prince de Ligne recalls the exploits of the great
Polish general, Sobieski, who saved Vienna from the Turks
in 1683: it was the Polish cavalry, charging down from the
heights at Kahlenberg, which routed the Turkish besieging
forces; from *Anecdotal Reminiscences of the Congress of Vienna* by
Comte Auguste de la Garde-Chambonas.

The Kalemberg is a lofty hill in the vicinity of Vienna from which
a broadly extensive view is obtained. The house (an old
monastery) is small, but neat and pleasing in appearance. Over
the portal of the entrance the Prince had caused to be carved
these words: *Quo res cadunt, semper linea recta.* 'Here,' said the
Prince, 'I find rest and relaxation; especially at present, for, no
matter what our own inclinations may be, there is a certain
stiffness which we are compelled to impose upon ourselves in
presence of so many crowned heads and important personages.
Here I can live my own life.'
    When we reached the extremity of the garden he opened a
door which led into a summer-house overhanging the Danube,
from which was a view of the whole city of Vienna. 'It was from
this spot,' he said, 'that John Sobieski began his glorious attack
upon the Grand Vizier.'

[95] Jan Sobieski, the dashing Prince and leader of the
Polish forces, addresses his men before the attack which
routed the Turkish forces encamped around Vienna; from
Eye-Witness Accounts of the Siege of Vienna collected by Karl
Rach. Translated by Richard Bassett.

The enemy which you see now is the same as that which you have
vanquished in countless victories. Although you fight in a foreign
land, remember you fight for your homeland. Your courage,
which will free Vienna, will protect the frontiers of Poland.
    Here you will gather the respect and honour of all Christen-
dom. You fight for God, not for King.

Mail-coach on the Wienerberge by the Spinnerin-am-Kreuz column

[96] Drinking *heuriger* (new wine) on the Kahlenberg in the 1920s; from *A Young Man Looks at Europe* by Robert Young.

A few days later we were drinking *Heuriger* in a white house on the slopes of Kahlenberg. There was a sprig of evergreen over the door of the house – final proof that the new unfermented wine could be bought in the courtyard. The sun was dancing on the plane-trees in the courtyard; and far below us lay Vienna, the old and the new Danube and the Stefansdom, which the Nazis once threatened to destroy. Behind us lay Kahlenberg and behind Kahlenberg lay the craggy hill which belonged to the Emperors of Austria when it was not safe for them to live too near Vienna.

It was hot in the room, in spite of the three feet of limestone and clay which separated us from the garden. The Föhn wind was blowing, making us lazy and giving an inconsequent turn to our conversations. We had tasted the Föhn wind in Innsbruck; here we were drenched in it. But it was more peaceful in the house than in the fields or on the winding, dust-covered road which leads to Vienna. And the *Heuriger* wine is always more tasty in the country.

[97] An anonymous observer records the Battle of Aspern, 1809; from *An Eyewitness Account of the Battle of Aspern* in the Heeresgeschichtlichesmuseum, Vienna, 1811. Translated by Richard Bassett.

(In 1809 an army led by the Archduke Charles defeated Napoleon in a bloody encounter by the Danube near Vienna. It was the first time Napoleon had been seriously defeated on land, and though some weeks later he gained the upper hand at the Battle of Wagram, Europe had seen that Napoleon was not invulnerable.)

A unit of French troops appeared in the morning in the suburbs and fought its way desperately to the Kärntnertor [*now the site of the Opera House*]. General Mesto, however, dispatched a squadron of Hussars – who drove the enemy back out of the walls. But in the Prater the pavilion was stormed by a regiment of French *Voltigeurs* and by evening shells were falling on the city. By 13 May, the French possessed the city.

However, barely a week passed before the Archduke Charles, with a cannonade, drove in the enemy's pickets and engaged him around the village of ASPERN. Though the enemy's northern front was guarded by the Danube, across which there was only one narrow bridge, a battalion of Gyulai Grenadiers stormed across, driving the enemy back at the point of the bayonet. The French fell back in considerable disorder on the village of Aspern, which was quickly captured.

It did not take long, however, before the enemy was reinforced and retook the village, but the Grenadiers, stiffened with a battalion of Jaegers under Major Schneider, forced the enemy to

Archduke Charles of Austria, with the colours of the 15th Infantry
Regiment, at the Battle of Aspern, 22 May 1809

abandon it again. Both sides, seeing the value of the village,
continued to contest the battle here. In every street the fight
raged; in every house; in every ditch. Carriages and carts were
obliterated by musket-fire before the battle was fought hand to
hand. Every wall was of strategic importance. The church tower,
tall trees, cellars – all had to be taken if our troops wanted to hold
the village. As soon as we had taken one road, the enemy retook
the others and forced us to withdraw. This murderous fight went
on for hours. By nightfall, the battle was still raging, with most of
the houses burning.

In another part of the battlefield, 400 cannon were in play, and the oldest soldier could not recall such violent fire. Hand-to-hand fighting seemed to spread all over the line. At every point, our generals could be seen at the head of their troops inspiring them by their courage and strength. The Archduke himself seized the standard of the Zach regiment of Grenadiers, which was beginning to falter but which rallied with renewed passion around his heroic example. Most of those around the Archduke were wounded. His adjutant, Count Colloredo, fell with a musket-ball through his head. Sword and bayonet were, however, to decide the rest of the day's action.

[98] The Italian opera singers enjoy a summer season at the Palace of Laxenberg in the 1780s; from *Reminiscences* by Michael Kelly.

Just after this startling event, the Italian company were ordered to prepare to follow his Majesty to his palace at Luxemburgh, and to remain there for the summer months. The palace is only a few miles from Vienna, and nothing can be more magnificent; it is surrounded by forests full of all kinds of game; the park, gardens, and grounds, truly beautiful, and in the centre of a rich and luxuriant country. The theatre was very pretty, and very well attended; for all had their *entrée* to it gratis, including the surrounding peasantry.

Italian operas were performed three times, German plays twice, and German operas twice in each week. I passed the time here most delightfully. Every performer of the Italian opera had separate apartments allotted to him, and his breakfast was sent thither. There was a magnificent saloon, in which we all met at dinner. The table was plentifully and luxuriantly supplied, with every delicacy of the season; with wines of all descriptions, as well as all kinds of fruits, ices, &c.; and every night, after the spectacle, an excellent supper. In the mornings I had nothing to do (there were no rehearsals,) but to amuse myself. The Emperor and his court went often in chase of the Airone bird – an amusement he was very partial to. Prince Dichtrestein, the Master of the Horse, was very friendly to Signora Storace [*Nancy Storace, a singer*], and did her the kindness to send her one of the court barouches to view the chase.

[99] The Ritterschloss at the Palace of Laxenberg; from *Travels from Vienna . . . in the year 1814* by Richard Bright.

In this small village there is a palace belonging to the Emperor, which is his favourite summer residence. A large garden and wood are laid out in what is called the English taste; there are, however, whole colonies of hermits, not to mention the villages of fishermen, the mosques of Turks, and the temples of heathen goddesses; but the traveller's attention is chiefly called to a building named the *Ritter Schloss*, or Knight's Castle. This may with propriety be styled an imperial toy, and bears the same relation to an infant emperor which a painted cupboard, well peopled with dolls, bears to an infant subject. It is a little building provided with numerous turrets and watch-towers, loop-holes, irongrates, and portcullises; and that the castle may never be without a guard, even when every man capable of bearing arms is called into the field, the sentinel is painted with all his armour in lively colours upon the gate. Within the court-yard is, of course, that necessary appendage a draw-well; and nothing is wanting in miniature, either in the audience-chamber, the banqueting-hall, the sleeping apartments, the chamber of justice, the chapel, or the dungeon. The treasury chamber of Vienna has been put under contribution to supply the *Ritter Schloss* with valuables for the strong room; the gallery of the Belvedere has furnished its armoury; and old churches and cloisters have resigned their relics to adorn its altars. By a dark passage we reached the dungeon. Here sat a figure motionless upon a stone step; it was a knight templar, doomed to perpetual exclusion from the light of day. He raised his arm, but he could do no more; it fell unnerved upon his knee. A second time he attempted, and a third, but in vain; and we left him to all the cruelties which his merciless persecutor could heap upon him. Escaping from these mimic horrors, we returned with pleasure to the garden, and, crossing the water by which the castle is surrounded, came to the arena devoted to the celebration of tournaments; an oblong space, around which is raised a gravelled terrace with railing, and at one extremity is the royal lodge. It is about fifteen years since all this was completed. The emperor frequently visits it, and three years ago the last tournament was held.

[100] The Semmering railway, oldest of the Alpine railways and completed in the 1850s, whose spectacular
viaducts and tunnels are still admired as a monument to
nineteenth-century engineering; from *Austria, her people and
their homelands* by James Baker.

But far more glorious scenery awaits us as we go farther south,
running through the vine district of Voslau, that produces the
excellent red and white wine known by that name. . .

In not so far bygone days the railway broke off, and we had to
go by diligence over the Semmering Pass, but since 1854 this
mountain chain has been conquered by the iron road, and one
can quickly be at the summit, 3000 to 4000 feet above sea-level.

Austria is famous for its remarkably beautiful mountain
railways; as the Arlberg and the new Tauren railways; but if
these are grandiose, we shall cross them both shortly, yet this
Semmering railway is hardly surpassed by them in strange
beauty and sudden surprises.

At Gloggnitz, one is still in the lowlands, with rich fields,
through which the river winds, and cultured uplands. Then
quickly we begin to ascend, and the marvel of this early
engineering feat begins to excite one.

We twist round hill sides, through tunnels, and getting
different views of scenes, now on a level, then far below, catching
glimpses of snow on the heights far above. We are rising up from
the level of vineyards to the pine level; the views embrace vast
stretches of landscape or deep, rocky ravines, with, as at Klamm,
a grand old castle ruin perched on its rocky height. Then we
crawl round on a dizzy viaduct that gives a grand glimpse down
through the pines to the rich valleys, and so skirt the vast, rocky
wall of the Weinzettelwand, perhaps one of the finest, if not most
dramatic, scenes on the route. A double tiered viaduct, 150 feet
high, takes us over the deep Kalte Rinne, that is a ravine wide
enough to give us time for a good long look at the very beautiful
view. Another viaduct, not of so dizzy a height, leads us on to
more tunnels, and we pull up at the Semmering Station.

Just a couple of hours from the plainland and crowded city
streets of Vienna, and here we are amidst the scent of the pines,
with peasant girls offering one Edelweiss blossoms. A trudge up
through the winding forest road quickly brings one to the villas
and hotels of the Semmering.

❧ Music and theatre-going ❧
in Vienna

At night two of the poor scholars of this city sung, in the court of the inn where I lodged, duets in falsetto soprano, and contralto, very well in tune, and with feeling and taste. I sent to inquire whether they were taught music at the Jesuits' college, and was answered in the affirmative. Though the number of poor scholars, at different colleges, amounts to a hundred and twenty, yet there are at present but seventeen that are taught music.

After this there was a band of these singers, who performed through the streets a kind of glees, in three and four parts: this whole country is certainly very musical. I frequently heard the soldiers upon guard, and sentinels, as well as common people, sing in parts. The music school at the Jesuits' college, in every Roman catholic town, accounts in some measure for this faculty; yet other causes may be assigned, and, among these, it should be remembered, that there is scarce a church or convent in Vienna, which has not every morning its mass in music: that is, a great portion of the church service of the day, set in parts, and performed with voices, accompanied by at least three or four violins, a tenor and bass, beside the organ; and as the churches here are daily crowded, this music, though not of the most exquisite kind, must, in some degree, form the ear of the inhabitants. Physical causes operate but little, I believe, as to music. Nature distributes her favours pretty equally to the inhabitants of Europe; but moral causes are frequently very powerful in their effects. And it seems as if the national music of a country was good or bad, in proportion to that of its church service; which may account for the taste of the common people of Italy, where indeed the language is more musical than in any other country of Europe, which certainly has an effect upon their vocal music; but the excellent performances that are every day heard for nothing in the churches, by the common people, more contribute to refine and fix the national taste for good music, than any other thing that I can at present suggest.

[102] Michael Kelly meets Gluck; from Michael Kelly's *Reminiscences*.

Gluck was then living at Vienna, where he had retired, crowned with professional honours, and a splendid fortune, courted and caressed by all ranks, and in his seventy-fourth year.

L'Iphigenia was the first opera to be produced, and Gluck was to make his choice of the performers in it. Madame Bernasconi was one of the first serious singers of the day, – to her was appropriated the part of Iphigenia. The celebrated tenor, Ademberger, performed the part of Orestes, finely. To me was allotted the character of Pylades, which created no small envy among those performers who thought themselves better entitled to the part than myself, and perhaps they were right; – however, I had it, and also the high gratification of being instructed in the part by the composer himself.

On morning, after I had been singing with him, he said, 'Follow me up stairs, Sir, and I will introduce you to one, whom, all my life, I have made my study, and endeavoured to imitate.' I followed him into his bed-room, and, opposite to the head of the bed, saw a full-length picture of Handel, in a rich frame. 'There, Sir,' said he, 'is the portrait of the inspired master of our art; when I open my eyes in the morning, I look upon him with reverential awe, and acknowledge him as such, and the highest praise is due to your country for having distinguished and cherished his gigantic genius.' . . .

For describing the strongest passions in music, and proving grand dramatic effect, in my opinion, no man ever equalled Gluck – he was a great painter of music; perhaps the expression is far fetched, and may not be allowable, but I speak from my own feelings, and the sensation his descriptive music always produced on me. For example, I never could hear, without tears, the dream of Orestes, in Iphigenia: when in sleep, he prays the gods to give a ray of peace to the parricide Orestes. What can be more expressive of deep and dark despair? – And the fine chorus of the demons who surround his couch, with the ghost of his mother, produced in me a feeling of horror, mixed with delight.

Dr Burney (no mean authority) said, Gluck was the Michael Angelo of living composers, and called him the simplifying musician.

[103] Michael Kelly meets Mozart, asks his advice about counterpoint, and later enjoys a musical *soirée*; from Michael Kelly's *Reminiscences*.

I went one evening to a concert of the celebrated Kozeluch's, a great composer for the piano-forte, as well as a fine performer on that instrument. I saw there the composers Vanhall and Baron Dittersdorf; and, what was to me one of the greatest gratifications of my musical life, was there introduced to the prodigy of genius – Mozart. He favoured the company by performing fantasias and capriccios on the piano-forte. His feeling, the rapidity of his fingers, the great execution and strength of his left hand, particularly, and the apparent inspiration of his modulations, astounded me. After this splendid performance we sat down to supper, and I had the pleasure to be placed at table between him and his wife, Madame Constance Weber, a German lady of whom he was passionately fond, and by whom he had three children. He conversed with me a good deal about Thomas Linley, the first Mrs Sheridan's brother, with whom he was intimate at Florence, and spoke of him with great affection. He said that Linley was a true genius, and he felt that, had he lived, he would have been one of the greatest ornaments of the musical world. After supper the young branches of our host had a dance, and Mozart joined them. Madame Mozart told me, that great as his genius was, he was an enthusiast in dancing, and often said that his taste lay in that art, rather than in music.

He was a remarkably small man, very thin and pale, with a profusion of fine hair, of which he was rather vain. He gave me a cordial invitation to his house, of which I availed myself, and passed a great part of my time there. He always received me with kindness and hospitality. – He was remarkably fond of punch, of which beverage I have seen him take copious draughts. He was also fond of billiards, and had an excellent billiard table in his house. Many and many a game have I played with him, but always came off second best. He gave Sunday concerts, at which I never was missing. He was kind-hearted, and always ready to oblige; but so very particular, when he played, that if the slightest noise were made, he instantly left off. He one day made me sit down to the piano, and gave credit to my first master, who had taught me to place my hand well on the instrument. – He conferred on me what I considered a high compliment. I had composed a little melody to Metastasio's canzonetta, 'Grazie agl' inganni tuoi', which was a great favourite wherever I sang it. It was very simple, but had the good fortune to please Mozart. He took it and composed variations upon it, which were truly beautiful; and had the further kindness and condescension to play them wherever he had an opportunity. . . .

Encouraged by his flattering approbation, I attempted several little airs, which I shewed him, and which he kindly approved of; so much indeed, that I determined to devote myself to the study of counterpoint, and consulted with him, by whom I ought to be instructed. – He said, 'My good lad, you ask my advice, and I will give it you candidly; had you studied composition when you were at Naples, and when your mind was not devoted to other pursuits, you would perhaps have done wisely; but now that your profession of the stage must, and ought, to occupy all your attention, it would be an unwise measure to enter into a dry study. You may take my word for it, Nature has made you a melodist, and you would only disturb and perplex yourself. Reflect, "*a little knowledge* is a dangerous thing;" – should there be errors in what you write, you will find hundreds of musicians, in all parts of the world, capable of correcting them; therefore do not disturb your natural gift.'

'Melody is the essence of music,' continued he; '*I* compare a good melodist to a fine racer, and counterpointists to hack post-horses; therefore be advised, let *well alone*, and remember the old Italian proverb – "Chi sa più, meno sa – Who knows most, knows least".' The opinion of this great man made on me a lasting impression. . . .

Storace [*later*] gave a quartet party to his friends. The players were tolerable; not one of them excelled on the instrument he played, but there was a little science among them, which I dare say will be acknowledged when I name them:

The First Violin	. . . .	HAYDN.
,, Second Violin.	. . .	BARON DITTERSDORF.
,, Violoncello	. . . .	VANHALL.
,, Tenor	. . . . .	MOZART.

The poet Casti and Paesiello formed part of the audience. I was there, and a greater treat or a more remarkable one cannot be imagined.

On the particular evening to which I am now specially

referring, after the musical feast was over, we sat down to an excellent supper, and became joyous and lively in the extreme.

[104] The first performance of *The Marriage of Figaro*; from Michael Kelly's *Reminiscences*.

Of all the performers in this opera at that time, but one survives – myself. It was allowed that never was opera stronger cast. I have seen it performed at different periods in other countries, and well too, but no more to compare with its original performance than light is to darkness. All the original performers had the advantage of the instruction of the composer, who transfused into their minds his inspired meaning. I never shall forget his little animated countenance, when lighted up with the glowing rays of genius; – it is as impossible to describe it, as it would be to paint sun-beams.

I called on him one evening; he said to me, 'I have just finished a little duet for my opera, you shall hear it.' He sat down to the piano, and we sang it. I was delighted with it, and the musical world will give me credit for being so, when I mention the duet, sung by Count Almaviva and Susan, 'Crudel perchè finora farmi languire così.' A more delicious morceau never was penned by man, and it has often been a source of pleasure to me to have been the first who heard it, and to have sung it with its greatly gifted composer. I remember at the first rehearsal of the full band, Mozart was on the stage with his crimson pelisse and goldlaced cocked hat, giving the time of the music to the orchestra. Figaro's song, 'Non, più andrai, farfallone amoroso', Bennuci gave, with the greatest animation, and power of voice.

I was standing close to Mozart, who, *sotto voce*, was repeating, Bravo! Bravo! Bennuci; and when Bennuci came to the fine passage, 'Cherubino, alla vittoria, alla gloria militar', which he gave out with Stentorian lungs, the effect was electricity itself, for the whole of the performers on the stage, and those in the orchestra, as if actuated by one feeling of delight, vociferated Bravo! Bravo! Maestro. Viva, viva, grande Mozart. Those in the orchestra I thought would never have ceased applauding, by beating the bows of their violins against the music desks. The little man acknowledged, by repeated obeisances, his thanks for the distinguished mark of enthusiastic applause bestowed upon him.

The same meed of approbation was given to the finale at the end of the first act; that piece of music alone, in my humble opinion, if he had never composed any thing else good, would have stamped him as the greatest master of his art. In the sestetto, in the second act, (which was Mozart's favourite piece of the whole opera,) I had a very conspicuous part, as the Stuttering Judge. All through the piece I was to stutter; but in the sestetto, Mozart requested I would not, for if I did, I should spoil his music. I told him, that although it might appear very presumptuous in a lad like me to differ with him on this point, I did; and was sure, the way in which I intended to introduce the stuttering, would not interfere with the other parts, but produce an effect; besides, it certainly was not in nature, that I should stutter all through the part, and when I came to the sestetto speak plain; and after that piece of music was over, return to stuttering; and, I added, (apologizing at the same time, for my apparent want of deference and respect in placing my opinion in opposition to that of the great Mozart,) that unless I was allowed to perform the part as I wished, I would not perform it at all.

Mozart at last consented that I should have my own way, but doubted the success of the experiment. Crowded houses proved that nothing ever on the stage produced a more powerful effect; the audience were convulsed with laughter, in which Mozart himself joined. The Emperor repeatedly cried out Bravo! and the piece was loudly applauded and encored. When the opera was over, Mozart came on the stage to me, and shaking me by both hands, said, 'Bravo! young man, I feel obliged to you; and acknowledge you to have been in the right, and myself in the wrong.' There was certainly a risk run, but I felt within myself I could give the effect I wished, and the event proved that I was not mistaken. . . .

Never was any thing more complete, than the triumph of Mozart, and his 'Nozze de Figaro', to which numerous overflowing audiences bore witness.

[105] Mozart's powers of improvisation are remembered by his friend the Abbé Stadler, who was then in his eighties; from *A Mozart Pilgrimage, being the travel diaries of Vincent and Mary Novello* transcribed and compiled by Nerina Medici di Marignano, and edited by Rosemary Hughes.

As we walked along together he [*Abbé Stadler*] communicated to me the following curious Anecdote: On my enquiring what were the most favourite pieces with Mozart when he was in private amongst his intimate friends, the Abbé said he usually played *extemporaneously*, but that his imagination was so inexhaustible and at the same time his ideas were so symmetrical and regularly treated that Albrechtsberger could not be persuaded but what they were regular pieces that had been studied beforehand — One evening when Mozart, the Abbé Stadler and Albrechts- berger were together, the latter asked Mozart to sit down to the Instrument and play something. Mozart directly complied, but instead of taking a subject of his own he told Albrechtsberger to give him a theme. Albrechtsberger accord- ingly invented a subject on the spot, and which he was quite certain that Mozart could not possibly have heard before; he also selected the most trivial features he could think of in order to put Mozart's ingenuity, invention and creative powers to the severest test.

This extraordinary Genius immediately took the theme that had been given him thus unexpectedly, and played for upwards of an hour upon it, treating it in all possible variety of form – fugue, Canon, from the most simple to the most elaborate Counterpoint – until Albrechtsberger could hold out no longer, but exclaimed in transport, 'I am now perfectly convinced that your extemporaneous playing is really the thought of the moment and that you fully deserve all the fame you have acquired from this wonderful talent.'

[106] Mozart's death, described by his sister-in-law Sophie Haibl in a letter to Georg Nikolaus von Nissen; from *Letters of Mozart and his family* edited by Emily Anderson.

I hurried along as fast as I could. Alas, how frightened I was when my sister [*Constanze, Mozart's wife*], who was almost despairing and yet trying to keep calm, came out to me, saying: 'Thank God that you have come, dear Sophie. Last night he was so ill that I thought he would not be alive this morning. Do stay with me today, for if he has another bad turn, he will pass away tonight. Go in to him for a little while and see how he is.' I tried to control myself and went to his bedside. He immediately called me to him and said: 'Ah, dear Sophie, how glad I am that you have come. You must stay here tonight and see me die.' I tried hard to be brave and to persuade him to the contrary. But to all my attempts he only replied: 'Why, I have already the taste of death on my tongue.' And, 'if you do not stay, who will support my dearest Constanze when I am gone?' 'Yes, yes, dear Mozart,' I assured him, 'but I must first go back to our mother and tell her that you would like me to stay with you today. Otherwise she will think that some misfortune has befallen you.' 'Yes, do so,' said Mozart, 'but be sure and come back soon.' Good God, how distressed I felt! My poor sister followed me to the door and begged me for Heaven's sake to go to the priests at St Peter's and implore one of them to come to Mozart – a chance call, as it were. I did so, but for a long time they refused to come and I had a great deal of trouble to persuade one of those clerical brutes to go to him. Then I ran off to my mother who was anxiously awaiting me. It was already dark. Poor soul, how shocked she was! I persuaded her to go and spend the night with her eldest daughter, the late Josefa Hofer. I then ran back as fast I could to my distracted sister. Süssmayr was at Mozart's bedside. The well-known Requiem lay on the quilt and Mozart was explaining to him how, in his opinion he ought to finish it, when he was gone. Further, he urged his wife to keep his death a secret until she should have informed Albrechtsberger, who was in charge of all the services. A long search was made for Dr Closset, who was found at the theatre, but who had to wait for the end of the play. He came and ordered cold poultices to be placed on Mozart's burning head, which, however, affected him to such an extent that he became unconscious and remained so until he died. His last movement was an attempt to express with his mouth the drum passages in the Requiem. That I can still hear. Müller from the Art Gallery came and took a cast of his pale, dead face.

[107] Anecdotes of Beethoven told by Mme Streicher, a former pupil of his; from *A Mozart Pilgrimage, being the travel diaries of Vincent and Mary Novello* transcribed and compiled by Nerina Medici di Marignano, and edited by Rosemary Hughes.

(In this extract, Mary Novello's narrative is complemented by her husband's brief notes of the same conversation.)

M.N. Mrs Streicher was intimate with Beethoven to a very great degree as she has above 50 notes written by him to her on familiar subjects. She amused us much by describing some of his peculiarities with his servants and sometimes driving them all out of the house in a body. He must have been a most wilful and disagreeable person as an acquaintance. In appearance she describes him as a beggar he was so dirty in his dress, and in manner like a bear sulky and froward, he laughed like no one else it was a scream, he would call people names as he passed them, yet for all this she thinks him an honest man but I doubt this for he was avaricious and always mistrustful. He delighted to pinch a person's hand till he hurt it, said no one could make a good crush that had not a good conscience; worried about the minutest things of his own, some counterpanes Mrs Streicher promised to get washed for him he teased her husband to death over, and even wrote to her to Baden a note set to music to the words of 'Where are my counterpanes?' Another time he visited Baden where she was, but instead of calling upon her threw his card in at the window, which as he was so odd looking a man, frightened her servant. He would frequently walk out in the fields for many miles and several times sat down to write, and having fallen asleep was wet through with the rain. His servants not liking him he was frequently much neglected. . . .

V.N. Eccentric and suspicious of the motives of all around him – a mixture of Sam Wesley and Rousseau – read a great deal (sometimes all Dinner) principally poetry – Goethe his favourite.

The only three musicians he liked were Handel, Sebastian Bach and Mozart – hated all etiquette or formality – wore shabby clothes – contempt for aristocrats and their formal parties – never shewed them the least respect – . . . Nephew he loved so much not turning out well – hurt him and hastened his

death. Tormented by Servants and no kind Lady to take care of
him; advised by Madame Streicher to marry, shook his head
bitterly (probably thought no Lady could love one who was so
deaf) – came full dressed in new Clothes, on New Years Day. . . .

She [Mme Streicher] attended his funeral stood in the spot in
the court yard where his body was deposited before the
Procession began – curious crowd. Streicher visited just before he
died – but was ill himself when the Funeral took place.
Purchased MSS at his sale – gave them to Madame who gave me
two pages of it.

Monument at the detached burying ground at Währing, of
pyramid form against the wall on the left side. Butterfly and
snake for eternity above, a Golden Lyre lower down and only his
name in large gold Letters (good taste). Large slab of granite
broken in two without any inscription is placed over his body.
When he was first buried a guard was placed every night for some
time lest his body should be stolen away.

[108] Martha Wilmot takes two of her children, Catha-
rine and Wilmot ('the Squire'), to the opera; from *More
Letters . . . Impressions of Vienna 1819–1829* by Martha
Wilmot.

The reason of this otherwise mad act was that there is a most
extraordinary and beautiful Opera at Vienna, performed
entirely *by Children*, some *younger* than Catharine, and none of
them above 16 or 17 – these act as men. Tis the prettiest thing I
ever beheld, the dancing is perfect, the glitter of the dresses and
the beauty of the scenery quite like magic. The piece is called 'the
triumph of Love' and after ten thousand frolic's of Cupid, and
gambols, the *flights* of children into the air, where they hang like
a *spiders nest* nobody KNOWS how, it all ends in the tiny Lover and
Loveress kneeling at the feet of Cupid, and being drawn gently
up into the air, where by slow degrees, you scarcely know how,
the whole space of Air is filled with *Clouds*, and groups of
Children hanging, reclining, perching amongst them, so fantastical and so beautiful and so *numerous*, that you don't know which
to admire most, the Collection of Children, amounting to some
hundreds, or the wonderful manner in which they perform the
parts allotted to them. I don't pretend to say what *the Squire* and

The Opera House, Vienna

his sister admired the most, but they were delighted, and as the whole thing was over *before* ten O'Clock, and as we sat in Ld Stewart's well carpeted box, there was but little risque of cold, and I am happy to say they are this day as brisk as *bottled* ale.

[109] Theatre-going in Vienna in the early nineteenth century; from Richard Bright's *Travels from Vienna . . . in the year 1814.*

In the evening, the theatre is the usual resource for the many who have no other more active engagement. The time and duration of the performances are very convenient. They begin about six, and conclude a little after nine. The play in Vienna is a recreation, – in London a fatigue. At Vienna you see the best national productions, and enjoy three comfortable hours; whilst in London, it is necessary to derange the whole occupations of the day, and at last to undergo many hours of fatigue and discomfort. The theatres at Vienna were all occupied by German companies; the Italian opera having been lately discontinued. There are five of them, one which communicates with the palace, and is called the Palace Theatre; and another called the Coertner-thor Theatre from its situation; is likewise within the boundary of the city. The other three are in the suburbs. In the two former, as well as in the chief theatre of the suburbs, the representations are highly respectable, and the language spoken is pure. In the two smaller theatres, the pieces are generally of an inferior character; and the German, even where it is not intended to imitate the low and vulgar dialect, is often extremely bad. The prices are all moderate, and the houses were generally well filled. The parterres; which correspond to the English pit, but where places may be previously taken; were full of strangers, the great majority men; officers and diplomatists negligently dressed, though generally bearing some star or cross in token of their rank or services. The greatest decorum prevails in the house during the representation; and England might, in this respect, again take a lesson, though the means employed detract much from the praises due to the result; for the police military; that is, police officers dressed in a particular livery, and wearing swords; are placed in all the avenues. I never saw them usurp any unpleasant authority; and the result certainly is, that a person who goes with a wish to hear the play, is not disappointed by the bursting out of those noisy quarrels, which scarcely fail to interrupt the performance in an English theatre.

[110] Theatre-going in Vienna at the turn of the century; from *The Vanished Pomps of Yesterday* . . . by Lord Frederic Hamilton.

(Lord Frederic Hamilton (1856–1928) served as a diplomat in Berlin, St Petersburg, Lisbon and Buenos Aires; was elected MP for South-West Manchester after he left the Diplomatic Corps, and later edited the *Pall Mall Magazine*.)

The Vienna theatres are justly celebrated. At the Hof-Burg Theatre may be seen the most finished acting on the German stage. The Burg varied its programme almost nightly, and it was an amusing sight to see the troops of liveried footmen inquiring at the box-office, on behalf of their mistresses, whether the play to be given that night was or was not a *Comtessen-Stück*, *i.e.*, a play fit for young girls to see. The box-keeper always gave a plain 'Yes' or 'No' in reply.

[111] The young Franz Schubert, enrolled in the Imperial Municipal Convent next to the imposing Jesuit Church, which was run by monks as a preparatory establishment for university students, writes to one of his brothers in 1812; from Schubert's *Gesammelte Briefen*, in the collection of the Musikverein, Vienna. Translated by Richard Bassett.

Let me get what I want to say off my chest at once and come straight to the point. I won't bore you be beating about the bush in my usual way. I've been giving a lot of thought to life here and have come to the conclusion that it's a pretty good thing, though in some ways it might be better. You will know from your own experiences that there are times when one could certainly do with a roll and a few apples, particularly when one has to wait eight and a half hours between a moderate-sized midday meal and a wretched sort of supper. This constant longing has become

more and more insistent and the time has come when, willy-nilly,
I must do something about it. The few *groschen* father gave me
vanished into thin air in the first few days. . . .

[112] An Austrian aristocrat's celebrated account of how
Schubert came across the poetry for his famous song cycle
Die Schöne Müllerin: from the Kreissle von Hellborn manu-
script, *c.*1827, in the collection of the Musikverein, Vienna.
Translated by Richard Bassett.

One day Schubert called on the private secretary of Count
Seczenyi, Herr Benedikt Randhartinger, with whom he was on
friendly terms. He had scarcely entered the room when the
secretary was summoned by the Count. He went out at once,
indicating to the composer that he would be back shortly. Franz
walked over to the desk where he found a volume of poems lying.
He promptly pocketed the book and, without waiting for
Randhartinger's return, departed.

The latter noticed that the volume of poems was missing as
soon as he came back, and called Schubert the following day in
order to recover the book. Franz put down his high-handed
behaviour to the interest which the poems had aroused in him,
and to prove that the removal had not been entirely
unproductive, he presented ̀the astonished secretary with the
manuscript of the first 'Miller' songs which he had partially
completed during the previous night.

[113] Robert Schumann imagines other great composers
in Vienna; from Schumann's *Gesammelte Schriften* in the
collection of the Musikverein, Vienna, written *c.*1835.
Translated by Richard Bassett.

(The composer Robert Schumann (1810–56) lived in the
Schonlaterngasse for a brief period during the 1830s. Though a
German, he found Vienna a comfortable home, as did many
other German artists and musicians.)

This Vienna, with its St Stephen's steeple, its delightful women,
surrounded by the innumerable curves of the Danube . . . with all

its memories of the greatest German masters, must be fertile ground for a musician's fancy. Often as I gazed at it from the mountain heights, I would imagine how Beethoven's eyes must have wandered restlessly towards the distant range of Alps; how Mozart, lost in thought, must often have followed the course of the Danube which seems everywhere to merge with the fields and woods; and how Papa Haydn must many a time have contemplated the spire of St Stephen's, shaking his head at the prospect of so dizzy a height.

Combine these pictures of the Danube, St Stephen's spire and the distant mountain range, suffuse them with the gentle Catholic fragrance of incense and you have a single picture of Vienna. And as we ourselves look upon this charming landscape, the sight stirs within us chords which would otherwise never have sounded.

[114] Changing musical tastes in Vienna during the nineteenth century; from *Vienna's Golden Years of Music, 1850–1900* by Eduard Hanslick, translated and edited by Henry Pleasants III.

(Eduard Hanslick (1825–1904) was born in Prague and studied both law and music at Prague University. In 1846 he moved to Vienna, where for forty years he both lectured in music and was the famous critic of *Die Neue Freie Presse*, devoted to the works of Schumann and Brahms, taking critical issue with Wagner, Liszt, Berlioz, Bruckner and Richard Strauss. The March Revolution of 1848, of which he writes below, saw the expulsion of Italian Opera from Vienna and a swing towards all things German.)

It has always been a valuable memory to me to have experienced the last years of pre-March (1848) Vienna. How trivial was public musical life at the end of the thirties and in the early forties! Sumptuous and trivial alike, it vacillated between dull sentimentality and scintillant wit. Cut off from all great intellectual interests, the Vienna public abandoned itself to diversion and entertainment. Not only did the theaters flourish; they were the chief subject of conversation and occupied the leading columns of the daily newspapers. Musical life was dominated by Italian opera, virtuosity, and the waltz. Strauss and Lanner were idolized. I would be the last to underestimate the talent of these two men . . . but it can readily be understood that this sweetly intoxicating three-quarter time, to which heads as well as feet were abandoned, combined with Italian opera and the cult of virtuosity, rendered listeners steadily less capable of intellectual effort.

The year 1848 marked the borderline between the old and the new Austria – not only in political and social matters but also in the literary and artistic life of the nation.

[115] Brahms playing his own music in 1862; from *Vienna's Golden Years of Music, 1850–1900* by Eduard Hanslick, translated and edited by Henry Pleasants III.

Brahms is already a significant personality, possibly the most interesting among our contemporary composers. In the form and character of his music he suggests Schumann, although rather in the sense of an inner kinship than of actual imitation or modeling. Only with the utmost difficulty could such an individual entirely escape the spirit of Schumann, which so undeniably permeates and determines the musical atmosphere of the present. His music and Schumann's have in common, above all else, continence and inner nobility. There is no seeking after applause in Brahms' music, no narcissistic affectation. Everything is sincere and truthful. But with Schumann's music it shares, to the point of stubbornness, a sovereign subjectivity, the tendency to brood, the rejection of the outside world, the introspection. . . .

It may appear praiseworthy to Brahms that he plays more like a composer than a virtuoso, but such praise is not altogether unqualified. Prompted by the desire to let the composer speak for himself, he neglects – especially in the playing of his own pieces – much that the player should rightly do for the composer. His playing resembles the austere Cordelia, who concealed her finest feelings rather than betray them to the people. The forceful and the distorted are thus simply impossible in Brahms' playing. Its judicious softness is, indeed, such that he seems reluctant to draw a full tone from the piano. As little as I wish to gloss over the minor shortcomings, just as little do I wish to deny how insignificant they are compared with the irresistible spirtual charm of his playing. This was most deeply effective in Schumann's Fantasy in C major, opus 17. . . . I cannot imagine a more profoundly, more genuinely effective performance of this remarkable piece than that which Brahms gave it. What pleasure it is to hear him play! The instant he touches the keys one experiences the feeling: here is a true, honest artist, a man of intelligence and spirit, of unassuming self-reliance! Brahms appeared to be in especially good form. By that I do not mean to say that every passage was ultimately immaculate or that in every leap he hit the mark unerringly. His technique is like a big, strong man, negligent in attire and given to loitering. He has too many more important things in his head and heart to be constantly concerned with his external personal appearance. But his playing is always compelling and convincing.

[116] The first performance of Bruckner's 8th Symphony in 1892; from *Vienna's Golden Years of Music, 1850–1900* by Eduard Hanslick, translated and edited by Henry Pleasants III.

The Philharmonic Orchestra devoted its entire concert to a new symphony by Bruckner. It is the eighth in the series and similar to its predecessors in form and mood. I found this newest one, as I have found the other Bruckner symphonies, interesting in detail but strange as a whole and even repugnant. The nature of the work consists – to put it briefly – in applying Wagner's dramatic style to the symphony.

Not only does Bruckner fall continually into Wagnerian devices, effects, and reminiscences; he seems even to have accepted certain Wagnerian pieces as models for symphonic construction, as, for example, the Prelude to *Tristan and Isolde*. Bruckner begins with a short chromatic motive, repeats it over and over again, higher and higher in the scale and on into infinity, augments it, diminishes it, offers it in contrary motion, and so on, until the listener is simply crushed under the sheer weight and monotony of this interminable lamentation. Alongside these upward surging lamentations we have the subsiding lamentation (after the model of the *Tannhäuser* Overture). Wagnerian orchestral effects are met on every hand, such as the tremolos of the violins *divisi* in the highest position, harp arpeggios over muffled chords in the trombones, and, added to all that, the newest achievements of the Siegfried tubas. . . .

Even before the performance we had heard such provocative reports of the extraordinary profundity of the new symphony that I took care to prepare myself through study of the score and attendance at the dress rehearsal. I must confess, however, that the mysteries of this all-embracing composition were disclosed to me only through the helpful offices of an explanatory program handed to me prior to the concert. . . .

And the reception of the new symphony? A storm ovation, waving of handkerchiefs from the standees, innumerable recalls, laurel wreaths, etc! For Bruckner, the concert was certainly a huge success. Whether Hans Richter performed a similar favor for his subscribers by devoting an entire concert to the Bruckner symphony is doubtful. The program seems to have been chosen only for the sake of a noisy minority. The test is easy: just give the symphony in a special concert outside the subscription series. This would be helpful to all concerned, save probably the Philharmonic Orchestra.

[117] An obituary for Johann Strauss the Younger, 1899; from *Vienna's Golden Years of Music, 1850–1900* by Eduard Hanslick, translated and edited by Henry Pleasants III.

When we buried Johann Strauss, Senior, fifty years ago, I remarked in an obituary that Vienna had lost its most talented composer. This was annoying to musicians and laymen alike. They refused to admit that a correct but characterless piece of concert or church music could reveal less talent, less in the way of natural resources, than a melodious, original waltz.

In this sense, I can only repeat the same point today, at the grave of the younger Johann Strauss. Vienna has lost its most original musical talent. The sources of his melodic invention were as fine as they were inexhaustible; his rhythm pulsated with animated variety; his harmonies and his forms were pure and upright. He named one of his waltzes '*Liebeslieder*.' The designation was applicable to all of them: little love stories of bashful courtship, impulsive infatuation, radiant happiness, and here and there a breath of easily consolable melancholy. Who could enumerate even the most charming of Strauss's numerous dance

Cartoon of Johann Strauss the Younger

pieces! It's too bad that each ball season, like Kronos, pitilessly devours its own children in order to make room for others. Thus it is that we are as little familiar with Strauss's earliest and best waltzes as though they dated from the time of Maria Theresa. They are not obsolescent; they have merely been crowded aside and neglected.

One waltz among the hundreds deserves to be named specifically: 'The Blue Danube.' As I once wrote many years ago, one has only to sound the first three notes of the D major triad and all cheeks instantly glow with enthusiasm. 'The Blue Danube' not only enjoys unexampled popularity; it has also achieved a unique significance: that of a symbol for everything that is beautiful and pleasant and gay in Vienna. It is a kind of patriotic folk song without words. In addition to Haydn's national anthem, which celebrates the Emperor and the ruling house, we possess in 'The Blue Danube' another national anthem, one which celebrates the country and its people. Wherever Austrians are gathered together abroad, this wordless 'Marseillaise' of peace is their national song and their symbol of recognition. Whenever Vienna or Austria is toasted at a banquet, the orchestra strikes up 'The Blue Danube.' Its melody has the effect of a motto.

Johann Strauss modernized, extended, and enriched the Viennese waltz created by his father. He made a school, and it has become almost compulsory. What is heard today in the way of waltzes is mostly rewritten Strauss. However hard they may try, our operetta composers cannot write two measures in waltz time without involuntarily copying him.

[118] Opera-going in Vienna before and after the First World War; from *The lure of Vienna* by Alice Williamson.

Before the war laid its withering black hand on our poor old world, the auditorium of the Vienna Opera House on a 'good' night of the high season was as dazzling a sight as you could find in the world of sophisticated society. A white and rose-crimson background, flecked with gold, and lit with a ruby gleam as of unseen fire: cameo clear and pearly pale in the rosy golden glow, row upon row of lovely forms and faces: white necks and arms with drapery of silk, satin, lace, velvet, delicately tinted as flower petals; and over all a glitter of diamonds such as the setting sun strikes along its path in a cascade. Riches, beauty, high birth! The fairest, most famous women of Europe: and the only dark splashes in the river of light, the wonderful uniforms of officers in 'crack' Austrian and Hungarian regiments. . . . The Imperial box was the heart of this brilliance, just as the royal crown is the heart of the Regalia in the blazing Jewel House show in old London's Tower.

In my day, the tragically romantic figure of the beautiful Empress [*Elizabeth*] had already vanished from the centre of the galaxy: but always there would be a glitter of graceful tiara-circled heads in that splendid box, even when the old Emperor [*Franz-Josef*] was absent. There would be arch-duchesses and princesses, and Royal guests from all over Europe and even Asia. And the orders on the uniformed breasts of soldier-dukes were as blinding in their rays as the diamonds on the necks of lovely ladies. . . .

Now, though the Opera House seems invariably filled to capacity, there are none of those light-signals, as diamond calls to diamond from across the cream-white, and rose-red and gold-splashed auditorium; there are no sun-burst rays that blaze from cascades of jewels. And the reason for this is simple enough: there are no diamonds: there are no jewels. The auditorium glows dully because in its row upon row of boxes there are no flower-petal effects of exquisite dresses lit with sheen of pearl and diamond. There are no more uniforms with jewelled orders. The lovely ladies (they are there, don't doubt it!) are mostly in black. The men are all inconspicuous civilians. If you and I go dressed in our simplest evening gowns, we feel half ashamed of our conspicuous elegance. And because of this monotonous dusk, with its dark shadows, the stage – when the curtains roll away – is a thousand times more striking than when Vienna came to the Opera gorgeous and bejewelled.

Somewhere those diamonds and pearls of the past must still exist; for rare jewels survive all the cataclysms which destroy their one-time owners. Kings, queens, emperors, tsars, and tsarinas pass forever, far beyond our sight in the beautiful, sad pageant of history, but their diamonds, their pearls, their rubies, and emeralds, and opals, remain worldly of the world forever. They are in other lands and other hands, but they have not crumbled into dust. As you and I sit in a box for which we have paid next to nothing in 'real money,' though incredible sums in Austrian kronen, we wonder for a moment where the vanished constellations of jewels are scattered, whom they are delighting, whom they are making miserable. But it is only for a moment that our thoughts stray. They are caught back by voices, and violins, and a glory of sound beyond all price, all jewels: and as our ears hear, so our eyes seem to *see* the music as rainbow light, shimmering as no diamonds of the past ever shimmered in the great days of the Vienna Opera House.

While the music holds us, we – the audience – are all gods and goddesses in our own right, and we are on the heights of Olympus where money doesn't count, and there's no such thing as poverty. Even when the curtain drops between acts we are happy and successful and excited, though not quite so exalted in our minds. And, especially if it is a Wagner night, when we have long hours of enchantment to look forward to, we sometimes remember to be hungry.

You see, we have had to be in our places at the somewhat unearthly hour of five, or five-thirty, just about the time when English people would be having tea, and even Americans would not mind a glass of lemonade or ice cream soda, to say nothing of anti-Volstead refreshment. As for the Viennese, I believe that beautiful music actually makes them hungry! Anyhow, there is a step from the sublime pretty nearly down to the ridiculous between the acts of a long opera in Vienna.

Yes, it *is* funny to see every one sauntering about, munching thick ham sandwiches or fat cakes oozing cream, and bolting the last crumb (or the last *but* one, because the last often sticks to a nose or chin!) as the warning bell rings for the next act!

However, this funny part is charming, at the Opera, and so characteristic of Vienna and the Viennese! All are true music lovers. You and I know that, even from the absent-minded, dreamy way they eat those sandwiches! . . .

I think if the great dead composers come back to hear what Vienna is making of their music, they must be well content: just as the great composers who are still with us are well content: for instance, Richard Strauss. A country that has lived through tragic storms of emotion can appreciate him as the smiling, jewelled beauties and ornamental officers could never have appreciated him before they fully learned to *feel*.

[119] The artists and composers of turn-of-the-century Vienna; from *Memoires* by Alma Mahler. Translated by Richard Bassett.

(Alma Mahler, a remarkable lady who moved among all the artists and musicians of turn-of-the century Vienna, married Gustav Mahler in 1902 in the Karlskirche. Her early years, like her later ones, were not without romantic attachments, however, to other members of that most remarkable circle. She was at times the feminine sun around which all stars turned.)

The architects Joseph Olbrich, Joseph Hoffman, the painters Gustav Klimt, Carl Moll, Josef Engelhart, Kolo Moser, the sculptor Strasser and many others, left the Kunstlerhaus and founded the Vienna 'Secession' which for a long time was to engage our thoughts and feelings.

The first clandestine meetings of this circle were held in the new house of my stepfather, Moll. Klimt was to be the first president. As a very young thing I got to know him at these meetings. He was without doubt the most gifted of them all: thirty-five, in the full bloom of his life and strength, beautiful in every way and even then a celebrated figure. . . . I owe him many tears and, through them, my maturity. My so-called good upbringing had only destroyed my first love. He was attached to a hundred places, women, children; and yet he still pursued me even when my family took me to Italy on holiday.

I remained deaf to all his pleas that I should visit his atelier. Nonetheless I trembled when I saw him, and so it remained for many years a form of engagement. . . . When I was twenty, I met Gustav Mahler, my first husband. He had already been director of the Vienna opera house for four years. He was a Christian though he had, unlike many Jews, in no way allowed himself to be baptized for opportunist reasons; even though to be Court opera director it was necessary to be a Catholic. He seldom passed a church without entering it, though his devotions provoked arguments with me. He loved excessively the mysticism of Catholicism. I was at that time opposed to Jews who believed in Christ . . .

Though Klimt was my first great love, I was a mindless child, absorbed in music and sheltered from life. I studied composition at that time with Alexander von Zemlinsky. It was, or course, to be taken for granted I should fall in love with this ugly man. He was a hideous gnome; small toothless unwashed, reeking of the coffee-house . . . and yet his spiritual strength and sharpness made him enormously fascinating.

When I was taking lessons with Zemlinsky, I also met Arnold Schoenberg. He was Zemlinsky's favourite pupil and even at that time he would say: 'The world will one day have much to say about him.' For his part Schoenberg adored Zemlinsky to such an extent that all his early works were dedicated to him. Through him I met Alban Berg whose songs, though pretty, were not original. It is significant, I think, about Berg that when torn between either going to Pfitzner or Schoenberg for lessons he finally came to Schoenberg through missing his train for Strasbourg and Pfitzner.

[120] Gustav Mahler as seen by the young conductor Bruno Walter; from Bruno Walter's *Thema und Variationen*. Translated by Richard Bassett.

Mahler was by no means alien to pity or unable to share joys. He could espouse a cause and be thoughtful of others, be ready to aid, and feel sympathy. He knew the meaning of friendship, but there was not within him a steadying stream of warmth. It would spring forth or cease, and though he clung to his friends to the end of his days, I used to think this relationship a rather 'intermittent loyalty'.

Mahler assigned to me some of the operas he had prepared. Among them was *Tannhäuser*. I felt that the performance, except for one role, was not lacking in musicality. How surprised I was when I read the following morning a furious attack on me in the *Neues Wiener Tagblatt*. It was the first time in my life that I had been so violently abused. I could not 'even direct a band of riflemen', in the eyes of one critic.

Mahler told me at once that these attacks were part of a campaign, against him. Those relentlessly opposed to him had closed ranks. It must be said that Mahler's violent actions, his peremptory manner in questions of art, his engagements and dismissals and his fight against tradition and age-old customs had helped to swell the ranks of his enemies among the artistic personnel . . . Some were philistines and others were 'scoffers', a

Gustav Mahler

particularly numerous breed in Vienna. They all hated Mahler but an attack against him would have mobilized all his supporters. By attacking me, his appointment of a young inexperienced conductor, these supporters would not be mobilized. Mahler and I were attacked but there was nothing Mahler could do to help me.

[121] The Vienna Opera House described by Bruno Walter before the First World War; from his *Thema und Variationen*. Translated by Richard Bassett.

The magnificent edifice on the Opernring was surpassed by the very similar Paris Opéra only in its site. There the façade of the building dominates the grandiose sweep of the Place de l'Opéra, while the Vienna house stands soberly in the line of the Ringstrasse and even the opposite side of the wide avenue has no gap that would add to its effectiveness.

A careful observer will be somewhat oppressed, too, by the vertical aspect of the building, detracting from the otherwise proud impression it makes. It is said that the architect Van der Null was promised that the street level would be lowered, and that he hurled himself from the balcony of the finished building when that promise was not kept and the noble proportions he had envisioned were so irreversibly damaged.

The exterior of the building nonetheless impresses one by its beauty while the interior – the grand stairway – has no equal among any of the opera houses I know. Aristocratic was the house and courtly its traditions. Among the latter when I came to Vienna was a Court carriage service made available to the female artists, who were called for at their houses and driven back again after the performance, a privilege which was only abolished in the days of the republic.

❧ Life, customs and morals ❧
in Vienna

[122] A seventeenth-century Turk describes the Viennese; from *In the Empire of the Golden Apple* by Evliya Celebi. Translated by Richard Bassett.

The air here is delightful, always evoking spring, so that everyone enjoys good health. The men, who live rather ascetically, may be thin but they live to a great age and are very fit.

These Germans all wear black coats and French shoes. Because of the delicious air, their skin is white like camphor and their well-formed bodies are soft, like the flesh of an ear-lobe. Often the exquisite German boys have such a light skin that they appear very pale.

In contrast to the young girls, the married women all display their bosoms which shine white as snow. They tie their dresses in a different way, towards the centre, which makes their ugly costumes appear even more out of shape. Thanks to Allah, the bosoms of these women are not like our ladies and as large as wash-tubs, but small like apples.

The girls go everywhere with exposed skin and loose hair. Because the air and water are so fresh, they have a beauty and affection which is like a sun of gold.

[123] The women of Vienna as seen by Mary Novello in 1829; from *A Mozart Pilgrimage, being the travel diaries of Vincent and Mary Novello* . . . transcribed and compiled by Nerina Medici di Marignano, and edited by Rosemary Hughes.

The women of Germany have not improved upon me this second visit. It is true they are pretty in the common acceptation of the term: small regular features and fair skins, but they want air and carriage; the *trottoir* makes them all walk as if they had tight shoes on and though they stare with the vulgarity of the milkmaid, if you address them they are shy and at a loss. As for the peasantry, after 12 or 14 they really become frightful and are more like men than women in dress and appearance. In Vienna you see some women rolling barrows with stones, conveying up mortar and working on the scaffolding amongst the men, and some of the loads they bear would astonish an Irish porter. Scarce a shoe is to be seen on one of them, but the men cover their feet unless in the fields when their shoes are strapped to their backs.

How few women I have met like my dear Theresa. The Miss H[enickstein]s [?] here are very like all other young women; monstrously insipid. They extend their eyebrows at the commonest remark as an expression of wonder (alias ignorance) sing common ballads and talk frequently on commonplace subjects – that the Princess is most charming, that the other is *mignonne*, that the Emperor walked one way and the Empress another.

[124] Viennese women viewed somewhat differently some seventy years later; from *At the Gates of the East . . .* by Lieutenant-Colonel J.P. Barry.

Nor is the effect produced on the visitor the product of any eclipsing beauty. If this be a composition of harmonious line, a design of classic proportion, of coldly perfect lineaments, of flowing curves not spoiled by emphatic amplitude, then the women of Vienna are not beautiful. The faces show few fine ovals. There is an absence of regularity in their lines. The features seldom fuse into a sculpturesque ensemble. The figure is not slender. The bones are somewhat heaped with accessory, but the curvilinear poise is comfortable and pleasing. You never see any of the willowy creatures that on English lawns look like bundles of fluff. The skin, however, is almost universally good, as it ought to be, reposing on a cushiony substructure of delicate – what shall we call it? – adiposity. The bloom of the tints owes nothing to the bloom of Ninon. There are more browns than blondes. The eyes are large, frank, animated, and even the chill blues are kindly. Of hair there is great wealth, but except in some fair women it is unlike the zephyry aureolo of tossed floss that frames the type of English beauty. Though the ladies of Vienna besides being *bien maniérées*, are also *bien gantées* and *bien chaussées*, the ungloved hand is plump, and, if the *jeune personne* will forgive the twinkle of colour that I am going to summon up to her eyebrows, I think the region just above the bow of shoestrings is more massive than is sanctioned by the examples of Phidias; and the movement, though healthy, elastic, and responsive to the calls of grace, is marked by a somewhat heavier tread. But the frigid perfection of physiognomical contour, the extrinsic apparatus of beauty is no match for beauty of expression that catches its illumination from the dazzling moods of lovable souls; for with this, the supreme gift of charm, the gracious Viennese people are handsomely endowed.

[125] The importance of rank in Viennese society, 1716; from the *Letters* of Lady Mary Wortley Montagu.

It is not from Austria that one can write with vivacity, and I am already infected with the phlegm of the country. Even their amours and their quarrels are carried on with a surprising temper, and they are never lively but upon points of ceremony. There, I own, they show all their passions; and 'tis not long since two coaches, meeting in a narrow street at night, the ladies in them not being able to adjust the ceremonial of which should go back, sat there with equal gallantry till two in the morning, and were both so fully determined to die upon the spot, rather than yield in a point of that importance, that the street would never have been cleared till their deaths, if the emperor had not sent his guards to part them; and even then they refused to stir, till the expedient was found out of taking them both out in chairs exactly at the same moment; after which it was with some difficulty the *pas* was decided between the two coachmen, no less tenacious of their rank than the ladies.

Nay, this passion is so omnipotent in the breasts of the women, that even their husbands never die but they are ready to break their hearts, because that fatal hour puts an end to their rank, no widows having any place at Vienna. The men are not much less touched with this point of honour, and they do not only scorn to marry, but to make love to any woman of a family not as illustrious as their own; and the pedigree is much more considered by them, than either the complexion or features of their mistresses. Happy are the shes that can number amongst their ancestors counts of the empire; they have neither occasion for beauty, money, or good conduct, to get them husbands.

[126] Mme de Staël, ardent political thinker and brilliant conversationalist, laments the dullness of Viennese society in 1808: from *De L'Allemagne* by Mme de Staël.

One of the principal disadvantages of Viennese society is that the aristocracy and men of letters never mix. Aristocratic pride is not the reason; rather, that there are few distinguished writers in Vienna, and its inhabitants read little; each moves in his own circle, for there are nothing but 'circles' in a country where ideas in general and matters of public interest have so little chance of flourishing. A result of this separation of the classes is that men of letters lack social graces, and that men of the world seldom acquire learning.

The strict rules of good breeding, which are in some respects a virtue, in that they often demand sacrifices, have introduced to Vienna the most tedious customs possible. All good society transports itself en masse from one salon to another three or four times a week. One wastes time on the *toilettes* necessary to these large gatherings; one wastes it in the street, one wastes it on the staircases waiting for one's carriage to arrive in its turn, one wastes it spending three hours at a table; and it is impossible, in such crowded assemblies, to hear anything said except the usual round of conventional phrases. This daily exposure of people to one another is a clever device by which mediocrity has dulled the powers of the mind. If it were an accepted fact that thought was a malady to prevent which a strict regime had to be maintained, nothing better could have been devised than a kind of recreation which is simultaneously stupefying and insipid: such recreation allows one to pursue no ideas, and transforms speech into the kind of twittering which can be taught to humans as well as to birds. . . .

In Viennese society one can enjoy the security, the elegance and the nobility of manners which the women have made supreme; but one lacks anything to say, anything to do, any goal or interest. They want each day to be different from the one before, without, however, wanting that difference to shatter the bonds of feelings and habits. Monotony during a retreat soothes the soul; monotony in high society exhausts the spirit.

[127] The importance of rank in Viennese society in the 1820s; from *More Letters . . . Impressions of Vienna 1819–1829* by Martha Wilmot.

As you cannot guess the system of Society here I will just let you peep behind the curtain a little. The pride of the Aristocracy is by no means greater, but it is more defined, than that of England, and therefore talents, tastes and every natural endowment of a superior cast (if you have the luck to find them) can *never* break down the barrier of rank or be admitted into its circles. The consequence is, ambition of that ennobling mental cast is quite unknown; I never heard of a *verse* to a young lady's eyebrow since I came to Vienna, and I believe such a phenomena would *convict* the person of insanity!! so far for the APPRECIATION of taste or refinement or fancy. A young englishman arriving at Vienna, if quite unknown, is driven to theatres etc. in very despair; if known and introduced into different houses, he has the honour to sit in their drawingrooms during quarter of an hour where *nothing* but french or german is spoken, and where the young ladies seldom appear, and go from one visit to another, all to be over by 8 O'Clock when it is supposed each has his private engagement, and this sort of thing lasts till near the Carnival, when gaiety begins. Then comes on balls thick and threefold, and woe be to him who does not *Waltz*, for tho' there is a blaze of beauty and the balls are quite lovely to look at once or twice, yet no girl will speak to a man who does not dance, and (the men say) very little to those who do. They dance uninterruptedly, and O what an exhibition it is. En attendant, strangers are stared at and, if not highly bred, quiz'd. The young men of our embassy give the *ton* to the english, and *they* are notorious for making no acquaintance with any young man who is not a Peer's son, and even *that* must be an Almack peer. But you will say, why not descend a little into more rational, sociable society? I answer, I have tried and seen both tried, and I do assure you tis the same thing on a more disagreeable scale.

[128] An Italian journalist sees rank in Viennese society as fossilized still further by the early twentieth century; from *Austria, her social and racial problems* by Virginio Gayda.

This haughty, magnificent Austrian nobility, which has, perhaps, no equal in Europe, is really composed of the proudest aristocracies of all races, with its genealogical roots spreading over the whole of Europe, from Russia to France, from Sweden to Italy, from Scotland to Spain. With all this it has not felt the need of expansion or of knowledge of the world; it has fused itself into a disdainful little circle, closely bound to the Court in time of need, impassive and indifferent to the changing times, unfriendly and opposed to things and people foreign to its kingdom.

Its intolerance begins at Court, the most rigid Court in Europe, with the most severe and glacial etiquette, where no one is admitted who cannot boast of noble descent for fourteen generations. Some decades since, an American Ambassador to the Court of Vienna, John Lothrop Motley, wrote: 'An Austrian might be Shakespeare, Galileo, Nelson, and Raphael in one person; he would not be received in good society if he did not possess the sixteen quarterings of nobility which birth alone can give him.' Even to-day the Jockey Club of Vienna – the most magnificent aristocratic club of the Empire, established to encourage horse-racing, and thus cement cordiality among its members – has only accepted till now, as an exception, five *bourgeois* names on its list of members.

It was not always so. Formerly the aristocracy of Vienna showed themselves in the streets among the populace with the utmost familiarity, but in those days Vienna was still unconquered by the smoking chimneys of her factories and by the middle classes. It was a gay and placid city, and its nobles could stroll about its streets as if they were the only masters.

The Austrian nobility all resemble each other; they have the same way of speaking, the same profile, the same spirit, and even the same gait, when – perhaps in reaction from the Prussians – they walk slowly, with long strides, with head bowed forward and shoulders slightly bent, like the Emperor. This class-uniformity, which has isolated the aristocracy almost automatically from the people, like a vein of hard metal which runs though a mountain without disppearing or losing itself, is seen in the large assemblies, in the gala receptions, which with all their magnificence, have something monotonous and symmetrical about them, and give the impression of an arrogant crowd descended from a common ancestor.

[129] Carnival in the late eighteenth century; from Michael Kelly's *Reminiscences*.

The people of Vienna were in my time dancing mad; as the Carnival approached, gaiety began to display itself on all sides; and when it really came, nothing could exceed its brilliancy. The ridotto rooms, where the masquerades took place, were in the palace, and spacious and commodious as they were, they were actually crammed with masqueraders. I never saw, or indeed heard of any suite of rooms, where elegance and convenience were more considered; for the propensity of the Vienna ladies for dancing and going to carnival masquerades was so determined, that nothing was permitted to interfere with their enjoyment of their favourite amusement – nay, so notorious was it, that for the sake of ladies in the family way, who could not be persuaded to stay at home, there were apartments prepared, with every convenience for their accouchement, should they be unfortunately required. And I have been gravely told, and almost believe, that there have actually been instances of the utility of the arrangement. The ladies of Vienna are particularly celebrated for their grace and movements in waltzing, of which they never tire. For my own part, I thought waltzing from ten at night until seven in the morning, a continual whirligig; most tiresome to the eye, and ear, – to say nothing of any worse consequences.

[130] Carnival in the 1820s; from *More letters . . . Impressions of Vienna 1819–1829* by Martha Wilmot.

All the balls that are given in the course of the year are given during the Carnival, which begins the 1ˢᵗ Janʸ and ends Ash Wednesday. This year the Archbishop would not allow it to begin so soon, and it lasted not quite 5 weeks. While it lasts the young people almost dance themselves to death, and then the last thing is a Ridout, where the *cram* and *mob* is suffocating, the dancing and music maddening. Twelve O'Clock strikes! It

Frenzied waltzers: a contemporary cartoon

announces the arrival of Ash Wednesday! The music makes a *sudden stop*, the sudden pause and quiet which follows is *awful* – it lasts a moment, when the buzz which succeeds is worse than the *honest* ball music and noise. This lasts till Morning, indeed Day is advanced when the Ghosts of the ball change their dresses and you may say the Carnival like another Pompeii is burried under the ashes of the irruption of Lent, for everybody goes to Church and goes thro' the ceremony of having ashes sprinkled on their foreheads and being told 'Dust thou art, and unto Dust thou shalt return.'

I do not enter much into the gaietys of the Carnival. You must know that nothing would be easier than for us to go to a ball *or two every night,* but as our dancing days are over and our childrens dancing days are not come, the stupidity from want of interest is very great, and the expence of dressing very great likewise . . .

[131] Balls for the lower classes in the 1830s; from *Vienna and the Austrians 1836–7* by Frances Trollope.

It is necessary to come to Vienna, and see with one's own eyes a ball of the kind, to which we were now admitted, to believe in the possibility of its existence. In a magnificent room in one of the Faubourgs, splendidly illuminated, and animated by a band of excellent music, we found about five hundred people, all exceedingly well dressed, in the very height of festive but orderly enjoyment. The rank of the men was that of shopmen or little shopkeepers, barbers, journeymen tailors, and the like. That of the women may be given comprehensively by the word '*grisettes.*'

The most remarkable features in this gay assembly were – first, the luxury, for I can use no lesser word, of the *locale*. The room was in no respect inferior to Almack's. Secondly, in the well-to-do-in-the-world air of the men, and the neat and very respectable appearance of the women. There were no chaperons, no old people of either sex among them; and the result was such as, if reasoned upon, might go far towards banishing old ladies from ball-rooms for ever. It was indeed quite evident that no such restraint was necessary in order to obtain all that the presence of old ladies is intended to ensure.

The most remarkable circumstance of all, however, was the peaceful, well-behaved tranquillity which pervaded the whole assembly. . . .

The dress of the females was for the most part of white muslin very delicately clean; some as décolletées as their betters, but many reserving the modest fichu still belonging to their class on ordinary occasions. A few aspired to the more questionable elegance of coloured gauze; and a robe of rich but soiled blonde, worn by one gay belle, afforded some amusement to our party, as it was recognised as having adorned the lovely lady of one of them – 'a princess and no less,' during the last year's carnival.

It appears that to these balls (of which, by the way, thirty are advertised as to take place at this same room during the carnival,) it is the custom for every young man of the class for whom they are given, who is about to be married, to bring his bride elect, so that we are to presume that a great part of the company were happy lovers. It is probably from consideration to the feelings of such, that no change of partners takes place during the evening, unless it happen that some partnerless cavalier should approach during the moments when a couple pauses to take breath, and invite the lady to take a *tour de waltz* with him. This is never refused by the belle, nor objected to by her swain, – which may fairly be considered as one among many proofs of Austrian bonhomie. . . .

You must not suppose, however, that this elegant display of grisette festivity is of the lowest grade to which the balls of the carnival descend; on the contrary, we have just been assured that all the washerwomen in Vienna are about to have a meeting of their own for the purpose of waltzing all night, an annual custom of respectable antiquity.

[132] Animal fights and bullfights staged as holiday entertainment in the late eighteenth century; from *Travels in the year 1792* . . . by William Hunter.

In the suburbs, there is a large amphitheatre, where, in imitation of the ancients, combats of wild beasts, and bullfights, are exhibited on Sundays and holidays. Curiosity prompted me to go there once, but I confess that I received no gratification. The boxes and galleries, where the spectators sit, are ranged in rows one above the other, and the lowest is raised considerably above the arena, round which are the dens, where the different animals are kept. The commencement of this spectacle presented a strange scene of confusion. A wolf, a bear, a wild boar, a fox, and a monkey, were turned out together. The monkey, being the wisest of the five, soon thought fit to run up a pole, which stands in the centre of the arena, to secure himself from the danger which awaited him below. The wild boar made an attack on the bear, which was very violent, but did not last long; for as the bear was retreating from the dreadful tusks of his adversary, he fell backwards into a small pool of water, about two feet deep, where he thought proper to remain to cool himself, whilst his enemy was grinning at him on the borders. The poor wolf and fox were hunted by dogs, and were terribly galled. This conflict being over, several bulls were turned out, and baited; after which a man entered on horseback, armed with a spear, with which he attacked one of them. But he was more than his match and after wounding him several times, when the animal was quite faint with loss of blood, he leaped from his horse, and, seizing him by the horns, ran a long knife into his brain. The beast instantly fell, and expired; and was carried off amidst the acclamation of the spectators . . . The last animal that was exhibited was a byson, and about a dozen large dogs, with jackets round their bodies to protect them from his horns, set on him at once. But he was so fierce and outrageous that he soon disabled them all . . . he tossed them one after another, over and over, till they were at last so disheartened that they would no longer renew the attack. I am told that, now and then, a fine lion is turned out, but that, on this occasion, the keepers always expect to lose at least one of their dogs . . .

I have been particular in my account of this spectacle, because it is to be met with in very few of the modern states in Europe. It is, in fact, a barbarous diversion, and might, I think, in this refined age, be dispensed with. It has, however, its advocates in this city, and I was surprised to see it so well attended, especially by the fair sex . . .

[133] Imperial sportsmanship – Archduke Franz Ferdinand goes shooting; from *Archduke Francis Ferdinand* by Victor Eisenmenger.

The Archduke, of course, arranged his hunt quite differently. He invited only three of his best friends. As all the boars had to pass his stand first, the guests had little chance for booty. Still, he let a few of the game pass without shooting at them so that the others might not go altogether empty-handed. Such consideration, however, he only showed when he was the host. When he was a guest, his reputation as a shot did not permit of it.

With great gusto he told of a boar hunt with the German Kaiser. As the Archduke was the guest, he had the first stand. Sixty boars were let out. Fifty-nine of them he knocked over, leaving them dead on the spot. The sixtieth, a young boar, came limping on three legs into range of Kaiser William. The other guests did not get anything at all. 'By Jove,' said the Kaiser, 'you are certainly a crack shot.'

From Prince Starhemberg he rented a fine wood-cock hunt in Helemonsödt near Lainz.

In all hunting grounds which he acquired the stock of game, through his great care and attention, increased unbelievably. He was a master in the arrangement and carrying out of battues. The kill was always splendid and he had the lion's share of it.

He even knew how to arrange hare-hunts so that he, as the solitary shot, was able to kill three or four hundred rabbits. The beaters were placed in a pear-shaped formation and beat up all the game toward him.

The owners of all big hunting grounds in Bohemia, Hungary and Galicia esteemed it an honour if he made a big kill there.

It is not surprising, then, that finally his shooting records mounted up incredibly. I do not remember the exact figures, nor do I know if some English lord does not surpass him in some details, but the following statements are a conservative estimate of the facts.

The total kill exceeds half a million specimens, among which are more than three thousand stags, not counting hinds and fawns. At Ringhoffer in Bohemia, during one hunt, he bagged 2140 pieces of small game which, apart from any other consideration, is an unheard-of physical feat. In Blühnbach he shot in one day 53 chamois without hitting one single doe, an achievement as unparalleled as the number itself. He wrote to me from Helemonsödt: 'I have had the incredible hunting luck to bag seven woodcock in one morning.' In Hungary, during one hunt, he shot, among others, two stags of ten points and one of eight.

Boasting, that favourite diversion of hunters, was never indulged in by him, nor was there necessity for it. In order to accomplish such records one must be a good shot and, as such, he had attained unparalleled perfection. It was a great pleasure to watch him. He invited me frequently to come to his covert or to walk with him so as to keep him company. On such occasions he liked to talk a good deal about his plans for the future. Whenever game came into range, he would interrupt himself in the middle of a sentence, shoot and then resume the conversation where he had left off. If I trained my field-glass on the game I could see that the red spot which marks the entrance of the bullet appeared with mathematical precision in exactly the proper place.

[134] On taking hot baths in Vienna; from Richard Bright's *Travels from Vienna . . . in the year 1814*.

The system established for private bathing in Vienna, from its convenience, deserves particular notice; for, besides accommodations at the baths, called the Diana and Emperor's baths, you may, at any time, by sending an order a few hours previously, be furnished from them with a warm bath in your own lodging. This is done by putting the hot water into small casks, formed of staves at least two inches in thickness, which are conveyed to any part of the city or suburbs upon carriages resembling our brewers' drays. A bathing vessel is brought at the same time, and placed in your chamber, and is filled from these casks, of which a sufficient number are left to be added to the rest, to keep up the temperature. When confined in these thick casks, the water will retain considerable heat for twenty-four hours. The apparatus is removed by the same persons who brought it; and the whole charge does not mount to more than eighteenpence or two shillings, according to the distance of your abode from the public baths.

[135] On housekeeping in Vienna; from *More Letters . . . Impressions of Vienna 1819–1929* by Martha Wilmot.

I must tell you that in expences we are disappointed – everything except luxuries is as dear as in England: dress, dearer, worse and a year behind us in fashion; *Tay* and *sugar* enormous. *However* there are glass konvaniences to be had in abundance, and fruit and flowers dirt cheap – parqué flours – *Carpits* if you chuse to give a daughters dowery for them, and if you do, the *Moths* eat them up to riddles in the summer. We happened luckily to bring a few knives with us which are *in*valuable, as is a small *tayput* – but the bedding!! no tongue can tell it, and as for a *double* bed, there is but one in Vienna (John Bloomfield tells me!) and that is Ld Stewart's, so English Turtle doves place two together to make believe tis one, and we have purchased *leather* sheets, exquisite things, one to serve as an under, the other as an upper blanket, for a blanket is not to be had for gold and precious stones. . . . Such a thing as bed curtain is not known, but then the turn out on the Prater of a Sunday Evening is Magnificent – 4, 6, 8 horses to *shell* like little carriages, footmen with streaming feathers. . . . Not a *drab* of a Hussy that has not better broderie about her tail than *my best* and parterres of artificial flowers round her head. And à propos of dress, while I was in London I did my best to procure you a patinet *half* handkerchief and could not, such a thing was not to be had; well, in the Prater I saw *scores* on the trollops! How is this to be accounted for I beg to know? English second rate dress is so common here that every milk maid has our prints, our ginghams, our muslins, even our tabinets, but *stuffs* are rare (I have *not* one), ribbons are dear, and as for shawls, y^r eyes are sickened of what looks like Turkish ones, but what is in reality Cotton.

[136] A German visitor finds the pervasive Viennese secret police presence oppressive; from *Journey on foot to Syracuse in the year 1802* by Johann Gottfried Seume. Translated by Richard Bassett.

There is scarcely a mention of public matters in Vienna, and you can visit public places for months on end, perhaps, before you hear one word which has any bearing on politics; such is the strictness with which they practise orthodoxy in politics no less than in religion. Everywhere in the cafés there is a reverent hush, as if High Mass were being celebrated, and no one dares breathe.
    Since it is my habit not to fly into a boisterous rage but instead to talk to myself quite calmly and quietly, my acquaintances several times gave me friendly warning that walls have ears . . . On one occasion my carelessness nearly landed me in trouble. As you know, I am no sort of revolutionary, since that always results in matters going from bad to worse; but it is a habit of mine to make a little more noise than is perhaps good for me about something I like. For example, the *Marseillaise* has always struck me as an excellent piece of music, and it so happens that, without thinking, I often hum a few bars of it – as indeed I might do with any other tune. This actually happened once in Vienna – admittedly in quite the wrong place – and very naturally it rather dampened things for those present . . .

[137] Martha Wilmot takes a somewhat lighter view of the Viennese police during Metternich's Chancellorship; from *More Letters . . . Impressions of Vienna 1819–1829* by Martha Wilmot.

The Police of Vienna equals that of Paris. As a proof of its minute attention to strangers, think of the Prime Minister, Prince Meternick, amusing a few select friends the other evening with *every thing* that passed in the interiour of a family of English travellors, more remarkable for their wealth than their refinement, and who little imagined that all their proceedings were reported to such a man and discussed in such a circle! He was off his guard probably at the time he *let the cat out of the bag for a little fun,* but I suppose we never cough, sneeze, nor turn a child into the Nursery *to blow its nose* without the events being reported to *Government!* The letters by post are read of course, but this one is to go by a Courier, so I write without caution. The effect of all this is wonderful security and peace in the town – a beggar is never to be seen, nor is there any appearance of poverty.

[138] Viennese holidays in the early twentieth century; from *Vienna Yesterday and Today* by J. Alexander Mahan.

In no place in the world are there so many holidays as in Vienna. The people improve all opportunities and excuses for making them. The Jews keep the holidays of the Catholics and vice versa. They also have many state holidays. Of the monarchy only the holidays survived the dissolution of the empire. Apparently the Viennese are not averse to adding the Fourth of July and Thanksgiving to their already long list. Christmas is a great day in all German countries. New Year's Eve is 'Sylvester's Eve' and lasts all night and well into the next day.

There is one holiday which is much honored in Vienna, that is almost unknown in other lands. It is the sixth of December and, on the evening before, a personification of the devil, called Krampus, is supposed to visit and punish all bad children. While in the act he is chased away by the bishop, St. Nicholas . . . [An old custom is] the *Veilchenfest* which we shall now explain.

No sooner had the snow vanished than the more adventurous of the inhabitants scattered along the Danube and among the sunny slopes of the hills seeking the first violet. When it was found the fortunate searcher marked the spot and ran like a winged Mercury never stopping till he stood before the Duke in the Hof. The news caused the wildest excitement. Trumpets blared, cymbals clanged, drums rattled and hurrahs of ecstasy resounded from the *Schottentor* across *Stephansdom* to the *Badstuben,* rousing the hibernating population to a glorious fête. Everybody young and old, rich and poor, who possessed two capable feet, put on best bib and tucker and hurried to the Hof. The Duke donned his brightest regalia and led the exultant throng to the

violet, where the prettiest maiden of the town was elected Queen
of the May and honored with the privilege of plucking the
blossom. After this ceremony the May-dance was held then and
there.

[139] Winter in Vienna, 1716; from Lady Mary Wortley
Montagu's *Letters*.

It is now the very extremity of the winter here; the Danube is
entirely frozen, and the weather not to be supported without
stoves and furs; but, however, the air so clear, almost everybody
is well, and colds not half so common as in England, and I am
persuaded there cannot be a purer air, nor more wholesome,
than that of Vienna. The plenty and excellence of all sorts of
provisions are greater here than in any place I was ever in, and it
is not very expensive to keep a splendid table. It is really a
pleasure to pass through the markets, and see the abundance of
what we should think rarities, of fowls and venison, that are daily
brought in from Hungary and Bohemia. They want nothing but
shell-fish, and are so fond of oysters, they have them sent from
Venice, and eat them very greedily, stink or not stink.

[140] Transport in Vienna during the winter; from *Travels
from Vienna . . . in the year 1814* by Richard Bright.

The climate of Vienna, during the winter of 1814–15, was nearly
as changeable as that of London: from the middle of December,
however, till the middle of February, there was sufficient frost to
keep the ground almost continually covered with snow. The
thermometer was often at 25° of Fahrenheit, during the day, and
at midnight seldom below 20°. At this period the streets of
Vienna were crowded with sledges, the greater part of the
wheeled carriages having disappeared; even the hackney
coaches had been taken from their wheels to be hung upon
sledges. The horses' heads were adorned with plumes, and, as
they passed over the hardened snow without occasioning any
sound, it became necessary to provide them with bells, which
gave warning of their approach. From 50 or 100, arranged in
order, upon a piece of leather or velvet, placed upon the horses'

shoulders, produced a lively and agreeable jingling sound on every motion of the animal. The scene afforded by these sledges is much more gay than that produced by an equal number of wheeled carriages; there is always some emulation in adorning them with plumes or coloured cloths; and amongst the nobility, the vanity of possessing rich and beautiful sledges was once carried to such excess, and produced such large expences, that it was discouraged by the court.

[141] The pleasures of a Viennese winter; from *More Letters . . . Impressions of Vienna 1819–1829* by Martha Wilmot.

My chilly thaw has taken such good effect that the frost and snow is almost vanished, but we enjoyed three days of very great amusement before it took its departure. You are acquainted with the Schwartzenberg Garden as the scene of such misery to W^m and me during our dear Blanche's illness in the month of April. You must change the scene to deep Winter; trees all crackling and sparkling with frost and snow; the ponds where the children threw bread to gold fish sporting in the sunbeams to a solid mass of ice, and on this ice fancy many of the ballroom beaux and bells sporting instead of gold fish. The young men and boys skating and the young ladies seated in little traineaux gliding along before their cavaliers, who pushed them forward on the light fantastic toe. Amongst this group fancy not only Catharine and Blanche frisking, but my *sober self* flitting thro' the air like a bird on the wing, or like Matty Wilmot a few years ago in old Russia,[1] and the very last day Wilmot making his first attempt at skating. Do not ask me why he did not begin sooner, or why we did not *all* begin sooner.

[142] The Viennese view of their city; from *Vienna* by Hermann Bahr.

In Europe everyone knows a lot about Vienna – how it is always Sunday there, always the Capua of the spirit where man lives

---

[1]Martha Wilmot and her sister Catherine spent the years 1803 to 1808 in Russia as protégées of the Princess Dashkov.

half in poetry and one is regaled by the names of waltzes by Lanner and Strauss.

Such imagery is rubbish. Things already sound different when you know Metternich said, 'Asia begins on the Landstrasse,' or that Kurnberger wagered that only foreigners talked about Viennese *gemütlichkeit*, and multiplied South German laxity with Slav untrustworthiness, adding to the equation the spiritual and material ill-government of centuries of Dalai-Lama-like absolutism.

This city, however, is still loved. Listening to its inhabitants, you feel you must flee, but no one does. The Viennese grumble and winge, but they remain. They do nothing to change Vienna or themselves. Anyone who tries to do so is a mortal foe.

The Viennese are extremely unhappy people, hating Vienna but unable to live without it. The city is condemned but also pitied; criticized but also expected to be praised. The Viennese are always grumbling, always threatening – but woe betide anyone who offers to help. Then the Viennese arm themselves.

[143] The Viennese character described in a letter from Georg Trakl, the celebrated Austrian writer, to his sister, October 1908; from Georg Trakl's *Collected Letters*. Translated by Richard Bassett.

Dear Sister,

Thank you for your letter. Every line, page and word from Salzburg is a treasured memory of a city I love before all others.

The Viennese, on the other hand, are most disagreeable. They are a people whose unreliability, stupidity and even wickedness is concealed beneath a veneer of unpleasant bonhomie. I find nothing more unpleasant than this reinforced concrete of cosiness! On the trams, the conductors bow and scrape; in the restaurants, etc., it is the same. One is everywhere greased up to in the most charmless way. And the aim of all these attacks? A tip. I've come to the conclusion that every tip must be taxed in Vienna. May the Devil take these shameless cockroaches! . . .

[144] Another view of the Viennese character; from *The Habsburg Empire* by Henry Wickham Steed.

The Viennese standpoint is, simply, to avoid unpleasantness, to take life easily, sceptically, and to get out of it as much thoughtless enjoyment as possible. Abroad, Vienna has a reputation for 'gaiety,' dating, perhaps, from the Congress of 1815. Of this reputed gaiety, the critical stranger sees little. He sees a whole population trying to be gay, but little spontaneous merriment. Centuries of absolutist government working upon a temperament compounded of Celtic versatility, South German slackness and Slav sensuousness, have – thanks to the constant efforts of the authorities to turn attention away from public affairs and towards amusement – ended by producing a population of *dilettanti*, disposed to take nothing seriously save the pursuit of pleasure. The result is depressing to those not born to the Viennese manner or capable of assimilating the Viennese standpointlessness. The Viennese themselves hold their city incomparable – as indeed it is, after its fashion. Their pride in it and in themselves as its inhabitants is intense, far deeper-rooted and livelier than the pride of the Parisian in Paris. For this pride there are many valid reasons. No European capital has so Imperial an air, none finer boulevards, none a more magnificent park at its gates or more delightful surroundings. First impressions of Vienna are usually seductive. The combination of stateliness and homeliness, of colour and light, the comparative absence of architectural monstrosities and the soft Italian influence everywhere apparent, contribute, together with the grace and beauty of the women, the polite friendliness of the inhabitants and the broad, warm accent of their speech, to charm the eye and ear of every travelled visitor. Then, in a brief space, the spell is often broken. Disillusionment, of the kind that overtakes a guest during too long a *tête-à-tête* with a handsome hostess who is handsome but nothing more, sets in and sometimes inclines strangers to harsh and hasty judgment. The defects of the city are felt to outweigh its attractions. The population appears soulless, its easy-going character amorphous, its politeness hollow, its honesty dubious and its vanity insufferable. The very architecture of Viennese buildings seems to stand in no relation to Viennese life save, perhaps, the Baroque which, with its apotheosis of unreality, somehow suits the character of a people that has latterly adopted with snobbish alacrity the unintelligible canons of 'modern art.' This disillusionment may last until the stranger discovers in some odd corner of the city a veritable Viennese and finds that beneath the appearance of gaiety there is much quiet, hard work, beneath the superficial politeness much real courtesy, alongside of childishness, great shrewdness and knowledge of mankind, and, amid scepticism and carelessness, an amazing richness of talent. . . .

The problem of Vienna as, indeed, the problem of Austria and of the Monarchy is how to adjust appearances to reality and to bring more sincerity into life.

[145] *Schlamperei*; from Edward Crankshaw's *Vienna*.

The municipal vice of Vienna is a sort of laziness, an easy-going spirit which quickly degenerates into slackness. The quality is recognised by the Viennese, who are not hypocrites, and called by them *Schlamperei*. It is shared by the highest and the lowest, causing the former to lose battles, the latter to forget errands – both for insufficient cause. This is not the virtuoso carelessness of the Southern French, the languid procrastination of the Span- ish, nor the militant unreliability of the Italian. It is something quite charming, frequently annoying, ultimately disastrous, and for ever catching its victims unawares.

Nor was the ruling house immune from the weakness of its children. One finds what is probably the first considerable act of Habsburg *Schlamperei* occurring in the summer of 1315, when the two brothers, Frederick and Leopold of Habsburg, lost the chance of an offensive against Louis of Bavaria in order to get married, although nothing less than the Crown of the Holy Roman Empire was at stake. And, dropping down the centuries, the war of 1914 would at least have been postponed (with the chance when it came, of having it unambiguously nailed to Prussia) had it not been for *Schlamperei*. For instance, it should have been known, and doubtless in some responsible quarters it was known (though not in the chambers of the Hofburg), that the unfortunate Archduke Francis Ferdinand would never come back alive if he went to Sarajevo. He was sent there, just the same. . . .

We begin, however, to get a wrong perspective. Touching

lightly on a minor vice of the Viennese, which is also the source (or the corollary) of so much charm and poise, we find it pointing the way to treachery and carnage. But in its everyday appearances that vice is transformed into an amiable weakness, unfateful in visage, unspectacular in effect. And even in its farthest-reaching mood its action is by no means always cruel. The old bureaucracy, with Franz Josef at its head, which governed the late Habsburg Empire was described by Viktor Adler as 'Absolutism modified by *Schlamperei*'; and without that modifying spirit, very analogous to the spirit of muddling through which has so strengthened our own country in its possessions, the Dual Monarchy would have foundered long before it did. It is not too far-fetched to say that it only foundered in the end because one half, the Magyar half, shared the Prussian incapacity to learn how to take things easily. Taking things easily is the mark of the civilised spirit and at the same time the unmistakable stamp of decadence.

[146] The origins of the croissant; from *The Vanished Pomps of Yesterday* . . . by Lord Frederic Hamilton.

In 1683 the Turks invaded Hungary, and, completely overrunning the country, reached Vienna, to which they laid siege, for the second time in its history. Incidentally, they nearly succeeded in capturing it. During the siege, bakers' apprentices were at work one night in underground bakehouses, preparing the bread for next day's consumption. The lads heard a rhythmic 'thump, thump, thump,' and were much puzzled by it. Two of the apprentices, more intelligent than the rest, guessed that the Turks were driving a mine, and ran off to the Commandant of Vienna with their news. They saw the principal engineer officer and told him of their discovery. He accompanied them back to the underground bakehouse, and at once determined that the boys were right. Having got the direction from the sound, the Austrians drove a second tunnel, and exploded a powerful countermine. Great numbers of Turks were killed, and the siege was temporarily raised. On September 12 of the same year (1683) John Sobieski, King of Poland, utterly routed the Turks, drove them back into their own country, and Vienna was saved. As a reward for the intelligence shown by the baker-boys, they were granted the privilege of making and selling a rich kind of roll (into the composition of which butter entered largely) in the shape of the Turkish emblem, the crescent. These rolls became enormously popular amongst the Viennese, who called them *Kipfeln*. When Marie Antoinette married Louis XVI of France, she missed her Kipfel, and sent to Vienna for an Austrian baker to teach his Paris *confrères* the art of making them. These rolls, which retained their original shape, became as popular in Paris as they had been in Vienna, and were known as *Croissants*, and that is the reason why one of the rolls which are brought you with your morning coffee in Paris will be baked in the form of a crescent.

[147] The Viennese coffee-house; from *The World of Yesterday* by Stefan Zweig.

(Stefan Zweig (1881–1942), novelist, dramatist and poet, chronicled life in turn-of-the-century Vienna, describing carefully the world which for many of his generation disappeared with the First World War, never to return.)

Viennese coffeehouse is a particular institution which is not comparable to any other in the world. As a matter of fact, it is a sort of democratic club to which admission costs the small price of a cup of coffee. Upon payment of this mite every guest can sit for hours on end, discuss, write, play cards, receive his mail, and, above all, can go through an unlimited number of newspapers and magazines. In the better-class Viennese coffeehouse all the Viennese newspapers were available, and not the Viennese alone, but also those of the entire German Reich, the French and the English, the Italian and the American papers, and in addition all of the important literary and art magazines of the world, the *Revue de France* no less than the *Neue Rundschau*, the *Studio*, and the *Burlington Magazine*. And so we knew everything that took place in the world at first hand, we learned about every book that was published, and every production no matter where it occurred; and we compared the notices in every newspaper. Perhaps nothing has contributed as much to the intellectual mobility and the international orientation of the Austrian as that he could keep abreast of all world events in the coffeehouse, and at the same time discuss them in the circle of his friends. For, thanks to the collectivity of our interests, we followed the *orbis pictus* of artistic events not with two, but with twenty and forty eyes. What one of us had overlooked was noticed by another, and since in our constant childish, boastful, and almost sporting ambition we wished to outdo each other in our knowledge of the very latest thing, we found ourselves actually in a sort of constant rivalry for the sensational. If, for example, we discussed Nietzsche, who then was still scorned, one of us would suddenly say with feigned superiority, 'But in the idea of egotism Kierkegaard is superior to him,' and at once we became uneasy: 'Who is Kierkegaard, whom X knows and of whom we know nothing?' The next day we stormed into the library to look up the books of this time-obscured Danish philosopher, for it was a mark of inferiority not to know some exotic thing that was familiar to someone else.

[148] Café life in the 1930s; from Edward Crankshaw's *Vienna*.

On the boulevards of Paris, and indeed elsewhere, it is customary to sit on a chair at a little table on the pavement and 'watch the world go by'. This is known as the charm of café life: but the real charm of café life is something other. It consists of sitting comfortably in congenial surroundings and talking, or meditating blankly, or reading the world's press on wicker frames, or looking up trains in a trans-continental Bradshaw, or having one's friends drop in on one, or dropping in on one's friends, or even writing – against the slow buzz of conversation with the cigarette smoke curling up into one's eyes and the tin tray on the marble slab rattling at every movement and the coffee cooling to lukewarm and then to coffee-cold, the deadest cold known to mankind. . . . if all that can be done on the pavement, well and good; in Vienna, as a rule, it is better done indoors: the seats are softer and the tables larger. A good Viennese coffee-house is as comfortable as and no more talkative than the solidest of London clubs. There are times, naturally, when one likes to sit on the pavement, as on a warm summer evening when the bright lights blaze against the gloaming with a pleasingly theatrical effect; but often it is too cold for this kind of occupation and the habitué anxious to watch the world go by can always sit snugly in an upholstered and centrally heated corner, gazing through the heavy plate glass which takes the place of the fourth wall. In summer, when it is hot, these great windows are bodily removed, and then one sits as in the cool recesses of a deep, deep loggia, or cave, watching the serious-minded tourist frying between sun and simmering granite setts. Within and about one are all the accessories of a pleasant life, rounded off by many sorts of coffee, from the finest mocha in the world, through the Turkish variety in copper vessels (the sole contribution of *that* Orient to the amenities of civilised life – unless one counts Rahat Lakhoum?), to the characteristic, local and opulent *mélange* with its dollop of whipped cream. With each cup of coffee will arrive newspapers on frames and two small glasses of cold water. These will be renewed at every opportunity, and thus, sipping the waters of alpine snows (Vienna's water-supply *does* come from the mountains sixty miles away and is nowhere else surpassed), one may sit hour after hour for the price of a single drink, reading, talking, or considering what to do next – an occupation so pleasant that the temptation is to do nothing at all – ever.

[149] *Heuriger* inns and dancing schools; from *Down River* by John Lehmann.

Approaching the city on such an evening, you come first through the world of *Heuriger* inns, scattered through the winding alleys of the countrified suburbs. *Heuriger* means 'this year's wine' and a green garland hung on a pole outside an inn indicated that the sour, heady wine from the surrounding vineyards was ready to be drunk. To these inns, on a Friday or Saturday or Sunday evening, the Viennese crowded, bringing with them as often as not their packets of meat and bread which they laid out on the little tables – and under the trees if the night was fine. But the drinking of the new wine was not the only feature of the *Heuriger* inns; there was singing, and music as well, performed by the special *Schrammel* quartettes, which consist of an accordion player, a violinist, a guitar-player, and a tenor or bass to sing the favourite *Heuriger* songs. On such evenings the Viennese really let themselves go, the laughter and uproar grew wilder and wilder at some tables, lovers fondled and kissed one another at others, while the tenor went round singling out a table here and a table there for his attention with a special song.

At the same time, nearer in, in hundreds of little cafés, the workers and shopkeepers and commercial travellers were gathering, to talk or play cards or billiards or chess for hours through the night, the lingerers migrating to the early morning '*gulyas* stalls' when the doors were finally closed on them; in the *Volksheime*, the great centres of culture from which the whole Viennese workers' movement sprang, thousands would be attending evening classes; and to one of the innumerable *Tanzschulen* in each district the Viennese boy would be taking his girl to dance the oldest waltzes of Strauss and the newest foxtrots from London and New York. The Viennese love dancing as passionately as music, and one of their earliest ambitions is to take a course of lessons in one of the *Tanzschulen*. Each *Tanzschule* – which was a dancing-bar as well as a school – had its own atmosphere and its own public, from the most elegant in the Inner Town to those where sudden brawls with knives were a regular occurrence. In Summer, the huge dance-halls of the Prater were the most popular. And in Winter, in Carnival time, while the fashionable and pompous Opera Ball and Ball of Vienna were taking place in the Inner Town, each *Tanzschule* would be celebrating its own *Fasching* evening with masks of fancy dress.

[150] Inflation in the 1920s; from *Europe – Whither Bound?* by Stephen Graham.

This depreciation of the currency strikes the mind of the visitor to Vienna, and from it he deduces the general ruin of the country. He sees the shabby condition into which imperial palaces and State houses are falling, and talks with the aristocratic or cultured *nouveau pauvre* carrying his lunch of sausage and black bread to a gloomy apartment at the back of a fourth floor, and he feels the calamity that has fallen upon Austria. Austria with a nominal 2800 crowns to the pound sterling cannot last. How then about Poland with 4000 marks to the pound – an Allied country with a close understanding with France? But nobody in Vienna can understand how Poland lives. . . .

The expression 'starving Austria' is a propaganda phrase. She may starve, she probably will, but the time is not yet. Individual classes of workers starve until they get their wages raised. There have been many moments of struggle between the time when the tram-conductor earned forty crowns a week to the time when he earned several thousand. Ten-thousand-crown notes are not uncommon among the working classes, and 10,000 crowns will purchase more than you could buy in England for five pounds, or in America for thirty dollars. A working-man's dinner with a glass of beer costs about a hundred crowns, a city man's lunch of three courses, a hundred and twenty. The working class is accused of constantly holding up the community for money by means of strikes. The truth is that here the organization of Labour and the strike-weapon proved a highly convenient method for getting level with the money-printing press. . . .

The most characteristic places of Vienna to-day are the new *Wechselstuben* or exchange offices, which have sprung up every-where. Here are such crowds waiting to change their money that you have to wait in a line for your turn. Some of the large banks give a much better exchange than the little ones – and the better the exchange given the longer the queue. The large banks stop public business at half-past twelve, and after that hour is the opportunity of the bucket-shop. If you have little time, or if you lose patience, you run into one of the greedy little bureaus and help to make some one's fortune, not your own. This would not be of much importance for Austria if the people one met waiting in these banks were mostly American, British, French. The sad fact is that the people who are changing their money thus are nearly all Austrian or at least ex-Austrian subjects. The old Austrian empire has been divided into five parts, and each part has a different money which has to be exchanged whenever you come into another part. And there is a great difference in the values of the various moneys. Thus the Hungarian money is worth more than double that of Austria. The twenty, the hundred, the thousand-crown notes are almost identical in appearance and printing – a small imprint of a rubber stamp being in many cases the only distinguishing mark – but even from a waiter in a hotel you can get two thousand Austrian crowns for one thousand Hungarian ones. Roumanian lei are also much the same in appearance. Czech crowns and Serbo-Croat crowns are certainly different. But when your home is in Czecho-Slovakia and your place of business in Austria, and your aged father and mother in Hungary and your uncles and cousins in Croatia, you have a lively time with your money. And it plays prodigiously into the hands of those who have started changing-shops upon the public ways.

An interest in the rate of exchange has developed among the masses of the people, who turn to the financial column of the morning paper as Westerners do to football news or baseball results. There is considerable fluctuation in the values, and it is no doubt possible to make a living by speculation alone, and many people do so.

Bibliography

(Translators' names in parentheses
indicate translations done for this book.)

ANDERSON, EMILY (ed), *Letters of Mozart and his Family*, London, 1966
'An Eye-witness Account of the Battle of Aspern', manuscript in the
Heeresgeschichtlichesmuseum, Vienna, 1811.

BAHR, HERMANN, *Vienna*, Vienna, 1906. (Transl. Richard Bassett.)

BAKER, JAMES, *Austria: her people and their homelands*, London, 1913.

BAREA, ILSE, *Vienna, legend and reality*, London, 1966.

BARRY, J.P., A.B. M.B., *At the Gates of the East: a book of travel among historic
wonderlands*, London, 1906.

BEETHOVEN, LUDWIG VON, *Letters*, ed. Dr A.C. Kalischer, transl. J.S.
Shedlock, London, 1909.

BRIGHT, RICHARD, *Travels from Vienna through Lower Hungary, with some
remarks on the State of Vienna During the Congress in the year 1814*,
Edinburgh and London, 1818.

BRION, MARCEL, *Daily Life in the Vienna of Mozart and Schubert*, London,
1961.

BURNEY, DR CHARLES, *Musical Tours in Europe, 1772*, edited by Percy
Scholes, Oxford, 1959.

CASTELLI, I.F., *Memoiren meines Lebens*, Prague, 1861. (Transl. Richard
Bassett.)

CELEBI, EVLIYA, *Im Reiche des Goldenen Apfels . . . 1665*, ed. Richard F.
Kreutel, Erich Prokosch, Karl Teply, in the series 'Osmanische
Geschichtsschreiber', Graz, 1987. (Transl. Richard Bassett.)

COCKBURN, CLAUD, *In time of trouble*, London, 1956.

CRANKSHAW, EDWARD, *Vienna, the Image of a Culture in Decline*, London,
1938.

— *The Fall of the House of Habsburg*, London, 1963.

EISENMENGER, VICTOR, *Archduke Francis Ferdinand*, London, 1928.

GARDE-CHAMBONAS, COMTE AUGUSTE DE LA, *Anecdotal Reminiscences of the
Congress of Vienna*, London, 1902.

GASSICOURT, CADET DE, *Papers of an Army Apothecary*, Heeresgeschichtlichesmuseum, Vienna, 1909.

GAYDA, VIRGINIO, *Austria, her social and racial problems*, London, 1915.

GEDYE, G.E.R., *Fallen Bastions, the Central European Tragedy*, London,
1928.

GRAHAM, STEPHEN, *Europe – Whither Bound?*, London, 1921.

HAMILTON, LORD FREDERIC, *The Vanished Pomps of Yesterday; being Some Random Reminiscences of a British Diplomat*, London, 1922.

HANSLICK, EDUARD, *Vienna's Golden Years of Music, 1850–1900*, transl. and ed. by Henry Pleasants III, London, 1951.

HUDDLESTON, SISLEY, *Europe in Zigzags*, New York, 1928.

HUNTER, WILLIAM, *Travels in the Year 1792 though France, Turkey and Hungary to Vienna*, London, 1798.

KELLY, MICHAEL, *Reminiscences*, London, 1826.

KOHL, J.G., *Austria: Vienna, Prague, Hungary, Bohemia and the Danube, Galicia, Styria, Moravia, Bukovina and the Military Frontier*, London, 1843.

LANCASTER, OSBERT, *With an Eye to the Future*, London, 1967.

LEHMANN, JOHN, *Down River*, London, 1939.

LIGNE, PRINCE DE, *Mémoires*, Paris, 1798. (Transl. Richard Bassett.)

LONYAY, COUNT CARL, *Rudolf: the tragedy of Mayerling*, London, 1950.

MAHAN, J. ALEXANDER, *Vienna Yesterday and Today*, Vienna, 1928.

MAHLER, ALMA, *Memoires*, Vienna, 1960. (Transl. Richard Bassett.)

MALLESON, COL. G.B., C.S.I., *Life of Prince Metternich*, London, 1888.

MONTAGU, LADY MARY WORTLEY, *Letters*, London, 1789.

MORYSON, FYNES, *An Itinerary written by Fynes Moryson, Gent, first in the Latin tongue and then translated by him in to English: containing his Ten Yeers Travell through the Twelve Dominions of Germany, Behmerland, Sweitzerland, Netherland, Denmarke, Poland, Italy, Turky, France, England, Scotland and Ireland. Divided into III Parts*, London, 1617.

MUSULIN, STELLA, *Vienna in the Age of Metternich*, London, 1975.

NOVELLO, VINCENT and MARY, *A Mozart Pilgrimage, being the travel diaries of Vincent and Mary Novello in the year 1829*, transcribed and compiled by Nerina Medici di Marignano, ed. by Rosemary Hughes, London, 1955.

PODEWILS, OTTO CHRISTOPH VON, *Memoirs*, Berlin, 1908.

RACH, KARL, *Eye-witness Accounts of the Siege of Vienna*, Dusseldorf, 1968. (Transl. Richard Bassett.)

RUMBOLD, SIR HORACE, BART., G.C.B., G.C.M.G., *The Austrian Court in the Nineteenth Century*, London, 1909.

— *Recollections of a Diplomatist*, London, 1902.

SCHUBERT, FRANZ, *Gesammelte Briefen*, collection of the Musikverein, Vienna. (Trans. Richard Bassett.)

SCHUMANN, ROBERT, *Gesammelte Schriften*, 1835, collection of the Musikverein, Vienna. (Transl. Richard Bassett.)

SCHUSCHNIGG, KURT VON, *Farewell Austria*, transl. John Segrue and others, London, 1938.

— *Austrian Requiem*, transl. Franz von Hildebrand, London 1947.

SCHIERBRAND, WOLF VON, *The Polyglot Empire*, New York, 1918.

SCHNITZLER, ARTHUR, *My Youth in Vienna*, London, 1971.

SEUME, JOHANN GOTTFRIED, *Journey on foot to Syracuse in the year 1802*, Leipzig, 1804, (Transl. Richard Bassett.)

STAEL, MADAME DE, *De L'Allemagne*, Paris, 1845. (Transl. Prudence Fay.)

STEED, HENRY WICKHAM, *The Habsburg Empire*, London, 1913.

STOYE, JOHN, *The Siege of Vienna*, London, 1964.

TRAKL, GEORG, *Collected Letters*, Vienna, 1912. (Transl. Richard Bassett.)

TROLLOPE, FRANCES, *Vienna and the Austrians, with some account of a journey through Swabia, Bavaria, the Tyrol and Salzbourg, 1836–7*, London, 1838.

WALTER, BRUNO, *Thema und Variationen*, Zurich, 1947. (Transl. Richard Bassett.)

WILLIAMSON, ALICE, *The Lure of Vienna*, London, 1926.

WILMOT, MARTHA, *More Letters from Martha Wilmot: Impressions of Vienna 1819–1829*, London, 1935.

WRAXALL, N. WILLIAM, *Memoirs of the Courts of Berlin, Dresden, Warsaw and Vienna in the years 1777, 1778 and 1779*, London, 1779.

YOUNG, ROBERT, *A Young Man Looks at Europe*, London, 1938.

ZWEIG, STEFAN, *The World of Yesterday: an autobiography*, London, 1943.

Index

GENERAL INDEX